*Sensible Words*

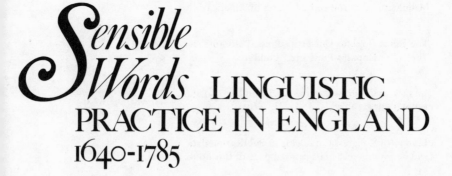

# Sensible Words LINGUISTIC PRACTICE IN ENGLAND 1640-1785

Murray Cohen

The Johns Hopkins University Press
Baltimore and London

Manufactured in the United States of America

The Johns Hopkins University Press, Baltimore, Maryland 21218
The Johns Hopkins Press Ltd., London

Library of Congress Catalog Card Number 77-1856
ISBN 0-8018-1924-5

Library of Congress Cataloging in Publication data
will be found on the last printed page of this book.

For
Betty

maker
of all kinds
of sense

# CONTENTS

# ACKNOWLEDGMENTS

Were I to consider all the circumstances that collected to make it possible for me to write this book, I might be led to autobiographical fragments that I could not live to assemble. Much then must stay unprinted, though not unthought. I recognize many sorts of indebtedness; indeed, I have an embarrassment of obligations. The year I spent in England initially surveying the original linguistic material that I describe here was made possible not only by a Humanities Research Grant from the University of California at Berkeley but also by the remarkable selflessness of my mother, Rose Cohen, and by the steady, loving support of my wife, Betty. The libraries at which I studied that year, in England and America, were unfailingly helpful, and their aid continues in the form of the permissions they have given me to reproduce pages from books in their collections. I am also indebted to the great project of reprinted materials selected by R. C. Alston and printed by The Scolar Press Ltd. The facsimile reprint series, *English Linguistics, 1500–1800,* for which they are responsible, is an invaluable resource, and without it I could not have turned my original notes into this book.

The amount, rarity, and obscurity of the materials I wanted to deal with made for frequent frustrations, and I am grateful to those who gave me the encouragement and opportunity to overcome them. The first chance I took to collect some of my sources was for a paper I presented to the fifth annual meeting of the American Society for Eighteenth-Century Studies. That essay, which became the basis of the first chapter of this book, appears in *Studies in Eighteenth-Century Culture,* vol. 5, ed. Ronald C. Rosbottom (Madison, 1976). Since then several friends and former colleagues and teachers have read different sections of this book as it came out in annual installments. For their advice, corrections, and comfort, I want to thank Frederic Amory, Don Ault, Stephen Booth, Stephen Greenblatt, Peter Manning, and Sheldon Rothblatt—that's an order that makes mere sense. Others worked through the whole manuscript and gave me the support I will remember as the happiest part of this project: Julian Boyd, Jackson Cope, Stanley Fish, Leonard Michaels, Richard Stein, and John Wallace. If the book matched the fine sense and good will of all these readers, it would be very good indeed. The staff at The Johns Hopkins University Press, particularly William Sisler and Barbara Kraft, made the publication process easier and the product better than either might have been.

Although my student days are long gone, I remain grateful for the "teacherly" example and intellectual integrity my teachers offered. I hope that the confidence they gave me to pursue and develop my own interests is well justified by this book. Two of them, Earl Wasserman and Jack Cope, gave me what I can say no more about: this book is an act in place of further speech. I want, however, to express my sadness that Earl Wasserman did not live to share with me either the pursuit of this project or the pleasures of its publication. Finally, I recall happily the active support of Jean and Herbert Levy, the dependencies of my son, Jonathan, born when this project could not even claim preformationist form, and, as always, the graces of Betty.

# INTRODUCTION

Intellectual histories often obscure their beginnings and start after
important first steps have been forgotten or buried. They tend to be
explanations of ideas—of modern science, romanticism, progress, plot,
and so on—with most credit conventionally going to those explanations
that account for more items, cover more time, connect more cultures, or
establish more continuity than others. Comprehensiveness and coherence
normally emerge as the standards of accuracy or as proofs of the historian's wisdom. But the crucial first step in any intellectual inquiry is the
decision to characterize the objects of study in one way or another;
explanation necessarily comes afterward. To credit the comprehensiveness of an explanation emphasizes a secondary intellectual activity. It is
the characterization that determines what we see—whether Pope's "Rape
of the Lock" is a mock heroic or a coterie poem, whether it is mythic or
sociosexual; whether *promise* is a verb, an embedded sentence, or a
speech act. Explanations merely organize and justify what we choose to
see. Yet most intellectual historians think that the choice of an idea is
obvious and that the explanation of that idea proves their worth. The
ideas ripe for explanation are those commonly mentioned in the writings
of a particular period ("utility" in the seventeenth century), in historical
accounts of the period ("romanticism"), or in the works of the most
eminent writers and those most important to the historian's own time
("progress") or to his own discipline ("plot").

These ideas are not the basic units of human expression, however.

They are actually explanatory terms so familiar that we imagine they are really out there, in history, people, and texts.[1] When intellectual historians explain an idea, they are often unknowingly analyzing a habit of their own thinking. Our methods of historical analysis, our selection of terms, figures, and sights (or cites), speak who we are by showing how we think and, even, what we do not know we believe. If we do not resist the blinders that the conventions of our own discourse put on us, we succumb to histories that put a premium on a continuous track (which may have some hurdles or some well-marked, gracefully curving detours) that finally includes us along the Way. Intellectual history of this sort is a form of self-validation; it works by subjecting the past to the terms or techniques to which we subscribe or by labeling the past as the beginning of what we have become. Most intellectual and literary histories join this colonialization of the past; they make history safe for our understanding. It may be that we can ultimately speak nothing other than ourselves, but it is nonetheless important to try to see through the shadows we cast when we look back (or dig under or peel away).

There is a moment in Claude Lévi-Strauss's intellectual autobiography, *Tristes Tropiques,* that isolates this problematic of seeking the Other and finding yourSelf. The author has come to Saõ Paolo to seek images and ideas other than those validated by French academic traditions. As he moves farther and farther from the city, he steadily leaves the all too abundant evidence of mingling and mutating cultures. He finds groups of people who have taken over and redefined the abandoned remains of modern society and who have interacted with and transformed the myths of contiguous tribes. He understands them in terms of their *difference from*—of one tribe's myth of origin from another's, of one group's use of a building from ours—but his analysis of difference is possible only because there is something ostensibly shared, something he can bring into relation.

Once, however, when his group is fatigued, sick, without an interpreter, and nearly provisionless, they come upon the few surviving members of a people who had never seen white or "modern" men and who had none of the implements or infections even benign anthropologists leave behind. These are "my savages" exclaims Lévi-Strauss, yet they mean nothing to him just because they are so absolutely Other: "They were as close to me as a reflection in a mirror; I could touch them, but I could not understand them."[2] As few other moments do so well, this one puts Lévi-Strauss's problematic project into focus: "I had only to succeed in guessing what they were like for them to be deprived of their strangeness: in which case, I might just as well have stayed in my village. Or if, as was the case here, they retained their strangeness, I could make no use of it, since I was incapable of even grasping what it consisted of. Between these two extremes, what ambiguous instances provide us with the excuses by which we live?" Lévi-Strauss hurries away from this encounter with what is totally strange, not to arrive breathlessly at what he already knows, but to set out on a wonderfully rich career of playing with the discontinuous relations between different groups.

If whatever we observe must be altered, as anthropologists have recognized by even that much participation, then we can never speak completely for what we are not. We can, however, look more closely at what and how we speak our minds and, as I try to do in this book, at the relationally distinctive modes of discourse and thought once practiced. We can at least compare the way in which similar sounding ideas or comparable intentions or techniques are distinctively assembled into the special shape of a people's knowledge at a particular time.

The change in the writing of history for which I am arguing depends, first of all, on a change in consciousness of what we are doing when we encounter the past. Histories need not try to make the past safe for historians; they could try to become familiar with the complexity, richness, and individuality of past practices. I set out, first, to avoid modern limitations of terminology and discipline; I did not expect to find confirmations of explanatory patterns that I had been taught. I was ready to find characterizations of the world unadapted to our own images. In approaching the past, I expected to meet comparative strangers, not domesticated pets. Second, I sought in the past neither the beginnings of the favored assumptions of modern discourse nor the conclusions of earlier starts; I wanted neither revolutions that separate "them" from "us" nor some earlier figures salvaged for our academic "hall of the tamed." Rather, I was prepared for difference as well as resemblance, discontinuity as much as coherence. In the following chapters, I contribute to an intellectual history of England in the years from 1640 to 1785 in a way that demonstrates the importance of these alternative premises. The claims I make here on the attention of readers are based, however, not on an exposition of the theoretical foundations of these ideas but on the practical contribution these pages make to our ability to respond to the life of those years.

To get closer to the period in which I choose to set out, we might look, briefly, at two varieties of intellectual history that have focused on the seventeenth century. The still-dominant form values, in one way or another, continuity. For most historians the seventeenth century is the best way to get from the sixteenth to the eighteenth, but most of the people who lived in it did not have the privilege of that perspective, much less the opportunity to endure the trek. The assumption of continuity necessarily undervalues (or overlooks) what might be distinctive or discontinuous. Instead of dealing with men who make the times in which they live, it treats history as if it were made for Man. It tends to honor figures who echo what is only about to be clearly said, to seek out for quotation words and allusions that sound alike, to establish extensive pedigrees for particular ideas. The assumption of continuity brings with it authority and credibility, since it seems merely logical to believe that ideas connect and develop. This belief is the source of our tradition of historical self-confirmation and an expression of our fear of diversity; it appears so strongly in intellectual histories of the seventeenth century because it is in that century that many historians find our beginnings.

The works of Richard Foster Jones, for instance, present us with a seventeenth century we could live in without sacrificing very much. Jones comforts us with a fairly familiarized past; he finds connected developments throughout, and he glorifies those intellectual revolutions and sanctifies those revolutionaries that mark the line separating those who did not think our way from those who began to. In his book *Ancients and Moderns: A Study of the Rise of the Scientific Movement in Seventeenth-Century England,* Jones writes that his subject is "that thought movement in the seventeenth century to which modern science in England traces its source."[3] That is only partly right: Jones discovers a track that leads to modern science, but his is not a study of a "thought movement" *in* the seventeenth century. He actually writes about an aspect *of* that period in which we recognize ourselves. For Jones the seventeenth century is a battleground on which the Baconians and the humanists fight it out; the Baconians trying to remove "the classical obstruction," the humanists defending themselves by a "blind reliance upon antiquity" (p. 268). His account of Hobbes, for example, results in a credit and debit sheet tabulating Hobbes's contributions and withdrawals from the "cause of modernity" (p. 129), and this "cause" is more important to Jones than any seventeenth-century fact.

In following footprints from the seventeenth century to the

twentieth, Jones comes to an unfortunate washout in the early eighteenth century. Unfortunate, that is, for the eighteenth century, not for Jones's concept:

> Thus science, having to thread its way between a humanistic literature and humanistic universities, found its growth retarded in spite of Newton's great discoveries... but its values were by no means extinguished. They persisted especially in that element of the population which derived from the Puritans. When this class rose to greater power in the eighteenth century, and the dogma of neo-classical criticism began to disintegrate, partly owing to science, romanticism began to take form, and those attitudes which flourished in the third quarter of the seventeenth century—utilitarianism, humanitarianism, democracy, and the like—resumed their onward march. (p. 272)

In improving or correcting Jones other intellectual historians have tried to recover the trail and to pursue the march through the eighteenth century.[4]

Jones's work with seventeenth-century language texts, especially in *The Triumph of the English Language,* is valuable for its range and authority, if not for its restrictive interpretive bias. The texts he surveys generally are overlooked completely by historians of linguistics, whose automatic concern is to seek what might be salvaged in seventeenth- and eighteenth-century work for the beginnings of the "real" science of linguistics in the nineteenth. Thus, Hans Aarsleff, in *The Study of Language in England, 1780–1860,* and Stephen Land, in *From Signs to Propositions: The Concept of Form in Eighteenth-Century Semantic Theory,*[5] whose works deal most interestingly with the linguistic material, select the figures whom they discuss according to their contributions to the prevailing version of linguistic study.

I began by distinguishing between two methods of intellectual history, or, actually, between two epistemologies expressed as ideas of history. The first method, exemplified by Jones or Aarsleff, does not, however, usually reflect on itself as a method, because it does not fully recognize the conceptual implications of its characterizations. It assumes its own logic of procedure; it values its own explanatory comprehensiveness. Nevertheless, the terms and divisions of this method are largely predetermined by the sense of order embedded in the goals of the study. The other form of historical inquiry assumes that history is not deducible from conventional ideas of sequential progress. It is not predisposed to grant that the seventeenth century marks the beginning of modern science because many writers in the eighteenth century saw it that way, or to assume that Bacon, Harvey, Boyle, Locke, and Newton are compatible representatives of seventeenth-century thought simply because they all championed the "advancement" of learning.

This second idea of history assumes that difference is as interesting and important as resemblance. This emphasis on difference does not say that resemblances are not important, only that pursuing them is not the primary method or the goal of historical knowledge. Recently, Thomas S. Kuhn, in *The Structure of Scientific Revolutions,*[6] and Michel Foucault, in *The Archaeology of Knowledge* and a number of other books, have argued for the study of differences in order to understand the nature of history. Their notions of "paradigm" and "episteme"[7] stress discreteness rather than connection, discontinuity rather than development.[8]

Kuhn is principally interested in the "revolutionary" aspects of the history of science; that is, in the "reconstruction of prior theory and the re-evaluation of prior fact."[9] Each of these distinctive reconstructions reinterprets history as well as the objects it studies. Newton's new emphasis on attraction not only altered the interpretation of atoms but also reevaluated all previous attempts to deal with or to avoid the problem. What the first variety of intellectual history does in the face of change is agree with the direction of history,[10] while Kuhn characterizes the process of history as one in which scientific thinking radically reevaluates itself. For Kuhn, the historian understands difference; he sees that a new paradigm changes the whole world. A paradigm is not an idea, but a new language requiring vast changes in both the *characterizations* and the *explanations* of phenomena.[11] A new paradigm brings with it "theory, methods, and standards together."[12] It is a transformation of vision, which cannot be observed in its integrity if historical units are interpreted as the goal of the sequence before or the bridge to the sequence following. The paradigm is a distinctive core of related ideas. Kuhn realizes that we see history the way we do because we look through the lens of our own paradigm. To see anew, we need a methodological transformation (a new "epistemological paradigm") in order to interpret history, not in regard to our need for tradition and continuity, but in regard to the distinctive character of events and changes in thought.

Kuhn likes the analogy between social and epistemological revolutions, but this restricts him to modified versions of the great-experiment or significant-moment theories of the history of science. Although Kuhn stresses the element of process in the shift from one paradigm to another, he still characterizes paradigms by particular names (Newton, Maxwell) or techniques (Leyden jar). Foucault's "epistemes," however, are not discrete world views, not the original contributions of great men, not summarizable collections of assumptions appropriate to a given period, and not "a motionless figure that appeared one day with the mission of effacing all that preceded it."[13] They are, rather, descriptions of how minds work, "the total set of relations that unite, at a given period, the discursive practices that give rise to" epistemology, sciences, and "formalized systems" (p. 191). In *The Order of Things* the classical episteme Foucault discovers is derived from an analysis of language, wealth, and natural history.[14] In *The Archaeology of Knowledge,* he defines an episteme as "not a form of knowledge or type of rationality which, crossing the boundaries of the most varied sciences, manifests the sovereign unity of a subject, a spirit, or a period; it is the totality of relations that can be discovered, for a given period, between the sciences when one analyses them at a level of discursive regularities" (p. 191). These "discursive regularities" are the "set of conditions in which the enunciative function operates, and which guarantees and defines its existence" (p. 144). An episteme, like Kuhn's paradigm, is a language with its terms distinctively described and its explanations peculiarly appropriate. It is not merely a vocabulary; it is a unique form of speech. Foucault's work does not seek the original or the average or the orthodox opinion of an age, for this would be to evaluate from an external position; he discovers, rather, new explanations by describing the objects he studies differently. Instead of looking through texts for particular names or allusions to establish expected development, Foucault defines the particular forms of knowing expressed in discrete historical orders of discourse. He does not ask what we can know about something but what is its basis of intelligibility.

The most important technique of historical study, for Foucault and for Kuhn, is the determination of how and why certain kinds of speech go silent or why some existing experiments are interpreted as never before. Both call for an uncommon subtlety that can discover how, why, and when epistemological barriers are formed. Such barriers are the habits of mind that, independent of "historical necessity" or simple causality or pure genius, select, organize, and represent what can be said or written or done. They are, in Foucault's terms, the "constraints of discourse" that operate through society's institutions, like writing, law, or medicine—all of which are "systems for the subjection of discourse."[15] The conditions determining what gets written, for instance, are evident in the shape of knowledge constituted (and instituted) by the texts—not, that is, simply in announced intentions or contemporary debates or collusions but in what particular forms of knowledge are possible at all (and what other forms are impossible or forbidden).

The historian who seeks a historical episteme or paradigm must not limit himself to one "kind" of writing or even to one discipline or institution, since his notion of kinds or institutions is likely to reflect the distinctive limitations of his own epistemology. For Foucault, especially, it is crucial to move among the various forms of human action, to draw together, for instance, ideas of writing, classifying, and exchanging (to become known by the names *linguistics, biology,* and *economics*). He obliges us to look at the documents and events of the past, not as illustrations of what, by virtue of their dates, authors, titles, or classifications, they are expected to "mean," but as independent, distinctively coherent expressions of a vision of the world different from our own.

This is what I have tried to do for language texts written in England in the seventeenth and eighteenth centuries. I do not read them primarily as contributions to the development of grammatical categories,[16] pronunciation,[17] rhetoric,[18] or universal language,[19] nor as examples of anti-Ciceronianism,[20] scientific method,[21] or utilitarianism.[22] I consider what they propose about language, how they present their ideas and represent their schemes, and what they say to and about one another. I followed them wherever they went—to medieval theories of language and to seventeenth-century mathematics, to Antoine Arnauld and to John Locke, to printing techniques and to debates about pedagogy, to proposals for teaching the deaf and dumb and to logic. I term these activities *linguistics* and the authors *linguists* in order to draw attention, by apparent anachronisms, to the special composition of the institutions I survey,[23] and I add, throughout the book, suggestions for refining and, in some cases, redefining, the languages of literature during these years as well.

The history of the establishment of epistemological barriers not only reconstitutes the distinctive limits of discourse—that is, each episteme's institutions and disciplines—but also prefers a description of particular compositions of thought to questions about source and influence. Seeking precedents and causes expresses a desire for continuity and substitutes documentations of possession or publication for arguments about the ability or readiness to know in a certain way.[24] One could contradict an argument about the *distinctive* importance of a historicist attitude toward language in the late eighteenth century, for instance, by pointing to the historical surveys of languages by, say, Scaliger or Wallis many years before. This resemblance of some surface features fades, however, before the vital differences between early and late ideas of change and the significance of linguistic development. The comparative order of thoughts and practices is, by this method, significant, whereas a resemblance between particular or peripheral ingredients is not. Similarly, references to linguistic relativism—the notion that different people speak and write differently—can be located throughout the seventeenth and eighteenth centuries; but in the earlier period such relativism was seen as a fault and as something to be overcome, whereas later it was valued as a national feature worth preserving, and this should dispose us to see not one idea differently highlighted, but two ideas. I am not looking for lines of influence or lineages of distinguished ideas but for descriptions of different ideas of language appropriate to their distinctive practices.

Whether the different historical characterizations of language practice that I have drawn are convincing depends, I think, on their ability to complement work done on other "disciplines" during comparable periods of time. The consideration of changes in literary languages, which I propose in the text, is just one possibility; if I had had the confidence to remark on other features of social, intellectual, economic, and scientific life during those years, I would have done so. I would argue, in any context, that the critical obligation is to deal with the entire variety of texts written, giving special emphasis to those that manifest the techniques of basic study. Significant epistemological changes do not occur when or because one person strikes a new thought or synthesis but when different ways of knowing become possible and when these new conditions for knowing alter society's institutions and disciplines. Influential innovation may, for convenience, be associated with particular individuals, works, or dates, but the institution of innovation depends on the acceptability of new ways of thinking and on the readiness of people to think in those ways. An excellent, if largely untapped, resource for this information is the school text, and the habits of pedagogy more generally.[25] Georges Snyders, in *La pedagogie en France aux XVII$^e$ et XVIII$^e$ siècles*, effectively locates the principles of pedagogy and its texts between philosophy and the conditions of social life. A history of pedagogy, then, would represent "tout ce qui, de la philosophie, peut, à un moment donné, dans des circonstances données, être proposé à la masse."[26] This history is not, however, a unilinear development of a single system, but a series of distinctively constructed "moments," each of which has "sa physionomie cohérente et sa force propre." Snyders's responsibility, he feels, is to represent these pedagogies as "confrontation, affrontement et synthèse" (p. 3).

It seems to me important, therefore, if we are to get close to the changing shapes of knowing, that we not make the history of ideas a hop, skip, and jump from prominent name to prominent name but look for its texture in the changing forms of basic texts. For this reason, I have concentrated on school texts and projectors' pamphlets in order to record, at the level of changing representations of language, the shifts in how and what a society thinks it can learn.

Basic school texts have a certain privilege in a discussion of language, particularly in the years I am discussing. English was being quite self-consciously discovered as a language, and, with the many-leveled investigation of the processes of human thought, the analysis of words attracted practically everyone's attention in one way or another. A critical description, like mine, of some of the approaches to and uses of language, must involve philosophy and pedagogy, linguistics and litera-ture, for these are all aspects of the same concerns. In an impressive and important work by Jean-Claude Chevalier, *Histoire de la syntaxe,* the author provides a critical survey of language texts that is simultaneously a contribution to the histories of grammar, pedagogy, and epistemology. Although he gives detailed attention to language texts and essays, "le coeur est une étude d'epistémologie historique . . . on a cherché à savoir comment se formait une notion, ici la notion de complément, et comment et pourquoi une discipline nouvelle s'établissait, ici la Syntaxe."[27] Although Chevalier trusts to the genius theory of epistemo-logical change, he nonetheless carefully studies the "mutations nécessaires de la pensée, de la pédagogie, des hommes" (p. 332), which reveal how new approaches and techniques come, in a complex and discontinuous way, to be accepted. He does not follow the track of time but the weave of ideas about grammar, and the distinct textures he discovers show us what could be thought at different times.

Chevalier, however, disagrees with Snyders and Foucault about the epistemological units and about specific characterizations.[28] My discriminations among forms of linguistic knowledge interrupt Foucault's "classical episteme" and differ from Chevalier's. These differences prove, happily, that shared intentions, or methodologies, do not identical performances make. The important point is that we are describing different things and, unlike historians who seem to select an explanation first, we comply with the shapes assumed by the texts we have embraced. Such compliance derives, not from an exhaustive survey or certified statistical charts, but from an analytic density that gets to what Foucault calls the archaeological level. Here we study not so much what was said but what assumptions made knowledge of a particular shape possible.

This level of analysis requires such close study of a variety of texts that I have limited myself, with few exceptions, to England. The epistemological barriers I see erected in language texts and, as I suggest, in literary languages, are not exclusively English phenomena. They seem to be evident, with some different distributions and displays, in France, as Chevalier has shown so fully and so well. Although it was often tempting to quote from Leibniz, du Marsais, Condillac, or Herder, I did not, for to do so would have been only to claim support, in too casual (and too derivative) a manner, for my description of English texts. I could not write at the same level of analysis or understanding about developments in France, Italy, or Germany, so I decided to make a more limited contribution, which would at least suggest the merits of the methodological integrity I have described.

My concentration on English texts (with the prominent exception of the widely distributed and translated work of Port-Royal) may account, in part, for some of the differences between my account of epistemological shifts and Foucault's. Then, too, the dimensions of his study are much more extensive, historically and institutionally, than mine. Foucault composes an ingenious triptych (pre-Classical, Classical, and modern epistemes), which neatly folds in on itself (in at least a couple of ways) and which also shines forth brilliantly. Each section, as befits the clever unity of the whole, is drawn with the others in mind. As a result, the differences I highlight in what corresponds to his central panel, the Classical (from the seventeenth to the early nineteenth centuries), he covers with one dominant shadow cast by discourse throughout these years. For Foucault—bold enough to cite texts wherever he finds them—Hobbes, Locke, Hume, James Harris, and Adam Smith (like Arnauld, Beauzée, Condillac, and Turgot) all share the same essential mental habits. My work, on the other hand, locates the significantly different assumptions and techniques that operate for them and their contemporaries. Our differences, as those between Chevalier and Snyders (or Foucault), are not of methodology but of content; they reside not in the principles of assembly but in the size and provenance of the frames.

Foucault's archaelogical history of words and things is determined, I think, by his sense of the modern. He intends, finally, to dis-illusion the pride we take in our inventions, especially the "new" institutions of critical discourse. He tries to extend the modern beyond the innovators whom we glorify (or vilify), to demystify the homage we pay to the topmost layers of modern interpretation—psychoanalysis, structuralism, Marxism, even demystification itself. He looks at what he calls the modern episteme not as something found, suddenly, by the eruption of the unconscious or the savage mind or by the upheaval that left an abyss, but as inherent, epistemologically and archaeologically, in earlier ideas of masturbation, monsters, medicine, and primitive cries. For his purposes, what is different from this extended idea of the modern is an equally extensive and massive idea of the Classical. What he sees coming before the frame in which he includes himself is a panel congruent with it. Perhaps because my interests are different, my picture seems different, too. I admire but do not presume to Foucault's immense achievement; I look at the practice of language in one of his epistemes not determined to find out what modern philosophy is or even who we are, but to describe the shapes knowledge took in those years and to suggest some relationships between these and the forms of literary language at the same time.

Time, like texts, is open to interpretation; indeed, it is only what interpreters make of it. I have tried to present the texture of language texts intimately enough to come close to how differently people thought about and practiced language in England in the years 1640–1785. I have chosen this frame and this composition because I intend to study the compatible shifts in literary language in terms of the relationship between the intentions of stylistic features and the shapes of reading.

In the following chapters, I summarize what I found in a variety of texts that, at first, self-consciously determined their own groupings. They portioned themselves not so much by expressions of collective agreement or enterprise (in fact, the groups more often contain some ostensibly and vocally antagonistic types) as by their basic assumptions and techniques of language study. In this sense my organization follows the historical units suggested by the linguists themselves. I begin with the first burst of English linguistic activity that takes the vernacular seriously as an academic and intellectual subject; I stop when writers have accepted the basic assumptions responsible for what is normally taken as the beginnings of linguistic science in the late eighteenth century. Chapter 1 opens with the sense of beginning shared by mid-seventeenth-century linguists and closes when their early assumptions about the nature of language are uncomfortably rejected and a new idea of language forms. Chapter 2 opens with early eighteenth-century linguists who share a new paradigm and reevaluate the practice of their predecessors in their new image, and it closes when another generation of linguists, equally self-conscious about the history of the study of language, traces its origins to those early eighteenth-century linguists. And Chapter 3 begins with a variety of mid-eighteenth-century attempts to provide either a philosophy of language or practical language texts. This distinction between linguistic functions hardens into division of linguistic kinds, and the chapter closes when the philosophers of language and the grammarians have little to say to one another.

My subject, however, is not this sequence in any developmental sense, but the discrete modes of linguistic discourse I found. Seventeenth-century linguists self-consciously discovered language not only as an object of scientific study but also as an instrument of knowledge. For everyone concerned with language in the middle of the seventeenth century, it seemed possible to organize, recover, or invent a language that represented the order of things in the world. The varieties of their interests led to visual grammars, shorthand systems, theories of signs, and universal languages. In all these efforts, the goal was not simply to analyze the elements of language but to show how these reflect the structure of nature itself.

In the last quarter of the seventeenth century, there were noticeable shifts in attitudes toward language. The rage for universal languages expended itself, interest in detailed interpretations of the physical elements of language—its letters and sounds—declined, and attention shifted from simply enumerating every part of language and nature to considering the ways of arranging the enumerated items. By the beginning of the eighteenth century, the idea of language study had shifted from the taxonomic representation of words and things to the establishment of the relationship between speech and thought. Seventeenth-century linguists sought to establish an isomorphic relationship between language and nature; in the early eighteenth century, linguists assumed that language reflects the structure of the mind.

The new view of language in the early eighteenth century constitutes a major epistemological change. If it has not been previously noticed, the reason may be that our habits of inquiry have prevented us from seeing it.[29] But it is clearly there, and, I think, it is important. Language texts of the early eighteenth century contain a new sense of history, a new set of "predecessors," a new idea of language, and new methods for studying it.

The new linguistic paradigm differed from the practice and principles of language study in the seventeenth century as Newton or Locke differed from Bacon. As Kuhn says, the "new Science" that preceded Newton rejected Aristotelian explanations in terms of essences and analyzed sensory appearances "in terms of the size, shape, position, and motion of the elementary corpuscles of base matter."[30] Newton's crucial addition to this mechanico-corpuscular analysis was the notion of "attraction." This addition of laws of relation to the concepts of atom and void signifies a paradigmatic change in man's apprehension of the world. Instead of characterizing things by the qualities of particles, Newton defined them in terms of their attractions and repulsions.[31] Locke's revolutionary analysis of human understanding depended on a strikingly similar insight. Locke, whose first responsibility was to retrieve words from their association with things, not only redefined them in terms of ideas but added to what might have been a mechanico-corpuscular theory of ideas the notion of relations between ideas (that is, between words). Locke did not simply reidentify words as ideas; he proposed a grammar of thought expressed in the logic of linguistic functions.[32]

Newton and Locke have conventionally been read, particularly by literary historians practicing intellectual history, as men who processed, packaged, and delivered the seventeenth century to the eighteenth. But this is true only if we want to see our own reflections in history, or want to imagine Newton and Locke as the children who become our maturity. This notion is contestable if we understand that history did not always have us in mind. I hope the chapters that follow demonstrate the difference between these two ideas of history.

The language texts I consider reinforce, and characterize in ways accessible to literary critics, the crucial change in consciousness that was taking place during the last years of the seventeenth century. This new idea of language, with its emphasis on language as thought—on words functioning syntactically and ideas operating logically—became so familiar in the eighteenth century that an equally important, though quite different, shift occurred toward the end of that century. The first epistemological change happened when one set of philosophical grounds for language replaced another; the second change resulted from the separation of philosophical grounds from the practical study of language. The consequence was a language that had become an object again—not an object that was structurally isomorphic to the order of things (the seventeenth-century situation), but a collection of native habits that could be compiled or used as evidence of forces like history, geography, and the progress of human societies, or could be studied rhetorically as effective and affective speech.

My story ends when our received histories of linguistics only begin taking language texts seriously. The result of these conventional histories has been a version of the past with too little intellectual activity and too much simplicity for persons to bear. I have tried to transform what has seemed to many a barren landscape into a strongly featured and well-inhabited territory.

*Sensible Words*

# CHAPTER 1

# Language and the Grammar of Things, 1640-1700

## Cave Beck and the Principles of Seventeenth-Century Linguistic Practice

Cave Beck's *The Universal Character* (1657) is not the most elaborate or the cleverest, and it is certainly not the best known, example of linguistic ingenuity in a century often cited for its fascination with language. It has been worth only a footnote to Bacon's linguistic proposals, Sprat's stylistic injunctions, Locke's warning about words, Dryden's redefinition of literary language, or Wilkins's grand universal language. Beck, son of a baker and, at the time of the publication of *The Universal Character,* master of the Free Grammar School in Ipswich, was apparently unattached to the groups that collected and communicated in the mid-seventeenth century for the purpose of reforming language.[1] Yet Beck's work is as representative as anyone's of the linguistic activity of the period, for the remarkable characteristic of all these linguistic works is that they share assumptions about the nature and practice of language.

Even Beck's "insignificance" testifies to the depth and extent of these assumptions.

The men in those learned groups gathered principally around Samuel Hartlib and John Wilkins in the years from 1630 to 1660 and reassembled, after the Restoration, to form the Royal Society.[2] Throughout those years, the common topics include not only proposals for altering the teaching of Latin, introducing instruction in English, inventing new languages, and correcting orthography, but also ideas for fixing pronunciation and assembling common words, phrases, technical words, proverbs, idioms, and archaic words. In addition, projectors tried developing the quickest shorthand, teaching the deaf and dumb, discovering the original language, promoting universal speech, organizing language mathematically, equipping the language for science, discovering the relationship between words and things. They also looked forward to providing English merchants with the advantage of a universal grammar, spreading the word of God, adapting education to language learning, communicating secretly or at a distance, interpreting Chinese characters and Egyptian hieroglyphics, and at last, repairing Babel. Remarkably, Beck's separation from the centers of projected achievement had no apparent effect on his intentions or his ambitiousness.

The subtitle of his book advertises Beck's range and presumption: *By Which All the Nations in the World May Understand One Another's Conceptions, Reading out of One Common Writing Their Own Mother Tongues. An Invention of General Use.* Some of Beck's friends, writing commendatory poems prefaced to his text, specify some of the claims of *The Universal Character.* One of them, Joseph Waite, leads us to expect:

> Th' Index of Speech, the dumb Interpreter;
> The Iliads in a Nut-shell; Tongues in Brief;
> *Babel* revers'd; The traveller's Relief;
> Ferry of Nations Commerce....
> . . . . . . . . . . . . . . . . . . . .
>
> The Chart of Dialects, right Cosmo-graphie.
> The Heavenly Orbs and we commune just so,
> We all their matters by Learn'd Figures know.
> Now see another Deluge come, and then
> The world, as was of old, new fac'd agen;
> Languages swallow'd up, the Ark a flote,
> Carrying within't something of every note.[3]

Classical scholars, users of shorthand, merchants, tourists, astronomers, teachers, preachers, the deaf and dumb, and everyone in God's creation were to profit from Beck's linguistic "Logarithmes . . . That teach by Figures to Uncypher minds, / And make our hands officious to help out, / Of tongues confusion, made at Babel's rout" (A5$^r$). Beck and his friends in Ipswich imagined that they might well be at the new center of the world, for they believed that all man needed to make creation right again was a universal language.[4] Renaming, in fact, could remake the world in the image of God's first activity.

Beck himself acknowledges four learned predecessors: Ricci, Bacon, Wilkins, and Comenius. Matthew Ricci, author of *De Christiana expeditione apud Sinas* (1615), introduced to Western Europe the first substantial discussion of Chinese writing and set off a century-long attempt to imitate what Ricci thought were ideographs in the invention of universal languages.[5] Bacon, often cited by seventeenth-century linguists, had already suggested that a real character, that is, one that directly and really expresses things, would be like Chinese characters.[6] When, in his *Essay towards a Real Character, And a Philosophical Language* (1668), John Wilkins summarized previous attempts at a "Real Universal Character, that should not signifie words, but things and notions," he draws his authority chiefly from "the Learned Verulam."[7] But the Wilkins Beck praises in 1657 is, principally, the author of *Mercury; or, The Secret and Swift Messenger* (1641), a book that collects the various means of communication, including not only ideographs and hieroglyphics but also musical notes, numerals, birds, shorthand, and bullets. In assembling these methods Wilkins encourages work on a system of similarly fixed, physical, and particular lexical symbols, which, though arbitrary, correspond to the order of things in the world. Beck's last source is Comenius, the Polish educator whose international travels promoting a visible language had the dominant influence on later seventeenth-century grammarians.[8]

In his intentions, scope, and sources, Beck associates his work with the great surge of contemporary linguistic activity. Although the particular system he recommends is not imitated and although Wilkins and George Dalgarno, with Wilkins a more prominent universalizing linguist, criticized his work,[9] Beck's *Universal Character* identifies those assumptions about the nature of language that prevail through most of the century. Only with the growing impact of ideas associated with the "messieurs du Port-Royal," especially with their influence on Wilkins and Locke, does the philosophy of language in England undergo a quiet, but profound, change. This additional bloodless revolution of the late seventeenth century was not completely registered in basic language texts until the early eighteenth century, and its effects will be the subject of the next chapter.

Beck, like his contemporaries, bases the study of language on four principles. The first is that words must be rationally organized. This is a remarkable point of departure. Of course it was obvious that people in different languages had been talking and writing in their own ways for a long time by 1657, and there was a popular and nationally approved grammar of a fairly common language, Latin.[10] However, as Bacon had argued while lamenting the "idols of the tribe," men's speech suffered from raging confusion, ambiguity, irregularity, and superfluity. For Beck, these faults prevented men from using English to encourage, simultaneously, commerce, science, and true religion. Latin was barely better, its grammar being hopelessly rule-bound and complex, making the language too time consuming to acquire. The only solution, says Beck, while acknowledging Ricci, Bacon, Wilkins, and Comenius, is a language everyone will understand by sight. It is as if the world were beginning again, and Beck, Adamlike, could reassign symbols to everything in existence. At this point Beck deliberately refrains from recommending a new set of symbols comparable to Egyptian hieroglyphics or Chinese ideographs, because such a solution would be too difficult to put into practice. Instead, he chooses to resignify existing words by an available, though arbitrary, universal sequence: Arabic numerals. This restraint earned Beck the disapproval of Wilkins and Dalgarno, whose systems admitted that things were more complex than numbers. But the difference between these men and Beck is a matter of sophistication and boldness, not one of assumptions about the relationship between signifiers and things.[11] They all agree that the first step to universal understanding is the systematic representation of words and their new symbols.

Beck's second principle is the importance of sequence in the system. Although other linguists make much more of the significance of order, Beck chooses Arabic numerals because of their universality and sequentiality. Most of The Universal Character consists of two parallel dictionaries, one alphabetical and the other numerical. Like all other mid-seventeenth-century language schemes, Beck's is basically lexical.

What is being organized are the items ("things or notions") in the world, and the process of systematization begins by identifying the parts. Beck's system is so simple because his symbols only count, whereas the more sophisticated identifying markers used by Dalgarno and Wilkins classify as they symbolize.[12]

The lexical-numerical system Beck projects is based on a third assumption common to seventeenth-century linguistic work: the most important parts of any system are its basic elements, the characters, marks, or numbers. This is evident simply in the instructions for using Beck's scheme, which require one to learn a language, not by rules and not by chance, but by the numbers and by the alphabet. Other linguists make the distinctive features of their systems "real" as well as organizational, but the impact on how one learns and uses language is the same. The importance of basic elements is apparent, too, in the grammar Beck includes in his book. Each word has a number, to which one can add vowels before to identify case, particular consonants after to indicate time, and other consonants before to mark inflections of the verb or kind of noun. One who is hardy is qp317, one who is hardier is qqp317, and then comes qqqp317. And Beck, mindful of his training and his responsibility to his students, illustrates his method by advising his readers: "leb2314 p2477 and pf2477" (honor thy father and mother). The basic unit of speech for Beck and the others is the word; grammatical functions are added on as accessories to lexical markers.

Beck's book represents a fourth principle of seventeenth-century linguistics, which is that language makes visible sense. Again, Beck's character system is not as bold as those of his contemporaries, who, from Comenius to Wilkins, try a number of schemes to get the nature of things into the shapes of their symbols. Beck trusts that his work will be visibly sensible; the dominance of numbers, the consistent marks for case, comparison, and other grammatical variations, and the orderliness of his tables are intended, clearly and distinctly, to represent words making sense.[13]

Even though I have claimed that Cave Beck is a representative seventeenth-century English linguist, he remains one of the least distinguished of the many men who made the study of language a principal concern. Beck rose to be rector of St. Margaret's in Ipswich and stayed there until his death in 1706. It is his lack of distinction, however, that makes his one published work so interesting. Perhaps Joseph Waite and Beck's other Ipswich friends, Nathaniel Smart and

Ben Gifford, were right: if Babel's curse were ready for redemption, Cave might be able to name the time. If a language could be designed to signify systematically every existing thing, and if the structure of that language were built sequentially and visibly from its elements, then man would know the nature of things by learning to speak and write.[14] To this project, Cave Beck contributes as significantly as anyone, and in the rest of this chapter, I will discuss the versions and revisions of his theme and suggest some connections between linguistic and literary practices.

## The Elements of Words and Things

One reason I began with Cave Beck rather than one of his contemporaries whose work (or reputation) seems more distinguished is that an impressive feature of seventeenth-century linguistics, in addition to its quantity, is the comparative obscurity of its practitioners. Although everyone (it seems) makes a contribution, the ones who have the greatest impact are schoolmasters.[15] Often, these are provincial scholars who boldly offer the idea of a lifetime or compile the lessons of a life's work. They agree that their language texts touch on the most critical issues, on God's word, man's speech, and the book of nature. In their texts they try to represent characters and sounds as the clear and distinct sources of meaning and to arrange words to reveal the structure of reality. Nor were those the only goals; if the physical elements of words and their orderly arrangement allow us to understand what the world is and how we know it, then, writes Comenius in his most popular schoolbook (*Orbis Sensualium Pictus*), the school "would indeed become a School of things obvious to the senses, and an Entrance to the School intellectual."[16] Charles Hoole, translator of the *Orbis,* writing from his Free School in Lothbury, closes his own preface with a prayer thanking God for "this gift of Teaching," which makes students proceed "as Nature itself doth, in an orderly way" (A7[r]), thus enabling them to serve church and commonwealth.[17]

The starting point for Comenius and Hoole, as for Beck, is the ordering of the basic elements—of letters, sounds, and pictures—in cooperation with children's senses. This was not the starting point in schools relying on Lily's nationally approved grammar. In these, the elements and tools of language were assumed to exist before actual schooling began, whereas in the reformed school, learning the elements was the necessary and natural origin of knowledge.[18] John Bird, in

*Grounds of Grammar* (1639), complains that "our old Grammar"—that is, Lily's—omitted the "Elementary Rudiment"—the letters, syllables, and words that must be learned prior to rules.[19] Rigorous opposition to Lily's rule-based grammar actually began with Joseph Webbe's *An Appeale to Truth, in the Controversie between Art and Use* (1622), but Webbe's elaborate scheme for learning Latin and English phrases collapsed under his directions for using it.[20] The lasting and persistent challenge to Lily came from linguists who, while also claiming increased efficiency for their systems, had a sure sense of the philosophical premises of their recommendations. Hezekiah Woodward, schoolmaster and Independent activist, is approvingly cited by Hoole and is one of the first Englishmen to spread the word of Comenius. In *Light to Grammar and All other Arts and Sciences. With a Gate to Sciences opened by a Natural Key* (1641), he instructs teachers who want learning to be "quicker and surer" to "make our words as legible to Children as Pictures are."[21] His premise is clear: "if the eye hath not seen that we are speaking of, it can make no report of it to the minde."[22] If words are to become the key to knowledge, then their shape and their acquisition must conform to what exists.

Whether by rearranging or reidentifying existing languages or by inventing new ones, the linguists seemed, even to themselves, to be rediscovering the rational principles of speech. Their determination to start the study and practice of language over again was aided by the absence of the study of English as an analyzed, organized language in the schools. The striking quality of these English grammars, and of the increasing number of Latin grammars in English, is that they treat English as if it were a foreign language, as if grammarians were organizing and clarifying a "new" language.[23] Every element of language is explained —the shapes of letters, the number and kinds of sounds, the formation of the plural, the use of interjections. In effect, the grammarians discover English as a language and go to work on its materials, origins, forms, and functions. Disagreements among the grammarians themselves have to do principally with systems of the parts of speech; but examples of their inconsistency, incompleteness, instability, and diversity indicate a lively struggle with the structure of language or, more precisely, with the relationship between reality and language.[24] The relationship between language and reality, the grammarians agree, must be sought in the physical parts of writing and speech—letters and sounds. Speech and knowledge emerge from what we see or can visualize.

Whether seventeenth-century English grammars are explicitly organized according to the materials of language—letters, syllables, words, and sentences—or according to its processes—orthography, pronunciation, etymology, syntax, and prosody—virtually all of them give initial and extensive attention to the materials, specifically to the shapes and sounds of letters and to the images of words.[25] Joseph Aickin, whose *English Grammar* (1693) comes well after the organized push for educational reform in the 1640s, still recommends Comenius's *Orbis,* for "such a work, wherein the pictures of all creatures, beasts, fishes, fowls, trades and occupations, and whatsoever is visible to the eye [are] presented to the senses" shows the natural way to learn to read.[26] For Aickin, since the senses convey "all things to our understanding, we ought to take a care to give the sense a true representation of all objects"—and those representations are words. Aickin thinks of the *Orbis* as a companion volume to his own text, which provides orthography and orthoepy (letters, sounds, and syllables), the parts of grammar Hoole admitted were lacking in the *Orbis.* Most of Aickin's work consists of representations and categorizations of English letters and sounds. His grammar provides physical descriptions of sounds, a symbolical alphabet ("What's like the half-moon? ☾ c C c see"), riddles, pictures, phonetic description, and lengthy tables of syllables. The combination of these techniques for visually displaying the organization of sounds and letters—the lists, columns, tables, diagrams, and illustrations—is a distinctive characteristic of seventeenth-century linguistic texts and complements Comenius's reliance on pictures.[27]

If words represent reality to our understanding, then, like existing things, they must consist of assembled elements. Reducing language to physical properties visually organized on the page justifies operating on words as objects. If the written and spoken language can be touched, tabulated, and visualized, then it can be secured, improved, perfected, and rationally taught. For Aickin, meaning is evident in language, and the distinctive features of linguistics are all the evidence needed to prove any proposition, assuming words are written "with proper and fit letters." Aickin's grammar, typical of grammars of the time, moves easily between its modest function as "An English Grammar for the English School" (Aickin himself was "Schoolmaster in Fisher-street, near Red Lion Square") and the philosophy of language and theory of language learning on which it was based.

Conceiving the minimal components of language to be the vocalization and visualization of letters is a habit not only of English grammars of the period but also of Latin grammars in English. Bird, in *Grounds for Grammar,* recognizes the primary importance of the rudiments of any language. Since a word is "a perfect voice or sound, made of one or more syllables" (p. 8), then English and Latin, having different sounds, must be rudimentally different. For an Englishman to learn Latin, he must know the literal systems of both languages equally well. Bird's responsibility, as he saw it, is to first supply a complete system of English letters. By starting with letters, Bird, like his contemporary grammarians, assumes that words consist of parts, that words are analogous to matter, and that, as with other objects, relationships between the parts can be sensed and visually represented.

In an anonymous grammar of 1688, *The Compendious School-Master,* the author begins with orthography, as is common, but dwells on it to an unusual and revealing degree. He delivers his "Words not by Tale, but by Weight, reducing them in due Place and Order into . . . regular Squadrons, and proper Divisions."[28] His ideas of order are completely letter-based. After carefully drawing and listing the letters, he divides his own prose into syllables "be-cause long Words are ea-si-ly read, when right-ly di-vi-ded" (p. 57). He adds "Pithy Proverbial Sayings" in what is, for him, a moral order: that is, "Alphabetically digested" (p. 78).[29] This comprehensive pedagogue, like his successor, Walter Shandy, emphasizes the importance of proper Christian names, that children "might be stirred up to ve-ri-fie the va-ri-ous sig-ni-fi-ca-tions of their Names" (p. 61). Such Shandean nonsense points precisely to what is implied by grammars that develop language from letters: the physical materials of language are the elements out of which meanings are made.[30]

These materials are tools, like any others, distinctively used to signify. Wilkins, in *Mercury* (1641), equates communicating by means of birds, bullets, and bells and suggests these systems as models for a universal language. Edward Somerset, in *A Century of the Names and Scantlings of Such Inventions as at present I can call to mind to have tried and perfected* (1663), provides a still more impressive catalog of signifying devices. He lists what and how to do things with signs, including a "cypher and character so contrived, that one line, without returns and circumflexes, stands for each and every of the 24 letters,"[31] "seals contrived to tell whatever owners want to know," and "systems for holding discourse without noise or notice even at night." He also offers a method for writing with needle and thread, knotted silk string, and fringes of a glove, as well as jangling bells, smells, tastes, touches, and holes in a sieve. Whether the correspondence be between original, essential signs and things or, as here, between arbitrary symbols and things, it is basically an item-by-item relationship between a linguistic (or symbolic) and a natural taxonomy.[32]

## Seeing Speech

Interest in pronunciation, which is usually closely associated in seventeenth-century grammars with orthography, points to a similar collection of assumptions about languages: English must be studied as if for the first time; the steps of any study begin with the basic parts of which any language is constituted; whatever is distinctive about English will appear in the classification of these constituent parts; and meaning derives from the basic parts of language. The study of pronunciation takes an important turn in the seventeenth century—toward phonetic specificity and visual descriptions; but unlike the phonetic spelling reformers of the late-sixteenth century, the new linguists seek in the physical nature of sound a natural or rational connection between speech and reality. Early in the century, in Robert Robinson's *Art of Pronunciation* (1617), the elements and parts of the voice are discussed in physical terms, every simple sound being given a letter. Robinson's work, however, is a more elaborate version of the phonetic alphabets of Thomas Smith and John Hart in the previous century.[33]

It is with John Wallis's *Grammatica Linguae Anglicanae* (1653) that the physical elements of speech are suggested as the basis of a complete linguistic description of existence. The first third of the *Grammatica* consists of a treatise subsequently published independently, *De Loquela,* and a summary of this opens the second section which deals with English grammar. The *Tractatus de Loquela* systematically describes the articulation of sounds and even provides a modest tabulated synopsis; but, more importantly, Wallis argues throughout the *Grammatica* that the distinctive vocal features of English sounds are the bases of letters from which one can construct words, sentences, and syntax. In sounds, there is meaning: not only are there sounds signifying qualities—such as diminution, and power—but, he suggests, there is a rough correspondence between sounds and meaning ('st' suggests strength or force; 'sp',[1] dissipation or expansion, and so on).

In *Essay towards a Real Character,* Wilkins expands Wallis's work by adding to it discussions of the pronunciation of Hebrew, Latin, and Greek. This sort of comparative study led him, he says, to the "essence of Letters," which consists "in their *Power* or proper sound, which may be naturally fixed and stated, from the manner of forming them by the instruments of speech; and either is, or should be the same in all Languages" (p. 357). Wilkins illustrates these essences both with a table giving "a rational account of all the simple sounds that are, or can be framed by the mouths of men" and with pictures of the "instruments of speech" forming these possible sounds along with the characters appropriate to them (fig. 1). Somewhat earlier Owen Price, in *The Vocal Organ* (1665), had also provided a scheme visualizing the physiology of sounds. Both schemes propose an articulatory phonetics based on an ordered, elemented, and evident arrangement of the speech organs.

These efforts to organize, visualize, and interpret basic sounds attempt to make language reflect the rudimentary composition and order of nature. Elisha Coles, in *The Compleat English Schoolmaster* (1674), insists that the agreement between sounds and letters is preliminary to more elaborate relationships between words and images and between one language and another.[34] The term he is fondest of is *syncrisis,* a principle "as Ancient as Nature itself,"[35] for it grounds what we are to learn against what we already know. Syncrisis justifies Coles's combination grammar-emblem book: *Nolens Volens; or, You Shall make Latin Whether you will or no ... Together with The Youth's Visible Bible: Being an Alphabetical Collection ... of such General Heads as were judg'd most capable of Hieroglyphicks* (1675). The related terms in that title—letters, grammar, pictures, truth—capture the integrated linguistic inquiry I am describing.

A more sensible example of the agreement between sound and sense is Christopher Cooper's *The English Teacher* (1687). Cooper is another provincial schoolmaster, "Master of the Grammar School of Bishop-Stortford in Hartfordshire," who associates his work with both a century-long tradition of attempts to bring English "to Rule"[36] and more recent efforts to understand "the Philosophy of Sounds ... the Nature of Characters" by "a clear, distinct, and particular explication of the Fundamentals, which must be as Rules" (A3$^v$). A more elaborate tabulation of sounds than appears in Wallis places letters "according to their Nature: 1. In respect of the Organs by which they are framed. 2. Of their sound.... 3. The several degrees of Apertion or closure." Cooper uses

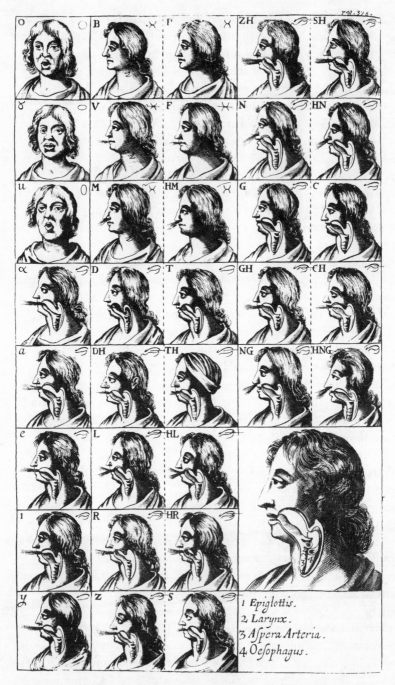

Figure 1. John Wilkins, *Essay towards a Real Character, And a Philosophical Language* (1668), p. 378. Reproduced by permission of the Bancroft Library, University of California, Berkeley.

this descriptive "ground-work of reading and writing . . . according to the true power of the letters" (p. 29) to reduce language to rule; visually, to lists of syllables—of beginning and ending consonants, of vowels, of alphabetized words illustrating the sounds of each letter. Alphabetizing is such an independently important principle that, in spite of Cooper's detailed descriptions of physical sounds, he alphabetizes words in which the "w" is silent (pp. 73–74). *The English Teacher* concludes with alphabetized lists of words having (1) the same pronunciation but different significations; (2) different sounds but the same spelling; (3) the same sounds but different spellings, and so on. All this—the sections on phonology and phonetics—precedes a grammar that Cooper leaves untranslated from his *Grammatica Linguae Anglicanae* of 1685.[37] His sense of priorities, of making as prerequisite to using, matches the working principles of seventeenth-century pedagogy: to make the method of teaching, the sequence of learning, and the structure of language compatible with the order of things.[38]

Cooper lays the groundwork: he reduces learning and language to the rule of a philosophy of sounds; he finds the possibilities of language in the "powers" of characters; he trusts that the stages of linguistic inquiry correlate with the process of learning; and he argues that all languages share the same principles. All these qualities show how closely aligned Cooper's work is with the various grammars, rhetorics, universal language theories, spelling and pronunciation guides, word lists, and educational tracts of the period.

### Shorthand and Signing

Common to all this linguistic activity is an assurance that language, spoken and written, can be visually represented. Sounds, letters, and meaning are, to these linguists, parallel systems of different elements of language. Therefore, we not only see the repeated use of tables, lists, and illustrations, but we find a burgeoning interest in shorthand and sign-language systems and in the origin and nature of characters. Proponents of shorthand systems in the seventeenth century exhibit the same diversity and rivalry evident in the grammatical battles. John Farthing, in 1654, met the challenge with *Short-Writing Shortened;* Elisha Coles competed with *The Newest, Plainest, and Best Short-hand* (in 1674); and George Ridpath's contribution was *Shorthand yet shorter*

(1687). The competitiveness is amusing, but it also indicates an intensity of commitment that can best be accounted for by the involvement of these shorthand systems with the liveliest and richest linguistic issues of the period. As early as Timothy Bright's *Characterie* in 1588, we find a lengthy table of English words reduced in number and to order by a "Table of characterie" based on the assumption that Chinese characters were ideographs.[39] In John Willis's oft-reprinted *Art of Stenographie*,[40] we find the quite explicit intention to connect the marks of the shorthand system and a theory of signification. During the century shorthand systems grew in number and assertiveness.[41] Some, like Willis's, were explicitly phonetic, and others relied on different rational systems; but all agreed that ideas can be visually represented, contained in the contours of lines on a page or evoked by the distribution of agreed-upon marks. Willis's figures "hath some agreement with the Signification of the word" (B4[v]), and the philosophical context of his abbreviated characters is explicitly stated in *The Art of Memory* (1621): since an idea is "a visible representation, bestowed by the Imagination in one of the places of a Repositorie, by the remembrance whereof we call to mind that which was thereby signified,"[42] then a shorthand, like any other character system, is an example of the transformation of propositions into pictures.[43]

Although most of the shorthand systems of the century are not similarly tied to sophisticated tracts, they all assume responsibility for convincing the world to accept a shorter, easier, plainer, and more precise system of representing meaning. They all give significant attention to the layout of their systems on the printed page. Samuel Botley, for instance, claims two marketable virtues for his handy little system, *Maximo in Minimo* (1674). First, his "Simbolicall Characters teach the art of Memory more exact than the Egyptian Hyerogliphicks."[44] They are designed to represent visually an ostensible view of the world (see fig. 2). Second, his system permits users to generate sentences by placing designated letters "about the chiefe substantive" (C2[r]). Botley asserts no more than he thinks he clearly understands: we name what we know, and sentences are functions of names.

Theophilus Metcalfe, in *Short Writing* (1645), claims only that no other shorthand "is grasped within so small a girdle, and so succinctly trussed up."[45] Francis Lodwick, in *A Common Writing* (1646), claims invention of "a kind of hieroglyphical representation of words"[46] (fig. 3). What these men share is confidence in the visual representability of

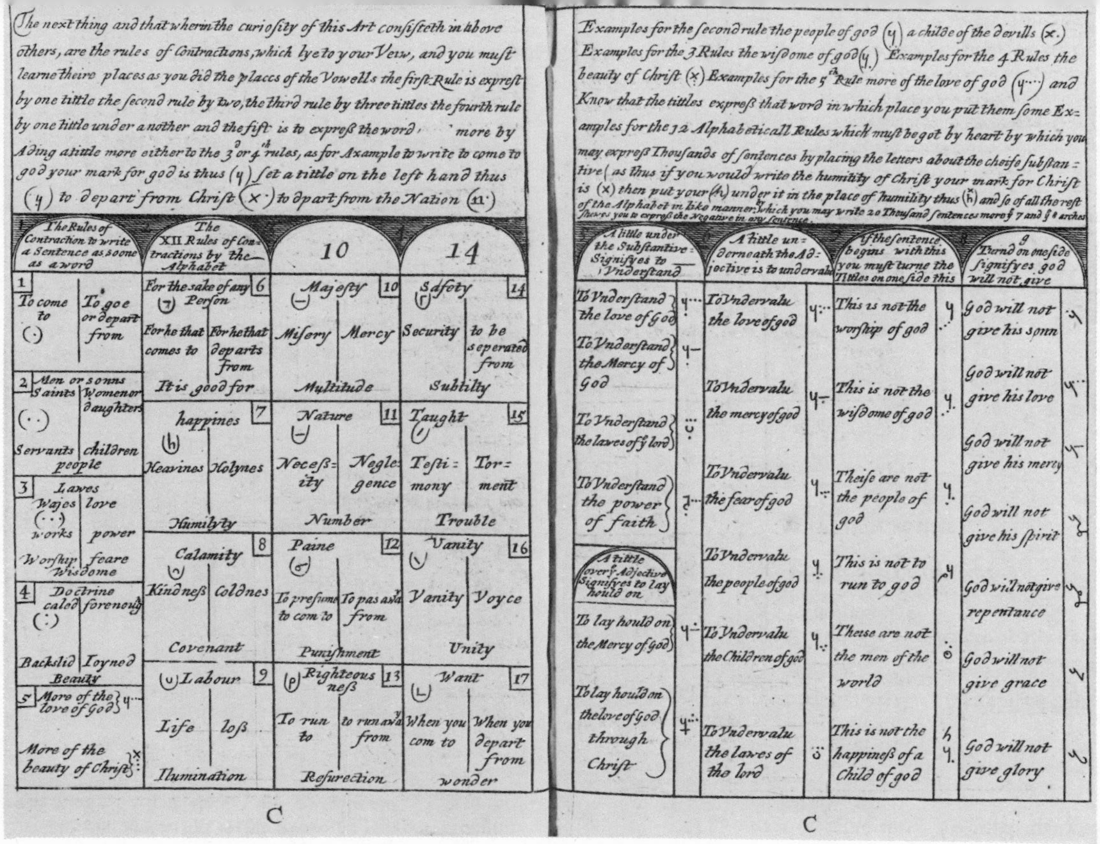

Figure 2. Samuel Botley, *Maximo in Minimo* (1674), B4ᵛ–C2ʳ. Reproduced by permission of the Bancroft Library, University of California, Berkeley.

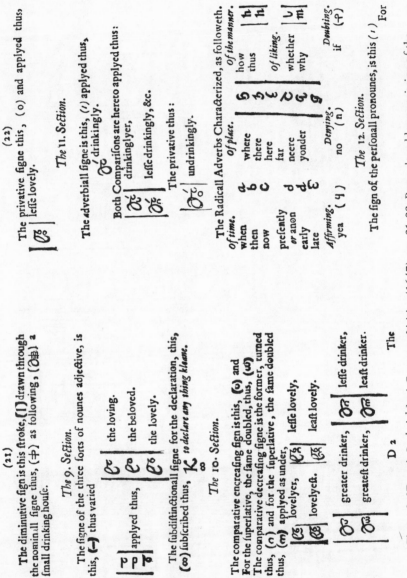

Figure 3. [Francis Lodwick], *A Common Writing* (1647), pp. 21–22. Reproduced by permission of the Huntington Library, San Marino, California.

meaning. Lodwick's notion that language is "the expression or outward presentation of the mind" (A2$^r$) appears not only in the form of a phonetic shorthand but also in his claims for a philosophical language based on "radical Characters" (A2$^v$) and a "universal Primer."[47] Such a combination of linguistic interests recurs in the careers of several writers (Wilkins and William Petty, among others).

The makers of these shorthand systems seek physical, visual, and precise representation of the forms and meanings of language; in their intentions and assumptions they are quite close to another group of seventeenth-century linguists—the makers of sign systems for the deaf and dumb. Among these "reformers," as among all the linguists we have noted, what is most striking is their competitiveness, the comprehensiveness of their intentions, and the recurrence of names and sources. Just as each grammarian intends to provide, at last, a complete analysis of language and, therefore, a basis for training a nation, so inventors of sign systems refer their cataloged gestures to a similar philosophic basis and claim for them similar educational effectiveness. George Dalgarno, in *Didascalocophus; or, The Deaf and Dumb Man's Tutor* (1680), reflects back on his earlier universal grammar, *Ars Signorum* (1661), claiming that that attempt to "remedy the difficulties and absurdities" of all languages should have been called "Sematology."[48] Sematology is "a general name for all interpretation by arbitrary signs," that is, it is the "art of impressing the conceits of the mind upon sensible and material objects" and thus the basis for any sign system whatsoever. Even accepting the "equally arbitrary and *ex institutio*" nature of all written and vocal signs, there must be a real basis for the effectiveness and coherence of sign systems, and that basis is the collection of rules found in "a Natural and Universal Grammar" (p. 18). Beneath the diversity of sign systems, he maintains, there is a rational and realistic connection between kinds of signifiers and the natural significations, and it is that connection Dalgarno pursues in his own universal grammar and in his sign system. The context in which he offers his handbook for the deaf and dumb is indicated by his citations to Seth Ward, John Wilkins, and John Wallis. Their various roles as preacher, pedagogue, and projector are evocatively caught by the ambiguous "or's" in Dalgarno's description of his goal as "that primitive and Divine, or purely rational Sematology, taught by Almighty God or invented by Adam before the Fall."[49] Every linguist and each linguistic work engages comparable philosophical terms and claims equally wide importance. Dalgarno traces the development of his own diverse linguistic inquiries from the study of Hebrew, which excited him "to do something for improving the art of Short-hand; that drove me before I was aware upon a Real Character; that again, after a little consideration, resolved itself into an Effable language" (*Works,* p. 163).[50]

John Wallis, to whose works on grammar and phonology I have already drawn attention, also figures importantly, and somewhat notoriously, in the case of one Alexander Popham, deaf and dumb. William Holder had presented evidence to the Royal Society in 1669 of his success in teaching Popham to speak and had followed this with *Elements of Speech: An Essay of Inquiry into the Natural Production of Letters* (1669). Wallis answered, claiming that his own success in teaching a Mr. Whaly, also deaf and dumb, to speak was actually the precedent for all such cases (*A Defense of the Royal Society* [1678]). Wallis bases his argument on the relevance of his *De Loquela* (1653), which taught, in detail, how the sounds of letters are formed. He also cites Dalgarno's reference to *De Loquela* as the source for his universal character (1661). Holder's claims, in *The Elements of Speech,* are quite like those of Wallis, Ward, and Wilkins; that is, he seeks a "Natural Alphabet ... to prepare a more easie and expedite way to instruct such as are Deaf and Dumb ... to be able to pronounce all Letters, and Syllables, and Words, and in a good measure to discern them by the Eye,"[51] by consulting "Nature at hand" (p. 21). Like Wallis, Holder organizes the "store-house" (p. 18) of sounds and uses a tabulated system of these as the groundwork for letters, syllables, words, and syntax. The debate between Holder and Wallis may have been motivated by a sense of injured pride, but, as with the many examples of linguistic rivalry in the period, it is carried on at an impressively substantive level, each party competing by providing a well-argued phonic-grammatic-pedagogic-semiotic system.[52]

### Visual Mnemonics

All the works and interrelated kinds of linguistic inquiry I have mentioned emphasize pedagogical techniques, most commonly a plan for some variety of visual mnemonics. The presentation of linguistics in visually convenient ways is motivated by theoretical assumptions and confirms, by the predicted success of the method, the truth of those assumptions. Usefulness is the test, not the maker, of principles. The student, in the process of acquiring the language, supposedly discovers the system the linguist has made. This compatibility assumes a correlation between the tools of expression and the determinants of what is expressible: how students acquire language determines how and what men think, how and what men think characterizes their moral natures, and upon their moral natures depends national worth (literary and otherwise). Although Bacon was the nearest prominent philosophical source of the importance of the relationship between the linguistic nature of thinking and the content of thought, the critical figure in the specific alliance between linguistics and learning is Comenius. Comenius, a contemporary of Bishop Wilkins and, like Wilkins, the center of a pre–Royal Society group eager to institutionalize a new systematic methodology, stands out because of his confidence that the proper acquisition of language must logically lead to the conversion of the world. Institutionalization of his syllabus precedes conversion because, he trusts, revelation is the consequence of using language correctly. For Comenius, proper language learning would lead to brotherhood, grammar to God. Once "the multitude, the variety, the confusion of languages" was overcome by means of "language absolutely new, absolutely easy, absolutely rational,"[53] then the progress to universal books to universal schools to a universal college to universal love would be easy and inevitable. The first step Comenius takes in this natural process is to establish the connection between the structure of language and "the course of things" (p. 183); and this could be accomplished in grammars and phonologies "by constantly expressing the nature of things with which [language] deals by the very sounds which it uses" (p. 184).

Comenius pursues his goal in ways with which we should now be familiar: by "containing all things which are necessary to be Knoune . . . with an exact Index";[54] by providing the key to knowledge in and as a book; by offering an "epitome" of language as prerequisite to the grammar of any particular language; by printing word lists so as to represent the "prime and fundamental notions of all learning, manners and piety";[55] by compiling a visual grammar and "encyclopedia" to prove "there is nothing in the understanding which was not before in the sense."[56] *Visible World,* Hoole's translation of Comenius's *Orbis,* proved a popular school text throughout the seventeenth century,[57] and its influence, as we have seen, extended even beyond its wide use. The *Orbis* begins, typically, with a phonology, associating letters with animal sounds and pictures; but most of it consists of pictures illustrating an ordered and carefully named universe beginning with Deus/God and continuing through the sequence of created things and actions. The book, Comenius writes, is "a brief of the whole world, and a whole language: full of Pictures, Nomenclatures, and Descriptions of things" (A3$^v$). Separate columns of English and Latin descriptions on the right-hand page are keyed by numbers to pictures on the left. The columns not only denote objects, professions, and actions but also give syntactic connections between the substantives. These connectives are printed in a different typeface from the named things, so there are four typefaces on the page, two in each column. The eye instructs the mind: we see a "little Encyclopadia of things subject to the senses" (A5$^v$), and we see that the things of the world and the names of those things exist in connected systems.

The eye sees more than Comenius intends, however. In representing Patience (fig. 4), for instance, Comenius illustrates a brief essay rather than simply picturing a list of qualities. He shows someone kneeling with an arm resting on an anchor that is attached to a ship being buffeted by winds and rain from dark clouds, while the clouds release lightning that strikes someone who wails beside a howling dog. The dramatic unity of the illustration corresponds to the integrated discourse of the enumerating commentary and to the syntactic relations revealed by the different typefaces. One of the definitions of what he intends in the *Orbis* captures this element of the work: the *Orbis* is "*a Picture and Nomenclature of all the chief things in the World, and of mens Actions in their way of living*" (A3$^v$). In that last phrase, Comenius suggests one of the most interesting, but unstressed, aspects of his book. *His* emphasis, like that of all his contemporaries, is on the significance of the elements of language—of letters, sounds, characters, words—as if meaning existed, naturally or rationally, in their systematic representation. But, as the integrated actions and connected speeches illustrated in the *Orbis* show, there is more to language than its lexical elements. Comenius, Hoole, Beck, Wallis, Cooper, and the others all admit the necessity of collecting words and sounds into a grammar, but their controlling principle is the priority and meaningfulness of the basic units of language.

## Truth as Correspondence in Language and Literature

The common feature of the linguistic works I have been surveying is the correspondence between the taxonomy of linguistic elements and the natural order of things in the world. I have stressed this aspect because it is central to each linguist's proposals, but as I have already noted, my emphasis subsumes two ideas of "nature." Some linguists in the seventeenth century tend to see the goal of their language work as the recovery, in the shapes and sounds of linguistic elements, of the essences of things in nature; others tend to define their work as reproducing, through mostly arbitrary symbols, the composition and coherence of things in nature. Linguists of the first group associate their plans with the seekers after Adamic naming, just as Comenius traces his interests back to his teacher, Johann-Heinrich Alsted,[58] and through him to Jacob Boehme.[59] The other linguists associate their proposals with those of the empiricists, just as Wilkins sees his work as a continuation of Bacon's recommendations for the advancement of learning.[60] The differences between representatives of the two groups are sometimes loud and vituperative, as in the short pamphlet debate between John Webster and Seth Ward in which Ward, from Oxford, accuses Webster, a practioner of Paracelsian physic in private practice, of Lullism and other mystifications.[61] However, more often the two groups make complementary practical contributions. There is a great deal of interchange and over-lapping between the Hartlib-Dury group and the Wilkins-Ward one, for instance, despite the Puritan, mystical, and continental allegiances of the first and the mostly Anglican, empirical, and native affections of the latter. That the Wilkins-Ward participants won the day and went on to form the basis of the Royal Society need not lead us to write the others off in a winner-take-all sweepstakes for the victorious ideas in history.[62]

The chief difference between these two versions of a correspondence theory between the taxonomies of language and of nature is that the Comenians looked back to an ideal they knew they could not recapture all at once, one that they had to qualify in order to make practical improvements, while the "Baconians" shaped the practical alterations they proposed according to an unprecedented ideal they often despaired of finally effecting. Even in the angry course of the Webster-Ward debate, Webster, who believes that he moves in the spirit of Bacon,[63] suggests possible curriculum changes the universities might make to come closer to the rediscovery of the original mysteries, whereas Ward defends the recently established curriculum as one already close to Webster's proposals and already engaged in the pursuit of a universal character.[64] Ward is more impatient with the sources (and vocabulary) of Webster's ideas about the project than with the specific directions of his thought.

*Language and the Grammar of Things, 1640–1700*

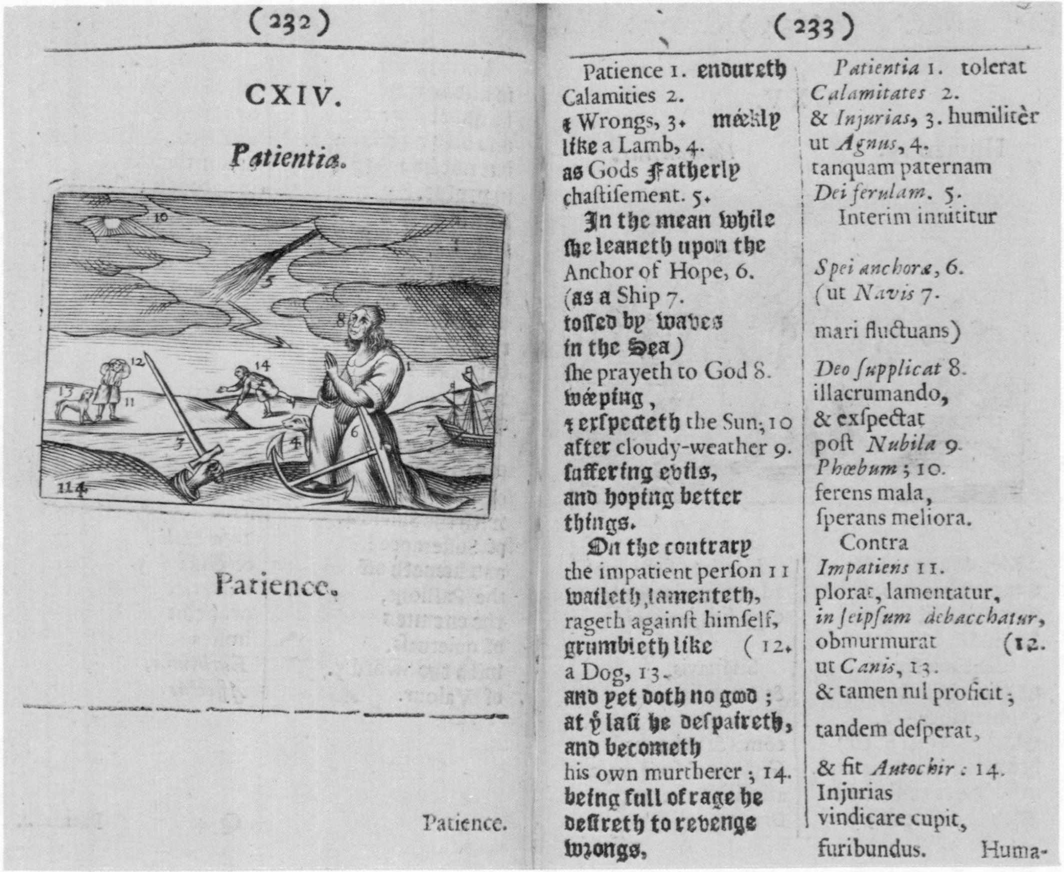

# CXIV.

## Patientia.

## Patience.

Patience 1. endureth
Calamities 2.
& Wrongs, 3. meekly
like a Lamb, 4.
as Gods Fatherly
chastisement. 5.
In the mean while
she leaneth upon the
Anchor of Hope, 6.
(as a Ship 7.
tossed by waves
in the Sea)
she prayeth to God 8.
weeping,
& expecteth the Sun, 10
after cloudy-weather 9.
suffering evils,
and hoping better
things.

Or the contrary
the impatient person 11
waileth, lamenteth,
rageth against himself,
grumbleth like (12.
a Dog, 13.
and yet doth no good;
at last he despaireth,
and becometh
his own murderer; 14.
being full of rage he
desireth to revenge
wrongs.

*Patientia* 1. tolerat
*Calamitates* 2.
& *Injurias* 3. humiliter
ut *Agnus,* 4.
tanquam paternam
*Dei ferulam.* 5.
Interim innititur
*Spei anchorae,* 6.
(ut *Navis* 7.
mari fluctuans)
*Deo supplicat* 8.
illacrumando,
& expectat
post *Nubila* 9.
*Phoebum;* 10.
ferens mala,
sperans meliora.

Contra
*Impatiens* 11.
plorat, lamentatur,
*in seipsum debacchatur,*
obmurmurat (12.
ut *Canis,* 13.
& tamen nil proficit;
tandem desperat,
& fit *Autochir;* 14.
Injurias
vindicare cupit,
furibundus. Humna-

Figure 4. John Amos Comenius, *Orbis Sensualium Pictus* (1659), pp. 232-33. Reproduced by permission of the British Library Board.

We can see a clear drift, historically, away from Webster's mystical assumptions and Comenius's justifications for reform and toward Ward's measured analyses and empirical methods,[65] paralleling, as I have begun to show, a shift in linguistic emphasis from the lexical to the syntactic. This change corresponds to an abandonment of revolutionary fervor, politically and socially, in favor of the restoration of the forms and figures of tradition. A closer parallel to this linguistic shift is the alteration in the languages of literature over the same mid-century period. While the boldest attempts were being made at representing in words the essence of nature, the most notable, and most notorious, poetic endeavours were being made to capture in verbal conceits and in the shapes of poems the presence of ideas. The metaphysical poem is an object of meditation that rewards, as modern critics well know, those who take the elements and shapes of the poems seriously enough to become the strenuous remakers of meaning in a cooperative effort to discover the poetic shapes of things known. Rosemond Tuve isolates the lexical basis of metaphysical poetry when she stresses, in *Elizabethan and Metaphysical Imagery,* its distinctive reliance on the image, and she summarizes her findings in words that bring early-seventeenth-century English poetry close to the contemporary linguistic activity I have been describing: the "purposes" of the Renaissance poet "are given body in suitable matter and made articulate through suitable form."[66] This evaluation of the perspicacious, universalizing, logical, and literally decorous image, close as it is to Ramus's logical taxonomies, complements the search by all the early English linguists for a representation of language that would suit the nature and order of things.

By the time of Wilkins's culminating effort, however, the dominant literary language of England had noticeably changed, as well. Like Wilkins, John Dryden seeks the nature of things more in their composition and coherence than in necessary or wittily contingent correspondence of linguistic and natural essences. His "purposes" are not distinctively represented in the physical shapes of his poems or in the peculiarities of his images. He mocks the metaphysical poets for their excesses, not only for the sort of linguistic wit that permits sexual metaphors to stand for traditional truths, but more generally for their habit of making meaning depend on the close correspondence of an image and a truth. "Absalom and Achitophel" begins engagingly, it seems, smiling at Charles's well-known sexual interests, since Charles, like David, "scatter'[s] his Maker's Image through the land" despite, or because of, the ungrateful "Soyl" the "Tiller" finds at home.[67] But, too soon, the moral implications of the poet's verbal wit strike us, as the fecund king winks at the murder committed by the natural son whom he begot with the (metaphorically witty) help of the Holy Spirit: "...inspir'd by some diviner Lust, / His Father got him with a greater Gust" (ll. 19–20). The poem enacts, for Dryden's contemporaries familiar with the poetry of the preceding generations, a literary and readerly version of the error committed by David/Charles. The attraction and the danger of metaphysical wit, poetically, and of sexual playfulness, politically, is that both tend to become ends in themselves, sources for indulgence in which the reader seeks out cleverer puns and the king assumes that "warm excesses" will purge "by boyling o'r" (l. 38).

Dryden alters his voice (and Charles/David's) and the nature of our reading experience by the end of the poem, as the king discards his easiness and his sexual exuberance in order to effect his true function directly. For him and for the poet there are social responsibilities that outweigh personal habits and a public language that supercedes private (or coterie) wit. No more will the king play fashionable games with words and call murder, "Youth," accept a modern sense of "patriot" (ll. 965–66), or tolerate a "Rebel" who is called the "Peoples Saint" (l. 974)—the stakes are too high to depend on mere names. Dryden too, by poem's end, has given up the metaphysical freedoms of the opening of the poem in favor of a language that is securer, plainer, and more direct. He still trusts that poems make readers, but the readers he wants are to be informed and not provoked, offered rhymes, for instance, that reinforce rather than brilliantly offend. Shortly before he wrote the poem, Dryden recommended rhyme, first, for the "help it brings to the memory" and, second, for its ability to "bound and circumscribe the fancy ... and bring forth the richest and clearest thoughts."[68] The intended reader of this kind of literary language is one who welcomes aids to clarity and familiarity, who relies on common rather than peculiar associations. Like Dryden's king who returns, finally, to what is "still" (ll. 991, 998, 1024) the "same" (l. 992) and true, the reader gives up the genial wit of the poem's first rhyme, "begin/sin," to return to the historically and politically precise statement of its last, "Restor'd/Lord."

Dryden chides his king carefully, of course, but also somewhat reluctantly, for both are giving up some of their natural resources. The king quells his native goodness (and randiness) to act up to his obligations for the good of the people, and Dryden surrenders some of poetry's richness (and intensity) to encourage surer laws of poetic expression, again, for the good of his readers.[69] Dryden does not read his poetic predecessors as aliens but maintains a high and admiring opinion of the Elizabethan dramatists especially; at the same time, however, he sees his writerly obligations in new terms and accepts the same burdens of public performance and responsibility that he places on his king. The "victory" of Dryden's literary language, like the dominance of Wilkins's version of the linguistic enterprise, is less a completed revolution than a drift[70] away from the strongest claims language can make to be isomorphic to reality. The modifications of Dryden and Wilkins both admit arbitrariness—Wilkins's invented signs are arbitrary, like words, but accurate and representative of the order of things, and Dryden's rhymes are devices that do not capture an essential truth but help constitute a memorable unit.[71] However, though their systems are arbitrary, both men still want to maintain a notion of truth as correspondence. Their mimetic theories draw the relation less, however, between particular things and specific words, as their predecessors had attempted, and more between the rules of relationship that account for coherence in speech and nature.

To get a clearer sense of this change in linguistic emphasis,[72] I want to look carefully at the common features of the problematic issues in linguistics during the last third of the century. The nature of these troubles will show us the first of the major shifts in linguistic consciousness that I want to point out.

## From the Lexical to the Syntactic

The first great change in the philosophy and practice of language in England, after its "discovery" in the seventeenth century, is brought about by growing interest in the syntactical, as opposed to the lexical, functions of language. The implications of this momentous change become clear only in the early eighteenth century (see Chapter 2), but the revolution is quietly taking place in the last part of the seventeenth century even in such works as the *Orbis*, in which an interest in "mens Actions in their way of living" indicates a need to deal with man's language in the way it operates. There are three reasons why the shift, ultimately so crucial, develops so quietly.

Syntax had always been a responsibility of the linguist, and it was likely that the assumptions governing the individual unit of language would be applied to interactions between units.[73] Second, the techniques for visualizing the orderliness of linguistic elements invited additional schemes for relating those elements.[74] Third, the emphasis on linguistic units, while it might have satisfied the need for adequate definitions of particulars and might have met the challenge to correlate words and things, could not account for the social functions of human speech or the poet's responsibility to act as public pedagogue.[75]

The taxonomies of letters, sounds, words, and things represented in seventeenth-century linguistic texts all contain principles allowing relation or combination of the parts. In the grammars that organize the vernacular, there is a natural and rational order in the growth of discourse out of letters, syllables, words, and sentences; in the pictorial systems there is an increasing visual complexity from images of particular sounds to representations of themes; and in the invented languages, there is a literal place for every sound, word, and thing in a thoroughly connected scheme. In all cases the decisive step is to clarify the elementary connection between language and things, as Beck does when he assigns numbers to words,[76] or as Comenius does when he brings every thing and notion to view. Equally true of each system is the idea that language builds from its meaningful elements and that such linguistic accretion amounts to syntax. Beck surrounds his lexical symbols with syntactic markers; Wallis suggests that the difference between English and Latin is a syntactic one ("Est enim tum in hac tum in modernis fere omnibus, a Graecae Latin-aeque linguae syntaxi immanis discrepantia");[77] Comenius attempts a series of visualized discourses rather than a set of inert emblems. But these indications of syntax are undeveloped and subordinated to universal, aural, literal, or visual precision. The treatment of syntax in the seventeenth century ranges from Aickin's claim that English syntax can be "absolved in three easie Rules" (A3^v) to James Howell's opinion, in *New English Grammar* (1662), that "it cannot be in the compas of the human brain to compile an exact regular Syntaxis" of the language.[78] The potential for the development of syntax, however, exists in the *operational* quality of the various language schemes, each of which considers the possibility of (and the need for) relating its parts. It is when the linguists assume responsibility for discourse as well as lexical marking that syntax receives new interest.[79]

The shift in emphasis from words and their symbols to sentences and their parts occurs in the last quarter of the century when, primarily in response to the *Grammaire générale et raisonnée* (1660) of Antoine Arnauld and Claude Lancelot, masters of Port-Royal, English linguists exchange a philosophy of language based on the correspondence of language to nature to one asserting the analogy of the function of speech to the operations of the mind. One exception, before 1660, to the English concentration on the relation of language to the grammar of things proves, by its oddity, this common concern. The work is *Herm'-aelogium; or, An Essay at the Rationality of the Art of Speaking* (1659), by Bassett Jones. Jones begins, typically, by "analogizing words with things,"[80] and he discovers just three parts of speech: words of being (that is, matter), words of motion (form), and words of quality (oddly, privation). He then launches into a specifically neo-Platonic discussion of these "gradual emanations of the same Naturing Nature" (p. 7). In this he is unusual, for he seeks a more active role for the mind than do his contemporary English linguists. Jones wants the study of language to reach a state "wherein the mind may practice her own power upon the nature of things" (A4$^r$). The differences between the world's languages, he writes, are simply variations in "vocality" and climate; in "point of syntax" (A6$^v$) they all agree. This distinction proves "the product of words to be more from nature; as of sentences from reason." In such statements, Jones suggests a new philosophy of language in seventeenth-century England, based not on the reality of words but on the rationality of speakers.

Jones's definitions are as obscure as they are distinctive. He tries to justify gender in strictly sexual terms, although with some things "the distinguishment of their sex [is] a knowledge peculiar only to Physicians" (p. 13). He defines words of motion as words "being actuated ... and modable according to the temporal inclination of the lover towards whatever being he therein can fansie perfection" (p. 74). To such active analyses of speech Jones adds some equally suggestive emblems, one of which shows modes and cases multiplying as a sign of universal social decay: Coelus, at the top of the page, typifies perfection, and Venus Caelestis, at the bottom, represents "the word of sense answering the direct natural motion of the verb ... as the Accusative case of the noun" (p. 88). Between these two are Venus Popularis, Venus Hortensis, Venus Terrestris, and Venator representing the ablative (or an "analogie with Romes political confederacy"), the genitive (or "answering the Circular motion"), and the dative. Jones's interest in the philosophical basis of syntax becomes progressively obscured by these schemes, but on his title page he advertizes the truth: "A Supplement to Lillie's Grammar, Philosophically, Mythologically, and Emblematically."

Although Jones quotes from the *Advancement of Learning* (to justify departing from "received partitions"), the precedent for his exotic linguistics is continental and learned, not English and popular. His work suggests a new rational basis for language. However, in the last quarter of the seventeenth century, a number of language texts, many of them attempting to represent grammatically Comenius's pictorial discourses, indicate a shift in emphasis from lexical symbolization to rational syntax. Mark Lewis, following Comenius, contributes a number of school texts in order to bring "down the Rudiments of Grammar to the Sense of Seeing."[81] He shares Elisha Coles's fondness for the term *syncrisis,* which becomes, in Lewis's *Vestibulum Technicum,* a printer's cue: "Each Part of Speech is distinguished by the Character it is Printed in (a Method never used before), and sufficient Grammar is brought down to the sense of Seeing, in regard of the thing signified."[82] Lewis's reliance on a visual key accommodates his reasons for reforming Lily. Lily erred by beginning his grammar with catalogs of general rules, by relying on the moral weight of examples drawn from classical authors, and by building a vocabulary word by word. For Lewis, such a submission to authority and to isolated lexical bits and pieces violates the proper pedagogy, which, by beginning with the sense of seeing, uses the same methodology to "learn things Natural, Artificial, Moral, and Divine."[83] His method also imitates the epistemology he accepts: "Whatever is in the world is matter and motion; thoughts are the Picture of this matter and motion, words are the Copy of our thoughts; as is the thing, so is the Picture. As is the Picture, so is the Copy; therefore every sentence must consist of a Substantive, thing or matter, called the Nominative Case; and the verb or motion of it, with so many more Substantives as do depend upon these; these cannot exist without qualities, which we express by Adjectives. Prepositions and Conjunctions are a kind of cement." (A4$^v$) In passages like this one, appearing throughout his work, Lewis connects the stages of the true epistemology (and, thus, the proper pedagogy) to the nature of existing things, so that learning properly and writing correctly reconstitute reality.

Lewis repeatedly compares language to a body—with substantives as the bones, adjectives the flesh, nominatives the cranium, accusatives the torso[84]—because he wants language, however arbitrary the specific relationship between *a* signifier and *a* signified, to represent naturally and completely "what God works by nature" (*Vestibulum,* p. 16). Lewis has an equally operational sense of language and of God—both are to be interpreted as functioning systems, not simply as static collections of emblems.[85] *How* God works is also how language works; the right method for acquiring language, therefore, "from the Senses to the Understanding, and from thence to the Memory" (*Essay,* p. 1), cannot help but train minds that would be, ideally, universally compatible and unproblematically orthodox. Since the "end of words and common things is divine knowledge" (*Apologie,* p. 37), the systematic visual representation of language has as much religious as scholastic power.

Lewis, unlike earlier seventeenth-century linguists, tries to accommodate a visual language to a logical syntax. The latter, he stresses, is the real basis of a general grammar. But Lewis remains uneasy about the inclusion of logic and syntax in his school texts: "Doubtless the Doctrine of Grammar is too subtle for Children; because it is communicated by Logical Definitions in the Etymologie, and by the signification of words in the Syntax, neither of which Children can reach, who cannot use Abstraction."[86] Lewis never resolves this conflict between his desire to give the rational grounds of syntax and his sense that it is beyond schoolchildren. He has this problem because, for him, logic and syntax are principles to be learned *about* language rather than, primarily, evident qualities *in* language. Only with Locke and the early eighteenth-century grammarians does this problematic aspect of language emerge as a natural consequence of grammatical description in English texts and therefore as a new core idea in linguistics.

Lewis's treatment of syntactic subordination is unique in the century, and his discussion of the relationship between punctuation marks and syntactic sense is the most elaborate.[87] Both of these distinctions indicate a shift away from the priority of characters, sounds, and taxonomies. Lewis brings syntax and punctuation together in his *Plain and short rules for pointing periods* (1675), in which he defines the grammarian's responsibility as the discovery of the syntactic structure, "Simple or . . . Compounded," of any "Proposition, Theme, or Matter."[88] In the *Grammaticae Puerilis* (1670), Lewis identifies the basis of a general grammar as the "one Rule of Speaking" in which "the Words stand in a Natural order."[89] Yet, in this unusual sense of the logic of syntax, Lewis is also inconsistent. He repeatedly praises Comenius's lists and pictures of "primitive words," since "words are the marks of things, and words being perceived, things are perceived" (*Vestibulum,* p. 16). The importance of Lewis's work lies in its contradictions, for these mark the transition from the philosophy of words as things to the theory of the rational structure of speech. They exemplify, too, a common debate at the time, a debate that had religious, political, and literary versions, between a closely literal, or lexical, hermeneutic and a more historicist one.[90]

Lewis's attempt to bring together Comenius's emphasis on lexical units and the logic of syntax (the "Rule of Speaking") is repeated in Samuel Shaw's *Words Made Visible; or, Grammar and Rhetorick Accommodated to the Lives and Manners of Men* (1679). The title tells the story: Shaw tries to put visualized words to work in the complex world of human discourse (as Comenius had done when he put words and their pictures to the service of "mens Actions in their way of living"). Shaw, who advertises himself as the "Philosophical Priscian" of his times, presents the court of King Syntaxis, King of the Grammar Common-wealth. The dialogue between the parts of speech and selected rhetorical tropes is often amusing, but Shaw's important claim is that "the most illiterate people in their most ordinary communication, do Rhetoricate by Instinct. . . .But that's not all; for men live Tropes and Figures as well as speak them."[91] The elaborately orchestrated relations between the parts of speech operate in every mind: "every individual mind is a system" of rhetoric. Shaw's work is a good example of a widespread change in English thought during the late seventeenth century. The shift from seeking the philosophy of language primarily in the nature of things to discovering in the system of language the logic of human reason appears, in Shaw, as the rhetoric of men's natures.

## John Wilkins and the Limitations of a Tabular Taxonomy

The works of Lewis and Shaw are expressions of the transition between two ideas of language, and both men are struggling with the differences. A more conscious and sophisticated attempt to span the two ideas of language is Wilkins's *Essay Towards a Real Character, And a Philosophical Language* (1668). Essentially, Wilkins shares the dominant assumptions about language in the century. His great work summarizes, improves, and fulfills the promise of the efforts of Beck, Lodwick, Seth Ward, Dalgarno, Hartlib, Comenius, and others. The point of departure for a rational language, writes Wilkins, is "the distinct expression of all things and notions that fall under discourse" (al[V]). He provides, in effect, a grammar of things. He organizes all existing things and all ideas into a

series of classified tables according to the proper "Method, to separate
the Heterogeneous, and put the Homogeneous together, according to
some rule of precedency" (p. 14). His "rule of precedency" is the
distinction between substance and accidents, which was the traditional
way of identifying the essential nature of particular objects. Wilkins's
reliance on this technique of classifying adds emphasis to the priority he
gives to identifying separate objects: "The first thing to be considered
and enquired into is, Concerning a just Enumeration and description of
such things or notions as are to have Marks or Names assigned to them"
(p. 20). Once each thing is marked, one may then make "some provision
to express Grammatical Derivations and Inflexions" (p. 21). For Wilkins,
as for Beck and the other universal language inventors, the first
responsibility is to fix the lexicon; considering the relations of words to
one another in sentences comes later, if at all.

The bulk of Wilkins's own work (that is, excluding William Lloyd's
"Alphabetical Dictionary") consists of a "Universal Philosophy" that is
a representation of natural philosophy. The "principal design aimed at in
these Tables" is to give "the primary sense of the thing defined" (p. 289);
but while claiming the success of this intention, Wilkins also admits that
he had hoped to do more. Although each thing and notion is ordered so
"that the place of everything may contribute to a description of the
nature of it," he would like to be able to mark, by a "transcendental
denomination," "every difference amongst the Predicaments" and
provide an "immediate form which gives the particular essence to everything . . . expressed." But the received theory of things does not admit
the former, and man's ignorance prevents the latter. In effect, Wilkins
admits he cannot make the "real" character he desires, one that strikes
the sense immediately and distinctly. Instead of a necessary and natural
correspondence between things and words, Wilkins offers a scheme that
reduces "all things and notions unto such a frame, as may express their
natural order, dependence and relations" (p. 1). It is the frame of the
system, not the markers themselves, that makes language meaningful;
and the relation of the parts, not their essential or independent reality,
characterizes human discourse. Wilkins, by admitting the limits of the
reality of his "Character," surrenders the assumption upon which his
strongest opinions are based.[92]

Wilkins's book, the most thorough linguistic work of the century, is
also the most honest. Not only does Wilkins notify us that what is "real"
about his language is the method used to organize it, but he also lists the

"kinds of things that are not capable of being provided for in a Character and Language, proposed for Universal use" (p. 295). These include titles of honor and office, law terms, clothes, games and plays, drinks, meats, tunes for music and instruments, and the "names of divers sects, whether Philosophical, Political or Religious" (p. 296). Wilkins, by excluding these areas of human life from his universal language, severely restricts the usefulness of his system for human communication, and this may be one reason why his ideas had little evident effect on the subsequent practice of language. Wilkins's work is not only the best but the last of the universal language schemes in seventeenth-century England.[93] Even as he concludes the search for the grammar of nature, other linguists, as we have seen, were discussing the reasons, not of words, but of discourse.

Wilkins also deals with grammar, but as a series of marks added to lexical symbols. This "Organical part" of language (as opposed to "Scientifical part") is "an enquiry after such kind of necessary helps, whereby as by instruments we must be assisted in the forming of these more simple notions into complex Propositions and Discourses, which may be stiled Grammar, containing the Art of Words or Discourse" (p. 297). Wilkins considered himself responsible for grammar because the actual use of his characters derives from their "order, dependence and relations." His goal, however, is to get rid of as many syntactic rules as possible. Since "words may signifie sufficiently and in some respects better without them . . . there is greater judgment shewed in laying them aside, or framing a Language without them" (p. 448). Neither option is possible, and Wilkins's own grammar consists of a reduction of etymological and syntactic variations to a bewilderingly complex minimum. The same thing should be said of the *Real Character* as of Comenius's *Orbis*—the method escapes the intention. Both linguists reduce language to its elements and then add to these radical objects (things, notions, and words) indications of their connections in sentences. These additions introduce a new set of questions: is speech more than the accretion of objects? Are the connectives "real"? Is there a philosophy of speech as well as of naming?

Wilkins's "Organical" grammar indicates both an awareness of these issues and a determination to avoid dealing with them. He tries to build discourse out of his lexical taxonomy first by reducing all nouns, adjectives, and verbs to radical substantives, and then by adding to them certain "Transcendental marks" to recapture case and mood. To these he adds "Grammatical Particles" like prepositions (fig. 5) and "Trans-

some *third thing* spoken of, which the Speaker confiders as being

| | | |
|---|---|---|
| *Higher* or *Lower* then that third thing, denoting a contiguity or nearnefs to it | | |
| 1. { *UPON* | Super. | |
| { *UNDER* | Sub. | |

VI. { *Nearer* to it, or *Farther* from it

2. { *ON THIS SIDE*    Citra.
   { *BEYOND*    Ultra.

In the *intermediate* fpace unto two other things, or *oppofite* to one of them.

3. { *BETWIXT, between*    Inter
   { *AGAINST, over againft.*    Adverfus.

For the clearer explication of thefe *Local Prepofitions*, I fhall refer to this following Diagram. In which by the *Oval Figures* are reprefented the *Prepofitions determined to Motion*, wherein the Acuter part doth point out the tendency of that motion. The *fquares* are intended to fignifie *reft* or the *Term* of *Motion*. And by the *round* figures are reprefented fuch *relative* Prepofitions, as may indifferently refer either to *Motion* or *Reft*.

§ III.

*pag. 311.*

Some

Figure 5. John Wilkins, *Essay towards a Real Character, And a Philosophical Language* (1668), p. 311. Reproduced by permission of the Bancroft Library, University of California, Berkeley.

cendental Particles" to indicate tropes. The mark for metaphor, for instance, when added to any character "will signifie the enlarging of the sense of that word, from that strict restrained acception which it had in the Tables, to a more universal comprehensive signification: By this, common Metaphors may be legitimated, retaining their elegancy, and being freed from their ambiguity" (p. 323). Thus, the character for "Streight" when marked for metaphor becomes "Upright," and "Crooked becomes "Perverse." Other transcendental markers signify kind and manner, place and time, cause, aggregate, instrument, gender, power, degree, and so on. Wilkins, although trying to make grammar simply serve enumerated things and notions, actually grants it authority over meaning in human speech. His transcendental markers signify, in effect, logic and rhetoric. What he designs as the "accidents" of his system overtake his "substances" by drawing attention to the modes of discourse, that is, man's logical and rhetorical uses of language.[94]

In the contradictions of his system, Wilkins expresses the changes occurring in English linguistics in the last part of the century. The major change, from linking language initially to the grammar of things to associating it primarily with a grammar of the mind, was due in part, I think, to the development of the typographic technology used to represent linguistic thought in England. Seventeenth-century English linguists, although giving priority to enumerating the elements of language, developed systems that represented the relations of those units. These relations were expressed in an operational, and not simply a static, taxonomy, and this, combined with the steady search for the conceptual content of language categories, accommodated rather easily to a new philosophy of syntax. But, to judge from the statements of eighteenth-century linguists, the major impact on the development of this new idea of language came from the adaptation of grammar to logic in France.[95] The Port-Royal linguists got credit for focusing a development already in process.

## The "Messieurs du Port-Royal" and the Logic of Language

For the "messiurs du Port-Royal" grammar illustrates logic, and both disciplines describe how the mind works. Arnauld, in La logique ou l'art de penser (1662), defines logic as the art of leading the reason ("conduire sa raison") to the knowledge of things, as much to instruct oneself ("tant pour s'en instruire soi-même") as to instruct others.[96] The self-reflexiveness of the definition is critically important, for the great effect of *L'art de penser* and the *Grammaire générale* (1660) on English linguistics was to help redirect the search for the rational basis of language from the order of things to the order of the mind.[97] Logic specifies the operations of the mind by forcing thinking beings to reflect on their own thoughts; it consists "dans les reflexions que les hommes ont faites sur les quatre principales operations de leur esprit, *concevoir, juger, raisonner,* et *ordonner*" (p. 37). It does not teach man how to think, "mais à faire des reflexions sur ce que la nature nous fait faire" (p. 38). Logic describes how all minds work, but to think about "les operations de nôtre esprit," one must consider language. It is in and through language that man's mind appears to operate:

> Que si les reflexions que nous faisons sur nos pensées n'avoient jamais regardé que nous-mêmes, il auroit suffi de les considerer en elles-mêmes, sans les revestir d'aucunes paroles, ni d'aucuns autres signes: mais parce que nous ne pouvons faire entendre nos pensées les uns aux autres, qu'en les accompagnant de signes exterieurs: et que mesme cette accoûtumance est si forte, que quand nous pensons seuls, les choses ne se presentent à nôtre esprit qu'avec les mots dont nous avons accoûtumé de les revestir en parlant aux autres; il est necessaire dans la Logique de considerer les idées jointes aux mots, et les mots joints aux idées.

The rational basis of language is embedded in language as it is. Even our solitary thought is discursive, so that self-reflexion is a form of verbal communication.

Arnauld admits that the best way to avoid the confusion of words evident in "les langues ordinaire, est de faire une nouvelle langue, et de nouveaux mots qui ne soient attachés qu'aux idées que nous voulons qu'ils représentent" (p. 86). Such a created language would be, for Arnauld, an arbitrary one in which sounds are assigned ideas and not a natural language in which there is a "real" connection between symbols and things. This distinction separates Arnauld from the English linguists who sought in the materials of language the elements of reality. But neither is Arnauld primarily interested in the invention of an arbitrary language of the kind that captured the imaginations of many English linguists. He does not imagine that there could be such a new language; indeed, "il ne faut pas entreprendre de définir tous les mots, parceque souvent cela seroit inutile, et qu'il est même impossible de le faire"

(p. 90). His purpose in suggesting the possibility is to introduce the distinction between real and nominal definitions. A real definition is one that gathers the ideas associated with the ordinary use of a word, whereas a nominal definition arbitrarily assigns a meaning to a word without concern for common usage.

Arnauld lists the advantages of nominal definitions, emphasizing their greater clarity, but he devotes even more space to their practical limits. First, it is impossible to give nominal definitions to all words; in fact, to define too much leads to the very confusion one seeks to avoid. Second, one should not change existing definitions unnecessarily; and, third, one should as much as possible accommodate oneself to common usage. A further restriction on the absolute clarity of arbitrary definitions is that words are used by men to communicate with one another. Although someone can create a private language for his own use, if he wants to live in the world of men, his nominal definitions must represent "non la verité des choses, mais la verité de l'usage" (p. 94). The difference between the truth of things and the truth of usage is that, in the latter, there are accessory ideas associated with the principal idea of a word. These accessory ideas necessarily accompany human discourse, because words mean more than they say. The words "You have lied," Arnauld argues, not only mean "You know that the contrary of what you say is true" but also convey from common usage ideas of contempt and outrage and convince one that the speaker would not hesitate to do harm. The speaker can also add accessory ideas by his tone of voice, facial expressions, gestures, and "par les autres signes naturels" (p. 95), all of which attach to our words ideas that diversify, change, diminish, and augment the signification. There are also accessory ideas permanently attached to words, so that the same principal idea can be expressed by words conveying different accessory ideas, as is the case with figurative language.[98]

Arnauld's discussion of nominal definitions represents his response to seventeenth-century attempts to make language rational. He inherits the sense of the limits of ordinary language and seems to accept the desirability of devising a new language; however, in the process of qualifying nominal definitions, he reintroduces all the problems of usage his predecessors sought to avoid by initially fixing (naturally or rationally) the elements of language. Arnauld's nominal definitions, finally, refer to meaning in complex human contexts, but there Arnauld finds logic. Arbitrary definitions cannot grant rationality to man, although their function in human discourse can reveal the rational activities of the mind.

He attacks Hobbes because the latter claimed that reasoning was simply the manipulation of names. For Arnauld, reasoning is independent of the names of things. Were Hobbes right, the French and the Arabs would think as differently as their words differ. Reasoning is not, then, "un assemblage de noms . . . mais un jugement solide et effectif de la nature des choses par la consideration des idées qu'il en a dans l'esprit, lesquelles il a plu aux hommes de marquer par de certains noms" (p. 43). A rational language already exists, not in words themselves, but in the analogy between the operations of the mind and the functions of language.

In *L'art de penser,* each of the four mental operations has a linguistic expression. Conceptions include things, the manners of things (mode, quality, or characteristic), and qualified things (adjectives). Part 1 offers, in effect, a discussion of common and proper nouns, pronouns, and adjectives. Judgments are "des propositions qui sont composées de diverses parties" (p. 103), and so depend on verbs. Reasoning refers to the synthesis or analysis of judgments, and so consists of a series of sentences (or an argument). Finally, ordering is the method used to arrange our reasonings about a particular subject; it is the art of discourse. Of these activities of the mind, the most important for Arnauld is judgment. It is the basis of all thought, expressing the distinctive operation of the human mind. Therefore, when he defines activities of the mind as parts of speech, he is stressing the syntactic rather than semantic functions of words. The sentence is the basic unit of linguistic meaning, and its rational structure reveals the structure of thought.[99] The linguist's responsibility, then, is to discover processes of thought by classifying kinds of sentences.

The *Grammaire générale,* by Arnauld and Lancelot, preceded *L'art de penser* by two years, but no English translation of the former appeared until 1753 (*L'art de penser* was translated in 1685).[100] These facts are unimportant, however, because the *Grammaire* summarizes the arguments of the logic and *L'art de penser* is as important to grammarians as to logicians. The *Grammaire* begins with a section on sounds and letters in which the authors criticize attempts to invent new characters or impose phonetic spellings. Most of the text discusses "des principes et des raisons sur lesquelles sont appuyées les diverses formes de la signification des mots."[101] These principles and reasons are the activities of the mind represented by the functions of language. Again, the most important operation of the mind is judgment, and the most important function of speech is the assertion. Reasoning is an extension of judgment, and conceptions are rarely expressed without judgments being made about them. Communication is the expression of judgments: "on ne parle pas seulement pour marquer ce que l'on conçoit, mais pour exprimer ce que l'on pense de ce que l'on conçoit" (p. 142).[102] Both the *Grammaire* and *L'art de penser* consistently emphasize the connection between language and thought, and the clarity and timeliness of their method helped Locke give English voice to a new idea of language in his own country.

## John Locke and Linguistic Action

The importance of Locke's *Essay concerning Human Understanding* (1690) to the remarkable shift in ideas of language in the late seventeenth century is due more to its popularity than to its brilliance or complexity.[103] To take the testimony (and, at times, the unacknowledged dependence) of eighteenth-century linguists, Locke's work, like that of the masters of Port-Royal, made clear the identity of the art of grammar and the art of thinking.[104] When read in the context of contemporary linguistics, both the significance and difficulty of book 3 ("Of Words") become apparent. Locke says he planned to proceed from the study of ideas to the analysis of knowledge, "but upon a nearer approach, I find that there is so close a connexion between ideas and WORDS, and our abstract ideas and general words have so constant a relation to one another, that it is impossible to speak clearly and distinctly of our knowledge, which all consists in propositions, without considering, first, the nature, use, and signification of Language."[105] His problem was to find a way of talking about words as ideas and knowledge as propositions (sentences), and the major contemporary significance of his solution was his agreement with the Port-Royal analysis of language as logic.[106]

Book 3 opens by rejecting two compatible ideas of language: that words are "natural" (as opposed to arbitrary) signifiers of things; and that words name particular things. Before he can discuss language Locke must explain, in effect, why he has not followed the example of other seventeenth-century linguists and started with taxonomies of things or words.

Locke gives three arguments against restricting words to particular things. These arguments summarize both the difference between his basic idea of language and that of his English predecessors and the closeness of his argument to Arnauld's. First, "it is impossible that every particular thing should have a distinct peculiar name" because "it is beyond the power of human capacity to frame and retain distinct ideas of all the particular things we meet with" (3. 3. 2). Second, even if such naming were possible, "it would yet be useless; because it would not serve to the chief end of language . . . . to communicate . . . thoughts" (3. 3. 3). Third, even if such a project were possible and communicable, it "would not be of any great use for the improvement of knowledge: which, though founded in particular things, enlarges itself by general views; to which things reduced into sorts, under general names, are properly subservient" (3. 3. 4). This is the new idea of language: words refer to ideas, not things; words are used to communicate our knowledge, not particular things, to one another; and knowledge is the result of the "ordinary proceedings" of the mind (3. 3. 9). Or, as Locke defines it in book 4, echoing the critical self-reflexiveness of Arnauld's definitions, knowledge is *the perception of the connexion of and agreement, or disagreement and repugnancy of any of our ideas*" (4. 1. 1).

According to Locke most human communication involves general, abstract, or universal ideas that are not in the "real existence of things; but are the inventions and creatures of the understanding, made by it for its own use" (3. 3. 11). These ideas are the mind's perceptions of itself operating on ideas of sensation, and their signification "is nothing but a relation that, by the mind of man, is added to them." Language, then, functions in the way the mind operates, and this assumption leads Locke, as it led Arnauld, to make a distinction between the real and the nominal. Locke, like Arnould, argues that there are real, but unrecoverable, essences only for simple ideas of objects with but one quality. Such ideas and words are not sufficient for human life, so man, to be able "to consider things, and discourse of them, as it were in bundles," must designate nominal essences (that is, abstract ideas with names assigned to them). The nominal essences of complex ideas depend on the workings of a mind that does not operate randomly or without reason. They are "always made for the convenience of communication" (3. 5. 7). If there is a rational language, it must reflect the general activities of thought. All words lead back to the mind that made them; and if communication is possible, it is because there is unity in the processes of thinking and expressing thought.

This correlation between thinking and speaking is necessary; but most men, "wanting either time, inclination, or industry" (3. 6. 30), think as ambiguously as they speak. The abuse of words results in mistaken ideas, and want of knowledge is responsible for the imperfection of words. However, were man to understand the logical operations of his own mind as it arranges particulars into species "for the convenience of comprehensive signs" (3. 6. 36), he would have as much power over language as Adam ever had. For Locke, as for Arnauld, a rational language already exists; it needs only to be expressed. Adamic naming, according to Locke, was not distinguished by an essential connection between word and thing, but by a correspondence between the order of ideas (the pattern of his thoughts) and the grammar of language: "What liberty Adam had at first to make any complex ideas of *mixed modes* by no other pattern but by his own thoughts, the same have all men ever since had. And the same necessity of conforming his ideas of *substances* to things without him, as to archetypes made by nature, that Adam was under, if he would not wilfully impose upon himself, the same are all men ever since under too. The same liberty also that Adam had of affixing any new name to any idea, the same has any one still...." (3. 6. 51). The difference between Adam and modern man is that there is already for each man an established language; we must adjust our ideas to the established language because the end of speech is communication with our fellows.[107] Even among the earlier linguists who had given up or rejected the traditional notion of Adamic naming, the search for a universal language still depended on a correspondence between words and things and was essentially a lexical and taxonomic enterprise. Locke strikingly redefines Adamic knowledge in syntactical and logical terms.

Communication, for Locke (and Arnauld), is not the mere exchange of words that are the names of ideas, but more importantly, the demonstration or intimation of a mental "action...relating to those ideas" (3. 7. 1). The words that connect the names of "things" (nouns, pronouns, adjectives, and verbs) are particles that relate not only "the parts of propositions, but whole sentences one to another, with their several relations and dependencies, to make a coherent discourse." Particles, then, are the grammatical functions that serve what Arnauld called the reasoning and ordering operations of the mind. Locke echoes Arnauld when he makes the effective expression of "methodical and rational thoughts" depend on words to show "connexion, restriction, distinction, opposition, emphasis, etc." (3. 7. 2). In what came to serve as a challenge to eighteenth-century grammarians, Locke notes that the study of particles is a part of grammar that has been "much neglected." For those linguists, particles become what Locke suggests they are, the key to the idea of language as a rational operation: "he who would show the right use of particles, and what significancy and force they have, must take a little more pains, enter into his own thoughts, and observe nicely the several postures of his mind in discoursing" (3. 7. 3). In language that is often imitated in the next century, Locke defines particles as "marks of some action or intimation of the mind," the "several views, postures, stands, turns, limitations, and exceptions" (3. 7. 4) of mental activity expressed linguistically.

Book 4 of the *Essay* distinguishes between kinds of knowledge and forms of reasoning, but throughout the *Essay* Locke retains the analogy between words and ideas, propositions (or sentences) and thoughts. It is this new idea of language that is picked out by early eighteenth-century linguists. In several places in the *Essay* Locke shows his affiliations with his countrymen's linguistic projects. He is eager to settle disputes by displaying objects themselves. Since names of substances are used to represent things, "their signification must agree with the truth of things as well as with men's ideas" (3. 11. 24). This being the case, "to define their names right, natural history is to be inquired into." Here Locke is close to Wilkins's philosophical tables. Later in the same chapter, Locke suggests a dictionary in which "words standing for things which are known and distinguished by their outward shapes should be expressed by little draughts and prints made of them" (3. 11. 25). Here Locke approves the idea of Comenius's *Orbis*.[108] But in eighteenth-century language texts, Locke is remembered for what distinguishes his views on language from those of his contemporaries.

A more detailed study of Locke could show the relationship of many of his ideas and attitudes to the long-standing claims among seventeenth-century linguists for an existing, retrievable, or created correspondence between words and things.[109] It would be easy enough to find traces of familiar ideas, but such an enterprise is likely to end up weaving robes that would add only to our comfort by reassuring us that the warp of ideas is close and continuous no matter what the design, use, or texture. That we can supply a genealogy for every idea does not mean that we ought to, even though many historians of ideas have machines ready to print out pedigrees for every project and coats of arms for every notion despondent about its detachment. Indeed, our readiness to turn what is different into what appears connected, to project the past indefinitely ahead, or to escalate analogy into identity amounts to no more than our determination to limit sense to a defense of what we believe we already know.

Such a habit gets us into more or less trouble depending on our subject. When we deal with texts around the beginning of the eighteenth century, we are likely to do a good deal of damage to what we can know since so important a redirection of intellectual life takes place then. When ideas and their practice are in transition, it is especially crucial that our methods of study not demand genealogies and continuities but, instead, remain open to difference and disruption. Locke, for instance, advertizes his *Essay* as an "essai" because it is a study in the problematics of understanding the sources and shapes of our knowledge. The conventional correspondence theory of truth, traces of which appear throughout his work, is not strong enough to dominate his inquiries. We see, in the problems he deals with and in the problems he has, a different philosophy of language, one that asserts, not the isomorphism of words and things, but the correlation between the structure of language and the activities of man's mind.

# CHAPTER 2

# Language and
# the Grammar of the Mind,
## 1700-1740

## The Distinctiveness of Early
## Eighteenth-Century Linguistics (and Literature)

In the first two decades of the eighteenth century, calls for linguistic
reforms continue but there is less of the revolutionary fervor and the
competitiveness characteristic of seventeenth-century linguistics.[1] The
issues seem much the same—the need for an English grammar true to the
genius of the language, the pedagogic importance of learning the native
language before a foreign one, and the appropriateness of fitting learning
to the natural sequence of language teaching (letters, syllables, words,
and sentences). Indeed, there is a clear, if temporary, grammatical
orthodoxy in this period, but one quite different from the common
principles of seventeenth-century linguists. The new stability of opinion
is evident in what the early eighteenth-century grammarians look back on
as the apparent coherence of recent linguistic history: Lily and his rule-
based grammar remains the enemy, but victory, it seems, has already

been won by the language revolution of the previous century. Seven-teenth-century linguists had stressed the differences between their work and that of earlier grammarians and had sought support from their contemporaries by forming groups to combat conventional errors. The associations of seventeenth-century linguists resembled the organizations —sectarian and scientific—common to intellectual life in the century, and they were indicative of the need to unite against a dominant, alien tradition. Early eighteenth-century linguists approvingly cite some of their predecessors—usually Wallis, Arnauld, Wilkins, and Locke—and compete, rather indirectly, with one another about who best presents the true principles.

The distinctive linguistic theories and techniques of the early eighteenth century are particularly important to us if only because they have not been observed before. Historical habit has massed these grammarians with a presumably uninteresting native tradition stretching from darkness in the mid-seventeenth century to glimmers of "real" linguistic light in the early nineteenth.[2] Similarly, the Augustan literary languages have been associated with the plain-speaking rigor of the Royal Society[3] or with the naive theories of visual representation imitating "Lockean literalism."[4] In fact, in both the linguistic and literary contexts there is a special character to the early eighteenth century.

In this chapter, I concentrate on the qualities and shape of the language texts, but I think that the general terms of my discussion are applicable to the literary developments of the period, as well. Antagonism to mere lexical ingenuity, for instance, persisted into a convention, as did the development of what might be called the syntactic basis of poetic language.[5] The shift, linguistically, from verbal taxonomies to syntactic structures becomes secured in this period, and it parallels, in literature, the clarification of the differences between a poetry of discrete image-units and a poetry of excursion and verse paragraphs.[6] The increasing attention paid to units of language larger than the sentence emerges in literature in the fascination with narrative generally and with prose fiction emphasizing plot particularly. The linguistic shift from things (or strictly referential ideas) to mental operations as the objects of words also has its literary and aesthetic corollary: the movement away from the imitation of objects to the representation of minds, from pictorialism to psychology. The change in linguistic analysis from a correspondence theory of meaning to a theory of logical universals recalls the compatible redirection of literary emphasis toward the psychology of style, most notably the sublime,[7] but more pervasively, the affective aesthetics of taste and sentiment. Recognizing in language texts these aspects of basic epistemological reorientation will allow us to see the literature of these years in terms of some distinctive features that have not often been reported in literary histories or in the responses to particular works. Such a comprehensive and close study of literary texts must await the work of many scholars, some of whom may be stimulated by this sort of close look at the techniques and theories of language study.

The period of agreement among early eighteenth-century linguists lasts until there seems to be no need to argue its principles any further. Then, in the 1730s, linguists, looking back, replace the commonly cited seventeenth-century authorities with the linguists of the early part of the eighteenth century. With this substitution, as we shall see at the end of this chapter, comes a significant deflation of what linguists consider to be their responsibilities in writing language texts. It is this division of responsibilities between practical instruction and rational explanation that becomes fixed in the second half of the century. The difference between ideas of language in the early and mid-century is not consciously conceptual but, to the later linguists, merely a matter of emphasis or fitness for a particular audience. However, the conceptual implications of their apparently minor organizational and definitional changes are immense. The significance of these ostensibly small changes makes an accurate and complete descriptive interpretation of the work of the early eighteenth-century linguists all the more crucial.[8]

The linguists I discuss in this chapter, then, participate in the two "quiet" revolutions that are the subject of this book. By stressing the similarities between their ideas and those of their selected predecessors and by adapting the earlier techniques of presentation, linguists at the opening of the century promote an idea of language which seems to develop naturally from their sources but which is, in fact, quite different from most of them. Later, mid-century linguists so clearly assert their "method" and so repeatedly suppress its rational justification and diminish their own claims that authority and agreement replace actual arguments. This new mood of language workers (including literary ones) adumbrates the emergence of significantly different ideas and texts.

*Language and the Grammar of the Mind, 1700–1740*

## Grammar and the Art of Expressing Thoughts

Although variations in the definitions of grammar are common throughout the seventeenth and eighteenth centuries, there was a noticeable tendency in the later seventeenth century to add "writing" to "speaking" in distinguishing the grammarian's art. In most seventeenth-century language texts, when the written language is studied, it is its elements, the very materials of language (its letters and sounds), that are described, interpreted, or reformed. The linguists of the early eighteenth century shift attention from characters to syntax, and they interpret writing as the art of discourse. Some seem troubled by their addition of "writing" to the traditional definition, partly because they see themselves as adapting rather than altering the work of their predecessors. Charles Gildon, in *A Grammar of the English Tongue* (1711), defines grammar as "the Knowledge or Art of Expressing our Thoughts in Words join'd together in Sentences,"[9] because the classical definition of grammar as the art of speaking ignores the fact that "a Mastery of it, is of more Consequence in Writing." He still holds himself responsible for a summary of received opinion about letters, their forms and sounds, since they are "evidently the Foundation of the Whole." However, at the end of a long note summarizing Wallis's *De Loquela,* Gildon disassociates himself from those who sought "to reform, or indeed make a new Alphabet ... against the Stream or full Tide of Custom" (p. 2). Such endeavors were "useless" and "singular." Gildon meets his obligation to the system of letters by offering three pages of tables displaying letter types—old English, Roman, Italian, Pipe office, Exchequer, Court hand, Running court, Chancery, Old Manuscript hand, Saxon, and Sampler letters. Letters, which for many seventeenth-century linguists had seemed the key to the meaning of the world, are here arranged in merely instructional, not interpreted or wittily imagined or pictorially reinforced lists.

James Greenwood, in *An Essay towards a Practical English Grammar* (1711), has other problems with the definition of syntax. His work depends on Wallis's *Grammatica* (1653); he even borrows substantial portions of Wallis's preface. Greenwood defines grammar as "the Art of Speaking rightly" and, like Wallis, associates natural, philosophical, rational, and Universal grammar with "the Philosophy of Letters and Speech."[10] Yet, Greenwood's chief interest in the *Essay* is to demonstrate the rational grounds of discourse, which is "the End of Grammar" (p. 35).

He consistently defers to Wallis, but at the same time, he substitutes an emphasis on etymology and syntax for his master's concentration on orthoepy and orthography. Gildon, attacking Greenwood in the *Bellum Grammaticale* (1712), approves Greenwood's use of Wallis but also points to his use of a quite different, and uncredited, authority, John Locke.[11] Greenwood, in fact, closely paraphrases Locke's discussion of the development of language from ideas and Locke's definition of the "Propriety of Speech" as "that which gives our Thoughts Entrance into other Mens Minds" (pp. 33–34).[12] Gildon rightly points to "Mr. Lock," his grammar, and Greenwood's own notes to prove that "Writing is the principal, if not the only End of Grammar."[13]

By 1724, when Thomas Wilson set out to "examin the present State of the Language,"[14] it was evident that the "Ars Loquendi" and the "Ars Scribendi" shared the same grammar, since "a Language is not bare Names and Words put together without Art and Reason; but Words in such Construction, that Persons, and common Things, and their Qualities, Actions, States, Agreements and Disagreements, may be understood according to their Numbers and Times. Words spoken without the Benefit of that rational Construction, are not Sense, or the Voice of Reason, but Confusion" (pp. 13–14). Wilson's distinction between words and names, on the one hand, and syntax, on the other, precisely captures the different emphases of seventeenth- and early-eighteenth-century linguists. For the former, the shapes and sounds of letters and words were, or could be made to be, analogous to meaning in the world; for the latter, linguistic significance depended on the system of language as it operates in human discourse.[15]

All the grammarians of the first quarter of the eighteenth century continue to include sections on letters and syllables and all agree with Lane, *A Key to the Art of Letters* (1701), that "the first and principal thing in learning of any language, is to get the true Pronunciation of the words."[16] However, they also agree that the principles of pronunciation are well known, chiefly through Wallis, and that its practice is the responsibility of schoolmasters who use the proper spelling books. Greenwood not only incorporates Wallis's preface into his own but he also apologetically puts his section on "Orthography, or Orthoepy" (p. 231) *after* his lengthy discussions of etymology and syntax.[17] He admits that pronunciation and spelling "ought to have been treated of first," but he despaired of settling all their particular problems before he got onto the more important parts of grammar. He appends a shortened version of Wallis's *De Loquela* to his *Essay* but recommends "some other way ... to render this Matter more easy and expeditious," namely, "a Book, that shall contain all the variety of Pronunciation, beginning with the Syllables and Words that are pronounc'd according to the most simple and natural Sound of the Letters, and thence proceeding gradually to Syllables and Words, that are pronounced otherwise than they are written" (pp. 231–32). This division of orthography and orthoepy from the main concerns of grammar is one consequence of the redefinition of "writing." Another is the attitude toward spelling in the period.

## Spelling Words, Not Speech

Spelling books organized as graduated lists of syllables and words already existed and became standard in the course of the first decades of the eighteenth century.[18] The difference between grammars and spelling books remained, as in the last century, more a division of labor than a distinction between ideas of language. Just as grammar books often shortened their sections on spelling and pronunciation in order to emphasize etymology and syntax, so spelling books usually had brief grammars appended to their bulky tables of syllables and words. Thomas Dyche's *A Guide to the English Tongue* (1707), the most popular spelling book of the century, is typical of the adaptation early in the century of inherited methods of representing the language. Its first part consists of twenty-six alphabetized tables ranging from the sounds of letters (*ay* to *zed*) to proper names of five and six syllables (*A-bei-miz-na-im* to *Zaph-nath-pa-a-ne-ah*). Like many handbooks of the last part of the seventeenth century, which alphabetically digested the language, Dyche's text organizes the spoken elements of language—in rhymed monosyllables arranged alphabetically by the rhyming sounds—as the first step to reading and writing. Dyche acknowledges "the many Works of this kind already Extant," but he is confident that his own book will be "more correct and useful."[19] It will be more correct because he has added accents to his tabulated words (and even made shifts in accent a reason for additional tables); and his guide will be more useful because his tables are "enlarged" (A4^v). Dyche believes he is contributing to reform already in progress, yet he adds an unusual goal in his preface. If students use his work well, the effect will be "that Children, tho' not so

capable of the Meaning of many Words, as the Latine Grammarian, who
knows their original, yet shall spell 'em every whit as truly and distinctly
as can be required." Not knowing the sources of words is no excuse,
Dyche felt, for not spelling words correctly and, more importantly, no
reason to change spelling to conform to current habits of pronunciation.

Unlike most of the spelling reformers of the late sixteenth and early
seventeenth centuries, Dyche and the other spelling-book composers of
a century later want words to reflect their native history. Unlike the
linguists of the later seventeenth century, these writers do not use the
irregularities and inconsistencies of spelling and speaking to justify
creating a new system or radically repairing the old. Spelling, for these
spelling-book authors, should reflect the origins and syntactic function
of the word. One example in this period of phonetic reform, *The Needful
Attempt to Make Language and Divinity Plain and Easie* (1711), stands
out not only because its title echoes the theological linguistics of the
previous century but also because it specifically contradicts the principles
of all other spelling books of the period. The *Needful Attempt* begins,
conventionally, by recognizing the frequent disparities between spoken
and written language, but goes on, uniquely for its time, to make the
written imitate the spoken. In this work exemplary speakers are those
who "speak most leisurely" for "the best and truest spelling ... comes
nearest to the best and commonest way of speaking."[20] After an introduction in familiar spelling comes "The English Grammar" in the
phonetic spelling. It will "bee an easi and shaurt Work" to change "our
present wai auf speling to our present wai auf speking" (p. 12), the book
argues, if we simply follow "dhe most usual wai auf speking" (p. 9). In
justifying phonetic reform, it commits two violations of accepted practice:
first it cites common speech as its model rather than, as Dyche does, the
"Custom of the best Speakers" (p. 103);[21] second, it assumes that the best
pronunciation is the easiest. Both assumptions conflict with the shift from
a philosophy of language in which words naturally or rationally signify
objects to one in which proper speech is that which best communicates
"Mens Minds." Implied in this historical development is the change from
a natural standard of pronunciation to a social one[22] and the change from
establishing the analogy of words to things to clarifying the relationship
between words and their origins or usage.

John Jones's *Practical Phonography* (1701), which was reprinted
three times in the next five years, clearly expresses the special features
of spelling reform in the period. Its most influential argument is its

insistence that "all Words which can be sounded, several ways, must be written according to the hardest, harshest, longest, and most unusual Sound."[23] He argues that "all Words were originally written as sounded" but "have since altered their Sounds . . . for Ease and Pleasure's sake." Therefore, he offers "an Universal Rule" of vowel and consonant shifts which, by reversing, will permit us to return to the visible letters of original sounds. The purpose of his work is not to recreate original spellings, but to justify the ostensibly odd habits of English orthography. Writing and spelling are his chief interests, and his "Alphabetical Spelling Dialogue" based on pronunciation leads to a justification of conventionally spelled words. Jones gives elaborate instructions for using his book, which moves from sounds to the variety of ways the sounds are written to the rules and reasons that govern the different spellings. Isaac Watts, in *The Art of Reading and Writing English* (1721), combines the work of Dyche and Jones by arranging "all the Words . . . in distinct Tables" and instructing his readers to write "according to the longest, the hardest, and the harshest Sound in which the Word is ever pronounced."[24]

These works by Jones, Dyche, and Watts strike a clearly moderate position between phonetic spelling and orthographic purity. Jones and Watts object, on the one hand, to codifying the language "az tiz spok," and, on the other, to trying to fix meaning in the shapes of letters. Jones comments, casually, that one might "easily invent an universal Language" that would be simple, sweet, and perfectly clear, but he knows that people could not "be induced to use it" (A2$^v$). Watts sensibly writes that excessive curiosity about minute orthographical features "is not worth the tedious Attendance of a reasonable Mind, nor the Labours of a short Life" (p. xix).[25] Their method is to justify the orthography of an acceptable national standard of speech and their pedagogical goal is to teach students how to read good books and write effective letters. Letter writers in this context are like private printers, and like them, they must learn how to exhibit the good sense of language.

## Pointing for Syntax

The language texts of the period, reflecting an effort to represent the obvious sense of the written language, include sections on punctuation, capitalization, and often, handwriting and type styles. These sections are significantly prominent. The second part of Dyche's *Guide,* which follows his abundant tables, provides brief rules for pronouncing and dividing syllables, and, equal in importance, a chapter "Of the Use of Capitals, Stops, and Marks in Writing" (p. 118). Lane's earlier grammar follows its brief opening section on sounds with directions for capitalization (p. 6), and even Jones concludes his sound-based spelling book with separate chapters on the "great (or capital) or larger Sorts of Letters" (p. 138) and the "Points (or Stops) or other significant Marks" (p. 141).[26] These discussions of marks become a prominent part of grammar because marks are judged to be crucial to the logical meaning of written and printed language. The fascination with marks among seventeenth-century linguists had mostly to do with their search for a method of representing reality on the page, but these eighteenth-century writers carefully redefine their attention to these devices. Repeatedly, in their sections on points and abbreviations, they distinguish their lists from those of shorthand-system makers, whom they consider to be technicians for special fields. Marks, for these eighteenth-century linguists, are not themselves significant; they are important because they indicate relationships between words or parts of a sentence rather than qualities of objects or cues for speaking.[27]

Punctuation marks, which Michael Maittaire discusses at the end of his chapter on orthography in *The English Grammar* (1712), are important "not only for the ease of breath, but also for the better understanding of the sense."[28] The first part of that definition is an inheritance from Lily and his predecessors, but the second part, on the relationship between stops and sense, indicates a new emphasis, introduced in the mid-seventeenth century but only common in this period. For Maittaire, punctuation marks serve to distinguish "the Syntax or Doctrine of Sentences" (p. 22). He defines the comma, for instance, as an "incision or fragment" that "distinguishes the imperfect senses and shorter constructions of each depending clause" (p. 192). Such definitions draw our attention once more to the major difference between seventeenth- and eighteenth-century ideas of language: in the earlier period the basic linguistic unit was the letter, sound, syllable, or word; later, it is the syntactical function. Maittaire offers the most detailed discussions of punctuating for syntactic sense, but it is in Hugh Jones's *An Accidence to the English Tongue* (1724) that we find the clearest expression of the working principle. Jones adds to the familiar four parts of grammar a fifth chapter on "English Discourse, or Speech," which he defines as a "Collection of Several Sentences concerning the same Subject ... divided into Sentences by four Stops."[29]

In most texts of the period, lists of other printed marks—such as hyphen, parenthesis, asterisk—are added to the four primary stops—comma, semicolon, colon, and period—because they too help divide the segments of sentences and make the syntactic structure visible. And, since figures of speech like ellipsis and pleonasmus are syntactical features, such marks help identify them as well. This new attention to syntactic units as equivalent to the significant portions of logic in a discourse resembles the elaborate variations being played on the heroic couplet at the same time.[30] Since writing is "the Picture or Image of Speech," writes Greenwood, it should include marks "adapted unto all the Material Circumstances of it" (p. 225). Parenthesis signifies additional parts of a sentence, "not necessary to perfect the Sense of it" (p. 226), and emphasis is marked by putting "Words into another Character, as the Italick ... or by beginning the Word with a Capital or great Letter" (p. 227). Greenwood even proposes that "there ought to be some Mark" for irony (he proposes <) to make sense as visual as possible.[31]

The emergence of debates about capitalization in this period also draws attention to the completion of the transition from the search to connect words with things to the assumption that the written language should be marked for syntactic sense. All the language practitioners of the early part of the century agree that capitals should be used to indicate emphasis, but this recommendation brings them into conflict with "Fashion," as Greenwood writes, especially the habits of printers. Gildon relates this problem to the efforts of Lodwick and Wilkins to use their "universal Alphabet" to make sounds, characters, and significance identical. Gildon has no hopes that people will "learn their Alphabet over again" (p. 58), but, possibly, such variations as the distinction between capitals and small letters could be made more significant, and more pleasing: "this Distinction is of great Advantage, and Beauty in mingling with a pleasing Variety the Capitals, and Small letters, in the beginning of Periods, proper Names, and to distinguish Names from Words of Affirmation, and all other Parts of Speech" (p. 57). Gildon, like his seventeenth-century predecessors, imagines a visual language, but one that makes distinguishing marks indicators of etymological and syntactic functions only. For Gildon, there is visual beauty in the page that consistently marks the different parts of speech. His view is taken up by printers in the first half of the century.[32]

Opposition to Gildon's view of capitals comes from Dyche, Watts, Greenwood, and Maittaire, among others, but all in the interest of a stricter sense of emphasis, truer to the actual stress of interrelated thoughts.[33] Maittaire does not want to capitalize all nouns, and, to prove his point, he pointedly uses the lower case for the first person pronoun. Gildon, who attacks Maittaire's *Grammar* in a postscript to his *Bellum Grammaticale,* picks out for satire the latter's "ridiculous Affectation of so absurd a Singularity, as always to write the pronoun I like the small vowel i; as if Distinction and Clearness were Vices of Speech, not Virtues" (pp. 62–63).[34] Maittaire's modest "i" remains an oddity among eighteenth-century books; and since the triumph of the written and printed language delivers the linguists to the hands, and sometimes the mercy, of printers, the only solution to the Gildon-Maittaire debate was to add additional markers for emphasis. Gildon himself suggests using different type styles for emphasis and points to "the Difference of Hands, or Figures of Writing or Printing, as the Roman, Italic, German, etc. in the Impression of this very Book" (p. 57). These different types are "usefully employ'd in the Distinction, either of certain Words, or certain Discourses, and Sentences, which conveys the Force and Energy intended by the Author to the Reader." Finally, Gildon's book does not look very different from Maittaire's. Although they disagree about the use of capitals, they both use print to show the relations between different parts of their language systems.

This competitive use of every aspect of the printing process for marking emphasis produces, as Gildon's ideas suggest, a visually rich page. Title pages, in particular, look like samplers of typeface, design, and size (fig. 6). Some emphasis comes from initial capitals, more from all capitals, still more from italic or gothic face, more again from size, and, if variations of kind and size are exhausted, color can be introduced. To judge from the pages of these books, almost nothing is unimportant; but the crucial point these crowded, confused pages reveal is the complexity of the relationship between differently stressed parts.[35]

## Syntactic Functions and the Relations of Ideas

The visual devices used by early-eighteenth-century linguists to alert

A

GRAMMAR

OF THE

English Tongue,

With NOTES,

Giving the Grounds and Reason of

Grammar in General.

To which is added,

A New PROSODIA;

OR,

The ART of English Numbers.

All adapted to the Use of

GENTLEMEN and LADIES,

As well as of the

SCHOOLS of Great Britain.

LONDON,

Printed for JOHN BRIGHTLAND, and Sold
by Mr. Gay in Lombard-Street, Mr. Sare at Grays-Inn, Mr. Brown
at Temple-bar, Mr. Mount on Tower-Hill, Mr. Barnes in Pall-
mall, Mr. Sprint in Little-Britain, Mr. Taylor in Pater-noster-
row, Mr. Strahan in Cornhill, Mr. Gundy in Westminster-hall,
Mr. Bettsworth on London-bridge, Mr. Clements in St. Paul's
Church-yard, and other Bookfellers of Great Britain and Ire-
land, 1711.

THE

APPROBATION

OF

Isaac Bickerstaff, Esq;

THE following Treatise being submitted to my
Censure, that I may pass it with Integrity, I
must declare, That as Grammar in general is on all
hands allow'd the Foundation of All Arts and
Sciences, so it appears to me, that this Grammar of
the English Tongue has done that Justice to our
Language which, 'till now, it never obtain'd. The
Text will improve the most Ignorant, and the Notes
will imploy the most Learned. I therefore enjoin
all my Female Correspondents to Buy, Read, and
Study this Grammar, that their Letters may be
something less Enigmatic; And on all my Male
Correspondents likewise, who make no Conscience
of False-Spelling and False-English, I lay the same
Injunction, on Pain of having their Epistles expos'd
in their own proper Dress, in my Lucubrations.

Isaac Bickerstaff, Censor.

Figure 6. [Charles Gildon], A Grammar of the English Tongue (1711), title page.
Reproduced by permission of the Houghton Library, Harvard University.

readers to the significance of their works contrast with the visual grammars and visualized languages of seventeenth-century linguists. In the earlier books, visual clues signified the actual nature or classification of the thing signified, so that, for instance, dots around a mark could indicate vowel sounds placed according to a picture of the relationship of physical sounds in the mouth. In the later books, attention to visual presentation has more to do with usefulness, convenience, and memorization. The grammars by Maittaire and Greenwood and the spelling books of Jones and Watts, for example, use typeface and size to distinguish parts of their books intended for different users, some being meant to read the Roman text, others the italic notes. These writers separate the practical grammar from its rational grounds by giving each a different portion of the page or a different typeface. The implication of this distinction, one crucial to the fate of language study later in the century, is that students can learn the language without acknowledging its rational justifications. The complete independence of language learning and philosophical discussion is loudly denied by the linguists of the early part of the century, but their practice turns out to be more influential than their stated principles.

Gildon represents the distinction between practical and rational grammar by the difference between text and notes. Such a separation permits "Children, Women, and the Ignorant of both Sexes" (A4ʳ) to read across the tops of the pages and affords "the reasonable Teacher" the "Reasons of Things" in the smaller type. This convenient division between the terms seventeenth-century linguists were determined to unite is defended on sensible gounds of usage, but there is a more important rationale, one that reveals the altered assumptions about the philosophical basis of language in the eighteenth century. For most seventeenth-century linguists the order of learning the language, reformed, revised, or invented, corresponded to the order of nature. In the last years of the seventeenth century, the philosophical basis of language moves from the nature of external reality to the structure of the human mind. By the early eighteenth century, this process is complete, and the physical separation between the rules of language use and the reasons for those rules is one consequence. The new philosophical assumptions are admittedly explanatory rather than presumptively descriptive.

Richard Johnson's *Grammatical Commentaries* (1706) supports a practical Latin grammar with extensive notes that provide the philosophical basis of language. His text begins with the definition of grammar common to seventeenth-century texts: "Grammatica est recte loquendi atq; scribendi Ars."[36] But his note, which goes on for four pages, corrects this once standard definition, at least for those who read these portions of the page, and offers an alternate definition, which clearly states the new grounds of grammar: "Grammar is the Art of Expressing the Relations of Things in Construction" (p. 3). Johnson, who advertises his work as an "Animadversion Upon the Falsities, Obscurities, Redundancies, and Defects of Lilly's System" (A1$^r$), distinguishes his interest in "Grammatical Systems" (p. 1) from Lily's insistence on "Rules . . . without any mention at all of the Relation of the Word govern'd" (p. 4). Johnson's "relations" are what his contemporaries usually called the "Reasons of Things"; they refer to *"Cause, Effect, Means, End, Manner, Instrument, Object, Adjunct,* and the like; which are Names given by Logicians to those Relations, under which the Mind comprehends Things, and therefore the most proper to discover them by, or speak of them to others." Johnson's use of logical terms to denote syntactical features shows his adaptation to the linguistic ideas of the masters of Port-Royal and John Locke.[37] Johnson works hard to save grammar from Lily's rules, which prescribed grammatical functions without observing the conceptual content of linguistic categories. The definition of a conjunction as a "Part of Speech that joineth Words and Sentences together" (p. 407) is, Johnson argues, not only inaccurate but inadequate since the conjunction does "not barely join . . . but so joins . . . as to shew the manner of . . . dependence" (p. 408). Similarly, the preposition should not be defined without naming "what other Parts of Speech it is set before, nor for what end." The correct definition would state that prepositions "are us'd to shew the Relation of Nouns Substantives in Discourse." True grammar reunites the structure of language with the arts of logic and rhetoric, "the Art of Speaking having such an Affinity with that of reasoning which it represents" (B2$^v$).

Johnson and his contemporary linguists repeatedly cite the distinction between the arbitrariness of words and the universality of syntax. In texts as learned as Johnson's, as modest as Lane's, and as market-hungry as Gildon's, admitting the force of custom serves as the prerequisite of the philosophical claims they all stress. For Lane, "late Master of the Free school of Leominster in Herefordshire, now Teacher of a private School at Mile-end-green near Stepney," the primary concern is the misery, toil, and perplexity common in the schools. His book refers to three causes of suffering: the putting of words before meaning, oppressing the memory with "Forein Grammars" (p. xiv), and depending on "Grammatical Propositions or Rules barely propos'd" (p. xv). Such habits are faulty because none help teach students "how to speak and write well in a Language, already known according to the unalterable rules of right Reason, which are the same in all Languages, how different soever they be" (p. x). These rules reflect the universals of mental functioning, and this theory of a logical psychology replaces the theory of correspondence, which supported the linguistic ontology of the previous century. The new concern is less with what words (or things) are than with how words (and ideas) function.

Lane's key to grammatical knowledge, in the phrase that reappears in many of the texts of the period, is "the Reasons of things" (p. xv). These reasons are incorporated in definitions which use terms drawn from logic:

> ... which I think (with submission to better Judgments) to be nothing else but Grammar, except [Aristotle's] superadded invention of Syllogisms, and some other things of less use, which he ingrafted upon the Stock of Grammar. And in my weak opinion the Art of thinking and speaking are not two but one Art; for Grammar first teaches us how to conceive of things in the order of Nature, and then how to express our Conceptions by speaking or writing: for we can never speak or write well, what we cannot rightly conceive; Speaking being nothing else but vocal Thoughts, and Thoughts but silent Speaking, and Writing the Images or Characters of them both. (p. xvii)

Much of this, including the adaptation of Aristotle, is drawn from the coordinated grammar, logic, and rhetoric of Port-Royal. For Lane, the philosophical basis of "rational knowledg" begins with thoughts, not with the nature of things. Although a word is simply "an Articulate sound that signifies something by the Custom of any Language" (p. 18), there are "but four kinds of Words, because there are but four kinds of things to be signified by Words" (p. 20). The perceived world consists of things and their aspects, the "Actions of things" and their attitudes; and the mind, perceiving this order, expresses its thoughts in an equally ordered language.

Gildon, in his *Grammar,* defends the new, reforming grammarians against the "revolutionaries" of the previous century who tried "to forge a New Language, and to alter the Orthography now in Use and settled by Custom" (A5$^r$). His sources for the "Rational Grounds of Grammar"

(A6$^r$) are Wallis and the masters of Port-Royal. He also cites Lane as a worthy grammarian, but one who "extended and tortur'd our Tongue to confess to the Latin." For Gildon, the accurate presentation of the "Use, Form, and Propriety of every Tongue" (p. ii) would, unlike the vain and whimsical inventions of the previous century or the Latinizations of his contemporaries, reveal the "inviolable rule, and right of speaking, and writing" (p. 2). Since all knowledge "draws its Original from the Senses, and our Perception, Judgment, and Reasoning" (p. 67) and since grammar is "the knowledge or Art of Expressing our Thoughts in Words" (A6$^v$), then "the several Classes, or Orders of Words are rang'd" (p. 68) under the activities of the mind. Words "proceed from these Notices of Things, and Beings, and their Relations to each other ... whence it seems pretty plain that the Words, which are to express our Sentiments of these Things, must bear some Proportion and Likeness to the Things they are to Express."[38]

Frequently in his grammar, Gildon feels the need to distinguish his claims for a rational language from those of seventeenth-century linguists; for him, there is "no real or natural likeness betwixt the Words, and operations of the soul of man; but only signs by compact, and agreement to signify our thoughts" (p. 69). For a "natural" relationship between words and ideas, Gildon substitutes a logical one: "the knowledge of what passes in the mind, is necessary for the understanding of the principles of grammar" (p. 71). Gildon derives his description of the three operations of the mind—perception, judgment, and reason—from Arnauld and Locke, and these are the grounds for "the general reason of all languages" (p. 97). From perception derive the first two parts of speech, the names of things and their qualities; from judgment comes the third part of speech—words of affirmation; and from reason comes the manners of words. Gildon cannot keep the three operations clear and distinct, but no more could Locke, and the problem for both is language as men use it. Human speech does not name without affirming or make affirmations without attitudes or manners. The "greatest Distinction" Gildon insists on is to "signify ... the Objects of our Thoughts, and the Form and Manner of them" (p. 70), yet even this "most general Distinction of Words" is complicated by the fact that words "do not signify the Manner alone, but in Conjunction" with the objects of thought.

Gildon has difficulty organizing the operations of the mind and the classes of words because the systems are not static taxonomies. Each system specifies classes that, in use, constantly interact. It is because of this dependence of communication on the syntactical operations of speech and the rational workings of the mind that Gildon, like Locke, gives such emphasis to particles. The part of speech corresponding to reason includes adverbs, prepositions, conjunctions, and interjections. The first two "signifie the Form of ... Objects"; the second two "signifie nothing but the very Operation of the Mind ... and mark the Motion of our soul" (p. 118). Such an emphasis on particles, as opposed to substantives or verbs, is common in the period. Even Johnson, whose *Grammatical Categories* shows no other restraint from elaboration or small print, finds he must stop when he gets to the problems of prepositions, for an explanation "would make a little Volume" (p. 408). And Hugh Jones, in his *Accidence to the English Tongue,* gives "the proper Particles of Connection" the responsibility of cementing the "whole Discourse ... together" (p. 67).

Greenwood, like his antagonist, Gildon, and his favorite contemporary authority, Johnson, associates Wallis's work with that of Wilkins and Locke. Linking Wilkins and Wallis with Locke minimizes the claims of the first two for an ontological connection between "the Character and the Names of Things." He stresses, instead, the implications of Wilkins's division of words into "integrals" and "particles." These two classes, argues Greenwood, identify both the operations of human understanding and the ordering of discourse. To make Wilkins agree with Locke, these eighteenth-century linguists ignored the former's desire to supersede ·custom. For Greenwood, particles are "as it were, the Nerves and Ligaments of all Discourse" (p. 69) since "the Mind is not always employ'd about single Objects only, but does likewise compare one thing with another, in order to express the Relation and Respect that Things have to one another" (p. 51). Particles, argues Greenwood in agreement with "the Great Mr. Lock," signify the operations of the mind connected "in one continued Reasoning or Narration" (p. 70). Clarity of reason, as of style, depends on "the Train ... the Dependence of ... Thoughts and Reasonings one upon another," and the words that signify these relations are drawn from logic: "Connexion, Restriction, Distinction, Opposition, Emphasis, etc." To define particles (and Greenwood is here in agreement with Johnson), one must study their "several Views, Postures, Stands, Turns, Limitations, and Exceptions" since they are "all Marks, of some Action, or Intimation of the Mind" (p. 71). Were particles adequately defined, we would know "the several Postures of the Mind" (p. 72).

*Language and the Grammar of the Mind, 1700–1740*

In the works of Greenwood, Gildon, Maittaire, and the others, the shift away from the ontological commitment of many of their linguistic predecessors is complete. The universal language projectors, the elementary grammarians, and the various shorthand and sign-system code-seekers of the seventeenth century had depended, for the most part, on substantives, in language and in nature. Even for Wilkins, Locke, and Mark Lewis, particles were as problematic as they were potentially significant. The substitution of a theory of logical universals describing the operations of the mind for a theory of correspondence between lexical and natural taxonomies appears in language texts in the new importance given particles (the ligaments of thought and ligatures of language) and in the priority of the verb over the noun (reflecting the logical dominance, since the time of Port-Royal, of judgment). Grammar becomes, preeminently, the syntax of connectives, and this characterization of language brings us close to one of the distinctive qualities of literary language in the period. The mere sight of objects means little to Pope, for simply seeing is likely to lead to just a collection of things, and the poetic result of a collection is the morally defective device of an undifferentiated series of objects ("Puffs, Powders, Patches, Bibles, Billet-doux"). Pope associates value, morally and literarily, with composition, with the well-connected series of verse paragraphs and the syntactic sophistications of cleverly coordinated couplets.[39] His finite variations on the couplet form invite readers to a play of rules, and this mental agility is principal proof that readers are with Pope on his poetic excursions.

## The New Pedagogy

The obvious agreement between Gildon and Greenwood about the philosophical grounds of practical grammar probably encouraged Gildon to attack Greenwood (and Maittaire) in the *Bellum Grammaticale*. The *Bellum* opens with understandably mixed feelings about the "mighty Bent, in the Buyers of Books, to Grammatical Essays" (p. 3). The author is of two minds: in the persona of someone criticizing all recent grammars, including the one Gildon wrote for Brightland, he charges them with pedagogical confusions; in the person of Gildon, who is eager to distinguish the virtues of his own work (under the name of "your Antagonist"), he succeeds in claiming superiority only by ignoring Greenwood's footnotes. For Gildon, this is simply a malicious technique, but it becomes an increasingly common response to grammars, like Gildon's own, that divide the page between practical and rational grammars. Such pages, instead of representing the rules of practical grammar resting on a rational groundwork, could be read as authorizing the independence of practical grammar.[40]

Gildon pulls Wallis, Arnauld, Locke, and Johnson on his side and criticizes Greenwood for keeping to "the old exploded track" (p. 24) while "your Antagonist has from Mr. Arnaud . . . given us the whole Rationale of the Thing" (p. 18). Gildon cleverly isolates the section of Greenwood's *Essay* that is most dependent on seventeenth-century assumptions, that is, in fact, a translation of Wallis's *De Loquela,* and even more pointedly, that portion of *De Loquela* that is most alien to the later grammarians—the identification of syllables with particular significations. He uses Greenwood's inclusion of Wallis's meaningful syllables to prove that Greenwood has not understood Bacon and Locke on the arbitrary connections between words and ideas. Gildon chides Greenwood for "quitting Nature, where she is not to be found, as in spelling" (p. 53). He attacks him for ignoring the fact that "Words are made to express the various Operations of the Mind" (p. 54) and for skipping "backward and forward, so that the Learner can make no gradual Rise towards a regular, that is, a sure and lasting knowledge" (p. 55).

Gildon's brief dismissal of Maittaire is selfishly motivated and perverse since they share the prevailing assumptions about language and mind. The material Gildon finds ready to be mocked in Maittaire is an absurd ink-horn vocabulary. Maittaire chooses his odd terms— heterostoichy, heterology, heteroclisy—in order to reunite grammar and philosophy by combining language and logic. Admitting the difficulty of giving a "just Idea of Things in the Definition of knotty and dry Grammatical Terms," he often calls in "the help not only of Logick but even of Metaphysick to discuss these minute Principles of Speech" (p. viii). Scattered throughout Maittaire's footnotes are analogies between language and geometry that echo some of the correspondences pursued by seventeenth-century linguists, including Wallis. Like Greenwood's reference to particles as the "Nerves and Ligaments" of speech, Maittaire's comparison is metaphoric, not literal. When Maittaire spins out his analogies, he does "not pretend to raise an exact and adequate proportion between Points and Letters, Syllables and Lines, Words and Schemes" (p. 5). Rather, he seeks an expressive, not a philosophically descriptive, parallel, and what he tries to express is the fact that the parts of speech "are by a necessary and mutual dependence so linked, that not one can be thoroughly understood without the knowledge of all the rest" (p. 60). Although Maittaire had already "compared Sentences to Axioms in Mathematics . . . where an adequate and perfect comparison is not pretended to," he goes on to consider the sentence "in allusion to a Mathematical Circle," as a "Period of so many words concurring towards the making of one full sense; the Verb is the Center, in which all those Words, like so many Lines meeting are united, from which they proceed, and unto which they tend, and bear a constant relation." Maittaire's disclaimer of exact correspondence between language and mathematics does not prevent him from profiting from the analogy; in fact, the distinction between identification and metaphor represents the difference between seventeenth-century philosophical explanations of language and those of Maittaire and his contemporaries.[41] The metaphoric nature of the analogy not only highlights this difference but also characterizes the new philosophical premise. For Maittaire, language works as the mind reasons, and this is an analogy between operations that use quite different elements, that is, conventionally connected words and thoughts.

Maittaire's illustrative analogies characterize a rather brief period of general agreement about the philosophical basis of language. A metaphoric sense such as his is unsteady at best, for there is always a tendency either to collapse the terms of the metaphor—in this case, mental and linguistic operations—into a real identity or to establish firmer barriers between them.[42] The desire to identify the terms, as, for instance, in seventeenth-century linguistics, is clearly antithetical to the intentions of the grammarians we have been discussing. However, their attempts to distinguish themselves from their predecessors contributed to the building of virtually permanent barriers. Although it seemed a good idea to separate the practical grammar from its reasons on the page, the effect was to suggest that the rational grounds were less significant, at least pedagogically, than the practical rules. Another interpretation of Maittaire's admittedly inadequate and imperfect comparisons is that they are as trivial as the type size in which they are printed. This is not Maittaire's interpretation, but, as we shall see in the next chapter, it is the view of many later eighteenth-century grammarians. Robert Lowth, whose *Short Introduction to English Grammar With Critical Notes* (1762) is one of the most popular grammars of the last third of the century, keeps the practical grammar in larger type atop the page but uses his notes to prove "the charge of inaccuracy brought against our Language as it subsists in practice."[43] Anyone interested in learned disquisitions on language, writes Lowth, can go to James Harris,[44] author of the philosophically erudite *Hermes: or, A Philosophical Inquiry Concerning Language and Universal Grammar.*

## The Method of Logical Grammars

It would be wrong to represent the changes in philosophical interests among the linguists either as a steady decline from the ambitiousness of seventeenth-century projects or progress toward the few dominant linguistic texts of the last part of the eighteenth century. To do so would blur the distinctive and important claims made by particular groups of linguists. It would be as misleading to interpret the early-eighteenth-century grammarians as pale imitations of their seventeenth-century predecessors as it would be to declare seventeenth-century linguistic philosophy dead with the stillborn appearance of Wilkins's *Real Character.* In order to recognize the significance of linguistic self-consciousness among the literary writers of Augustan England, for instance, we must determine the core principles of linguists who apply the philosophy of Arnauld and Locke to the practice of language.

*Method* is a word frequently found in the texts of these early-eighteenth-century linguists.[45] Questions of method are critical because, as for the innovative schoolmasters of the previous century, "Order in Teaching" contributes "mainly to Order in Understanding, so far as any thing is out of Order, so far 'tis out of the way of being understood."[46] The order, as with those earlier teachers, proceeds from letters to syllables to words to sentences. But, distinctively, the new pedagogy passes quickly over marks and pronunciation to get to etymology and syntax, for it is with these parts of grammar that human meaning becomes possible. Rather than finding or inventing the significance of the basic materials of speech, early-eighteenth-century linguists define meaning in terms of the functions of words in discourse. Greenwood, to Gildon's obvious glee, organizes his book to reflect the relative importance of the familiar parts of grammar. As we have noted, he puts his section on orthography and orthoepy last because Wallis had already settled the problems and because the rational basis of language appears not in spelling books but in the study of "the Relation and Respect that

Things have to one another" (p. 51). Gildon, in the *Bellum,* takes Greenwood's variant sequence as an opportunity to ridicule the lack of "Method and Order" (p. 9) in the *Essay.* However much the primary signifying function of language has shifted from semantics to syntax, the order of learning, Gildon insists, must be confirmed by the sequence of sections in language books.[47] The rational basis of language, in this version, is an explanation added on to the approved pedagogical sequence.

## The Shape of Logical Grammars

The correspondence between method and sequence is associated, as before, with techniques of printed visualization, but again there are crucial differences. Instead of the taxonomic illustrations common in seventeenth-century linguistic texts, we find printed keys controlling the eyes of readers and directing them to the best use of the books. The deliberate division of text and notes is the most noticeable example of this, but even grammatical lessons often read like instructions to a printer. Richard Johnson (*Grammatical Commentaries*) recommends not only his use of alphabetical lists but also his supervision of the printed format of his book: "And for the farther Ease of the Reader ... I have digested the Words treated of into Alphabetical Order, and for the most part set them out before the rest of the Matter in the beginning of the Line, or else indented them as was most convenient in point of room" (C1[v]).

There are more elaborate instructions for using a book, but none more ingenious than Jones, in his *Practical Phonography* (see fig. 7).[48] Jones, in promoting his book, reads like Comenius, Coles, and the many "syncretists" of the seventeenth century who also taught language by looking. For Jones, however, what students should see are not objects but the intricately organized pages of his book, which relates sounds to spellings. Jones instructs his students to memorize "the Examples of Rules in the Alphabetical Spelling Dialogue ... which will cause the Sounds of Words, as printed, or to be written, easily to recurr to your Mind" (p. 12).[49] The books themselves serve as the models of understanding, with understanding defined as the ability to build relations into a system.

In using the grammars of the period, those who read the notes with the text showed greater understanding than those who read the text only.

(IV) The main (and as 'tis thought the only *Exceptions*) to the *general Rule* being (I) That some sounds are never Writ tho sounded as, *eu, eeu, iu, iw, ú ú. uoo. uw, wu, yi, yu*, &c. (II) That some *Letters* are *Writ* that cannot be *Sounded*; as *two Letters* of the same sort in one Syllable, or *b* after *g*, &c. It has *two Chapters* showing you which they are so that the obstacles of the Universality of those *Rules* being removed (*as is aforesaid*) as to our *Language*: *The third Promise of Spelling so many Words in few days as to fail but in very few is answered*, especially considering that.

(V) It shows you to Spell all *Derivatives*, and *Compounds*; and when *silent final e is Writ*, when *not*; when upon addition thereto *it remains*, and when it is *lost*, or *changed to s*, or sounding *e* &c. which is all the Variety that happens to *it*; There are some other helps that we have not room to insert.

## An Account of the Third Part.

The *Neatness*, and *Newness* of this *Contrivance* is far beyond our *Description* without giving you a *Pattern* thereof which follows.

| ANSWERS. | | A. AI. | QUESTIONS | |
|---|---|---|---|---|
| The Sound of | Is Writ. | *Particular Alphabetical Rules.* | When is the Sound of | Writ. |
| a | aa | When it may be also sounded *a a*, as in these *Scripture-Names*, *Aaron. Balaam, Canaan, Isaac, Naaman*, &c. | a | aa ? |
| a | ad | When it may be also sounded *ad*, as in *adjacent* \| *adjoyn* \| *adjure* } Which are generally sounded *adjourn* \| *adjudge* \| *adjutants* } without the *d*. | a | ad ? |
| a | ae | In *Caer* in the beginning of Names of *Towns* and *Castles* in *Wales*, as *Caerleon, Caermarthen, Caernarvon, Caerwent*, &c. | a | ae ? |
| a | agh | In some *Irish* Words, as *Armagh, Bernagh, Caterlagh, Drogedagh, Usquebagh*, &c. | a | agh ? |
| a | ah | In the end of many *Scripture*-Names, as *Dalilah* \| *Elijah* \| *Jehovah* } And many more omitted here *Deborah* \| *Esaiah* \| *Nehemiah* } for brevity sake, but recited in *Dinah* \| *Hannah* \| *Sarah*. } the Book. | a | ah ? |
| a | aha | In — *Abraham*, which is sounded as with *a* for *aha*. | a | aha ? |
| a | ai | When it may be sounded *ai*, as in *Abigail* \| *bargain* \| *curtain* } Which are often sounded as *afraid* \| *Captain* \| *daisy*, &c. } with *a* only. | a | ai ? |
| a | al | When it may be sounded *al*, as in *almost* \| *calf* } And about 40 more, all which the Book men-*alms* \| *half* } tions Alphabetically, as it doth all such. | a | al ? |
| a | e | When it may be sounded *e* also, as in *Berks* \| *eleven* } And many more that the Book has. *Clerk* \| *phrentick* } | a | e ? |
| a | ea | In these, *Viz.* *changeable* \| *beard* } And many more that the Book has, *chargeable* \| *heart* } | a | ea ? |
| a | ua | In these, *Viz.* *guard, guardian*, &c. And many more, all which the *Book* has. | a | ua ? |
| ai | ayo | In — *Mayor*, which is sounded as without the *o*. | ai | ayo ; |
| ai | ei | When it may be also sounded *ei* in any part of a Word, but the end; where it is writ *ey*, as in *Conceit, deceit, heifer, veil, vein*, &c. The *Book* has all such. | ai | ei ? |

#### The forgoing *Pattern* explained.

The *Rules*, and *Examples* of this *Part* take in all Words used in the *English Language*, that are *Sounded* otherwise than *Writ*, and run all *Alphabetically* as *Dictionaries* doe from the Sound of *A* to that of *Z inclusively*.

The *Letters* that signify the Sounds of Words *as Spoken* are in the *left* Column (or *Row*) in each *Margin* under the Word *Sound*, and the *Letters* that signify how they are *Writ* in the *right* Hand *Row* (or *Column*) over against the *other*, under the Word *Writ*.

The *Alphabetical* Order mainly concerns the *Letters* that signify the Sound of Words, in the *left* Hand Column of each *Margin*; because it is by the *Sounds*, that you *must* learn to find how they are *Writ* in the other Column, tho these are in order also.

This is done, that you may find how any *Sound* is *Writ* by turning to the *Letter Sounded*. Thus you find the Sound of a Writ *Aa* in *Aaron, Balaam, Isaac*, &c; Writ *ad* in *Adjacent, Adjourn*, &c. Writ *ae* in *Caernarvon*, &c. and so in all Sounds to that of *Z inclusively*.

The *Sounds* or *Words* not to be found contain'd in, or under these *Rules* in the *Book* are to be *Writ* as *Sounded*; because (*as was said*) they contain all that are *Writ* otherwise than usually *Sounded*, tho in the *Pattern* we have instanced but in few *Rules*, and added but few *Examples* for want of room. Therefore you have an *Adequate* and complete *Art of Spelling* Never (we suppose) hoped for, or thought possible.

Nor *is that* all but the whole runs in *Questions* and *Answers*, which are under the Words *Questions* and *Answers* on the top of the *Columns*; nay it is so contrived, that one *Question* and one *Answer* serves quite thoughout only putting in the *Letters Sound ed* after (*Sound of*) and the *Letters Writ* after (*writ*) as you see in the following Three *Questions*, and the Three Answers made thereunto.

Q. When is the Sound of a Writ aa?
Q. When is the Sound of a Writ ad?
Q. When is the Sound of a Writ ae? &c.
Ans. The Sound of a is Writ aa when it may &c.
Ans. The Sound of a is Writ ad when it may &c.
Ans. The Sound of a is Writ ae in *Caer* in the &c.

So that there is no trouble to learn the *Questions* as in other cases, and no falling in any *Question*, because all run *Alphabetically*, that a *Master, Scholar* or one *self* may examine without the Book.

Now, it is the *Reading, Perusing*, and *Examining* by these *Rules*, and learning to *Read by*, and *Writing Copies out* of the *Examples* of these *Rules* in a peculiar manner directed at large by the *Book* it self, that perfects *Spelling*, and *Writing*, as is promised in the *Fourth* and *Fifth particular*. And

That of *Sounding all Words* rightly at the first *View* is now as *Easy*, as it was *Surprizing*; for it is only learning to *Read* by the *Examples* of these *Rules*, and Sounding them according to the Sound of the *Letter*, or *Letters* in the *first* Column which signifys the usual *Sound of Words*: *This performs the first promise*.

#### An Account of the Fourth Part.

This is a *Dictionary* distinguishing Words of the *same*, or *like Sounds* as is aforesaid; and *Performs the Sixth promise*.

*Note*, That to avoid even the *View* of Words ill Spelled, which may affect by errour, or otherwise; it is so contrived that the Learner has not as much as the *Sight* of any Word Spelled amiss as in *Common Spelling Books* that put the Words both ways; whereby as much room again is taken up, and the *Learner* amused: So that neither the *Questions*, nor such wrong *Spelled Words* take up any room, or cause any trouble

*Note*, That all Words that are to be *Writ* with great or *Capital Letters* in the *Examples* are so Writ, and others otherwise. that the *Learner* may always have the true *Sight* of Words as they are and not be prejudiced by any other *View* thereof

A 3

Figure 7. John Jones, *Phono-graphy* (1698), p. 3. Reproduced by permission of the British Library Board.

Students were to become more rational as they came to understand the rational underpinnings of the language system. The basic visualizing device remains the table, but these linguists do not use tables to represent reality, merely to clarify the system. Johnson, persistently animadverting on Lily, answers complaints of schoolmasters that his opponent's grammar did not fully describe declensions by tipping in a page displaying sets of examples: "a Draught of the Verbal formations, as would distinguish the Body of the Verb . . . from the other parts of it . . . and the Difference between the Active, and Passive so represented, as to be seen at one View" (p. 366).[50] Solomon Lowe, in *A Critique on the Etymology of the Westminster Grammar* (1723), admits that Lily's faults had been fairly exposed by Johnson but that the shortcomings of Richard Busby's *Rudimentum Grammaticae* (1688) also needed to be corrected. Lowe claims as the special distinction of the grammar he proposes that "all the doctrin of every great article . . . is drawn up so as to be taken in at one view, and presented, as in a picture, to sense and imagination, in order to assist memory and judgment."[51] In his work "the whole . . . rises to the view at once" (p. v), and this encourages students to see "the symmetry of the whole." For this pedagogic reform, Lowe requires the cooperation of his printer, since the "one great difference" of his whole work "consists in the disposing of the matter, or manner of printing." In practice Lowe uses small and large letters, type styles, brackets, and various other marks to illustrate the relations between parts of his systematic representation (see fig. 8).[52]

The use of illustrations that are organizational rather than symbolic fits the basic philosophy of language in the period: the reasonableness of language is its syntax (and its etymology, since that term usually included the parts of speech).[53] However, because the rational basis of language had become an explanation of its operation rather than an evident result of a full description, illustrations of the system of language could no longer simultaneously display its logic. Thomas Wilson, in *The Many Advantages of a Good Language* (1724), describes the most useful kind of grammar:

> For the Eight Parts of Speech containing the whole Number of Words within their Compass, their Agreements, Government and Connexions might easily be brought into their View; and the whole System of Language, both as Reason and Use made it, might be kept in the Memories of those that applied their Minds that way: And I will take leave to add, that no Man must now pretend to be a real Grammarian, or take upon him to make a true Judgment of the State

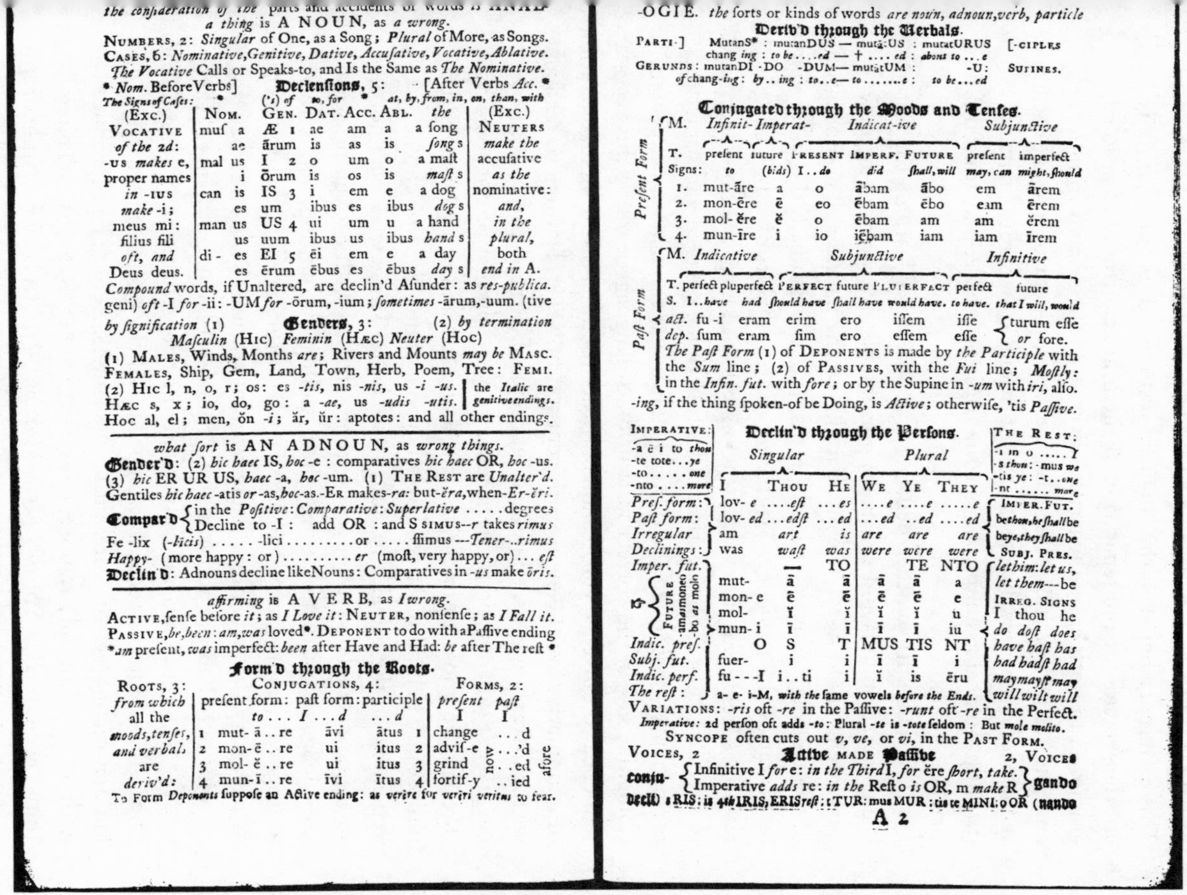
the conſideration of the parts and accidents of words is ANAL-
a thing is A NOUN, as a wrong.
NUMBERS, 2: *Singular* of One, as a Song; *Plural* of More, as Songs.
CASES, 6: *Nominative, Genitive, Dative, Accuſative, Vocative, Ablative.*
*The Vocative* Calls or Speaks-to, and Is the Same as *The Nominative.*
* *Nom.* Before Verbs] **Declenſions, 5:** [After Verbs *Acc.* *
*The Signs of Caſes:* * ('s) of · to, for * · at, by, from, in, on, than, with

| (Exc.) | NOM. | GEN. | DAT. | ACC. | ABL. | the | (Exc.) |
|---|---|---|---|---|---|---|---|
| VOCATIVE | muſ a | Æ 1 | ae | am | a | a ſong | NEUTERS |
| *of the 2d:* | ae | ārum | is | as | is | *ſong* s | *make the* |
| -US *makes* e, | mal us | I 2 | o | um | o | a maſt | accuſative |
| proper names | i | ōrum | is | os | is | *maſt* s | *as the* |
| *in* -IUS | can is | IS 3 | i | em | e | a dog | nominative: |
| *make* -i; | es | um | ibus | es | ibus | *dog* s | *and,* |
| meus mi: | man us | US 4 | ui | um | u | a hand | *in the* |
| filius fili | us | uum | ibus | us | ibus | *hand* s | *plural,* |
| *oft, and* | di- es | EI 5 | ēi | em | e | a day | both |
| Deus deus. | es | ērum | ēbus | es | ēbus | *day* s | *end in* A. |

*Compound* words, if Unaltered, are declin'd Aſunder: as *res-publica.*
geni) *oft* -I *for* -ii: -UM *for* -ōrum, -ium; *ſometimes* -ārum, -uum. (tive
*by ſignification* (1) **Genders, 3:** (2) *by termination*
*Maſculin* (HIC) *Feminin* (HÆC) *Neuter* (HOC)
(1) MALES, Winds, Months *are*; Rivers and Mounts *may be* MASC.
FEMALES, Ship, Gem, Land, Town, Herb, Poem, Tree: FEMI.
(2) HIC l, n, o, r; os: es *-tis*, nis *-nis*, us *-i -us.* | the *Italic* are
HÆC s, x; io, do, go: a *-ae*, us *-udis -utis.* | *genitive endings.*
HOC al, el; men, ŏn *-i*; ăr, ŭr: aptotes: and all other endings.

what *ſort* is AN ADNOUN, as *wrong things.*
**Gender'd:** (2) *hic haec* IS, *hoc* -e: comparatives *hic haec* OR, *hoc* -us.
(3) *hic* ER UR US, *haec* -a, *hoc* -um. (1) THE REST are *Unalter'd.*
Gentiles *hic haec* -atis *or* -as, *hoc*-as.-ER makes-*ra*: but-ĕra, when-*Er*-ĕri.
**Compar'd** {in the *Poſitive*: *Comparative*: *Superlative* ..... degrees
{Decline to -I : add OR : and S SIMUS--r takes *rimus*
Fe-lix (-*licis*) ......-lici ..........or ......ſſimus ---*Tener*-..*rimus*
*Happy*- (more happy: or) ..........*er* (moſt, very happy, or) ... *eſt*
**Declin'd:** Adnouns decline like Nouns: Comparatives in -*us* make *ōris.*

*affirming* is A VERB, as *I wrong.*
ACTIVE, ſenſe before *it*; as *I Love it*: NEUTER, nonſenſe; as *I Fall it.*
PASSIVE, *be, been*: *am, was* loved*. DEPONENT to do with a Paſſive ending
**am* preſent, *was* imperfect: *been* after Have and Had: *be* after The reſt *
**Form'd through the Roots.**

| ROOTS, 3: | CONJUGATIONS, 4: | | | | FORMS, 2: | |
|---|---|---|---|---|---|---|
| *from which* | preſent form: | paſt form: | participle | | *preſent* | *paſt* |
| all the | *to* ... | *I* ...*d* | ...*d* | | I | I |
| *moods, tenſes,* | 1 mut- ā..re | āvi | ātus | 1 | change | ...d |
| *and verbal,* | 2 mon- ē..re | ui | itus | 2 | adviſ-e | ...'d |
| are | 3 mol- ĕ..re | ui | itus | 3 | grind now | ..ed afore |
| *deriv'd:* | 4 mun- ī..re | īvi | ītus | 4 | fortif-y | ..ied |

To Form *Deponents* ſuppoſe an Active ending: as *verere* for *vereri veritus* to fear.

-OGIE. *the ſorts or kinds of words are noun, adnoun, verb, particle*
**Deriv'd through the Verbals.**
PARTI-] MutanS* : mutanDUS — mutatUS : mutatURUS [-CIPLES
chang *ing* : *to be....ed* — † ....*ed* : *about to* ...*e*
GERUNDS: mutanDI ·DO -DUM— mutatUM : -U: SUPINES.
*of chang-ing*: *by..ing*: *to..e*— *to* ........*e* : *to be*...*ed*

**Conjugated through the Moods and Tenſes.**

| | M. | *Infinit-* | *Imperat-* | *Indicat-ive* | | | *Subjunctive* | |
|---|---|---|---|---|---|---|---|---|
| *Preſent Form* | T. | preſent | future | PRESENT | IMPERF. | FUTURE | preſent | imperfect |
| | Signs: | *to* | (*bids*) | I..*do* | *did* | *ſhall, will* | *may, can* | *might, ſhould* |
| | 1. | mut-āre | a | o | ābam | ābo | em | ārem |
| | 2. | mon-ēre | ē | eo | ēbam | ēbo | eam | ērem |
| | 3. | mol-ĕre | ĕ | o | ēbam | am | am | ĕrem |
| | 4. | mun-īre | i | io | iēbam | iam | iam | īrem |

| | M. | *Indicative* | | *Subjunctive* | | *Infinitive* | |
|---|---|---|---|---|---|---|---|
| *Paſt Form* | T. | perfect | pluperfect | PERFECT future | PLUPERFECT | perfect | future |
| | S. | I..*have* | *had* | *ſhould have* · *ſhall have* | *would have.* | *to have.* | *that I will, would* |
| | *act.* | fu-i | eram | erim · ero | iſſem | iſſe | {turum eſſe |
| | *dep.* | ſum | eram | ſim · ero | eſſem | eſſe | { or fore. |

*The Paſt Form* (1) of DEPONENTS is made by *the Participle* with the *Sum* line; (2) of PASSIVES, with the *Fui* line; *Moſtly*: in the *Infin. fut.* with *fore*; or by the Supine in -*um* with *iri*, alſo.
-*ing*, if the thing ſpoken-of be Doing, is *Active*; otherwiſe, 'tis *Paſſive.*

**Declin'd through the Perſons.**

| IMPERATIVE: | I | THOU | HE | WE | YE | THEY | THE REST: |
|---|---|---|---|---|---|---|---|
| -a ē i *to thou* · -te tote...*ye* · -to.....*one* · -nto .....*more* | *Singular* | | | *Plural* | | | -i m o ..... I · -s *thou*: -mus *we* · -tis *ye*: -t..*one* · -nt ...... *more* |
| *Preſ. form:* | lov-e | ....*eſt* | ...*es* | ....*e* | ....*e* | .....*e* | IMPER. FUT. |
| *Paſt form:* | lov-*ed* | ...*edſt* | ...*ed* | ...*ed* | ..*ed* | .....*ed* | *be thou, be ſhall be* |
| *Irregular* | am | *art* | *is* | *are* | *are* | *are* | *be ye, they ſhall be* |
| *Declinings:* | was | *waſt* | *was* | *were* | *were* | *were* | SUBJ. PRES. |
| *Imper. fut.* | | — | TO | | TE | NTO | *let him*: *let us,* |
| FUTURE -amamoneo -bo *as* molo: | mut- | ā | ā | ā | ā | a | *let them*---be |
| | mon- e | ē | ē | ē | ē | e | IRREG. SIGNS |
| | mol- | ĭ | ĭ | ĭ | ĭ | u | I thou he |
| | mun- i | ī | ī | ī | ī | iu | *do doſt does* |
| *Indic. preſ.* | O | S | T | MUS | TIS | NT | *have haſt has* |
| *Subj. fut.* | fuer- | i | i | ī | ī | i | *had hadſt had* |
| *Indic. perf.* | fu---I | i..ti | i | ĭ | is | ēru | *may mayſt may* |
| *The reſt:* | a- e- i-M, with the ſame vowels before the Ends. | | | | | | *will wilt will* |

VARIATIONS: -*ris* oft -*re* in the Paſſive: -*runt* oft -*re* in the Perfect.
*Imperative*: 2d perſon oft adds -*to*: Plural -*te* is -*tote* ſeldom: But *mole molito.*
SYNCOPE often cuts out *v, ve,* or *vi,* in the PAST FORM.
VOICES, 2 **Active** MADE **Paſſive** 2, VOICES
**conju-** {Infinitive I *for* e: *in the Third* I, *for* ĕre *ſhort, take.*} **gando**
{Imperative *adds* re: *in the* Reſt o *is* OR, m *make* R}
**decli)** s RIS: is 4th IRIS, ERIS *reſt*: t TUR: mus MUR: tis te MINI: o OR (**nando**
A 2

Figure 8. Solomon Lowe, *Latin and French Grammar Reformed into a Small Compass* (1727), pp. 2–3. Reproduced by permission of the Librarian, Edinburgh University Library.

of our own Tongue, till without his Grammar, in all fundamental Points, he can view the whole System of it in his Mind.... (p. 15)

Such a system is not self-explanatory, and to understand the philosophy of language something must be added to representations of symmetry. This difference between the language system and its explanation is another version of the separation of the practical from the rational grammar. In both cases the spatial division of the system from its analysis has far-reaching effects on the development of language study in the century. The new linguists did not intend to separate linguistics from its philosophical assumptions but the form of their explanation did just that.

In seventeenth-century pedagogy, the child, by learning the letters or the pictured sounds and words or, presumably, by memorizing new characters would in essence or effect know the nature and composition of the world. The more he learned, his teachers assumed, the fuller would be his rational knowledge. Eighteenth-century habits of subdividing rational speech, not in terms of the materials of language but according to the increasing sophistication of its functions, delayed and sometimes permanently postponed the time when rational thought was expected.[54] Comenius saw in the correct institution of language learning the necessary sequence to universal (Protestant) brotherhood.[55] For the first generation of grammarians in the eighteenth century, however, learning to read and write correctly was based on, but was separable from, the reasons of language. Students and masters could choose whether or not to go back through the books to integrate texts and notes and to understand the philosophy behind illustrated symmetry. Commonly, this choice depended on the social status of the students. Those who were poor, foreign, or female were supposed to be satisfied with enough practical knowledge to get them through their reading, accounting, and letter-writing with some grace. The eighteenth-century student entered a course of pedagogy that was more likely to grant stature than secure belief.

Not only had the philosophical grounds of language changed, then, but the difference progressively resulted in the separation of reason from rules. Already in the second two decades of the eighteenth century, the familiar techniques of representing the language could be reproduced without, or with only remote, references to the "Reasons of Things." John Owen, in *The Youth's Instructor* (1732), offers an example of how independent practical language could be. Owen praises his book for "Containing More Words, and a greater Variety of very useful Collections, than any other Book of this Kind and Bigness."[56] Such a claim is not in itself unusual: many linguists competed for more complete lists or tables. But Owen's pride in quantity is the only distinction he advertises, and this is different. He has nothing to say about method or reasons, as if numbers were recommendation enough. He is also proud of a visual scheme for writing all the letters, "Mathematically demonstrating at one View, the exact Proportion each Letter ought to bear to the rest in Writing" (see fig. 9). The illustration is intriguing and, in its explanation, as complex as descriptions of seventeenth-century invented characters, but Owen is indifferent to the appropriateness of mathematics to language or to the significance of relations between the letters. The engraving, writes Owen, "may merit the Attention of the Learned in Painting, Sculpture, etc., as well as of the Learners in that Noble and very Useful Art of Writing" (p. iv). Characters, once the concern of philosophers, are here the curiosity of artificers; and the art of writing, once the ability to express thoughts, is here manual dexterity.

In the grammatical definitions of the 1720s and 1730s, there is a noticeable shift from ones that connect parts of speech to habits of perception to ones that isolate the classes of words. In the short "Compendious Grammar" that Owen includes at the end of his book, there is, typically, a summary of each chapter in the form of a question and answer dialogue. Owen's "Q" and "A" are condescendingly tautological:

Q. What is understood by Speech?
A. Speaking or Discourse.
Q. What is meant by Eight Parts of Speech?
A. Eight different Sorts or Kinds of Words used in Speaking.
Q. Why are there only eight Parts and no more?
A. Because every Word we use in Discourse is comprehended under one of these Parts. (N4$^v$)

Such dialogues are common to the grammar texts of these years, and they make clear their distance from the similar looking catechistical texts of a century before. Pedagogy has shed its philosophical responsibilities. John Entick's *Speculum Latinum* (1728), which sounds as if it might be imitating Lowe, or perhaps Comenius, turns out to mirror only its own definitions:

*Master.* What is Syntax?
*Scholar.* 'Tis the good Order, or Disposition of Words.
*M.* What mean you by Good Order, and Disposition of Words?

*Language and the Grammar of the Mind, 1700–1740*

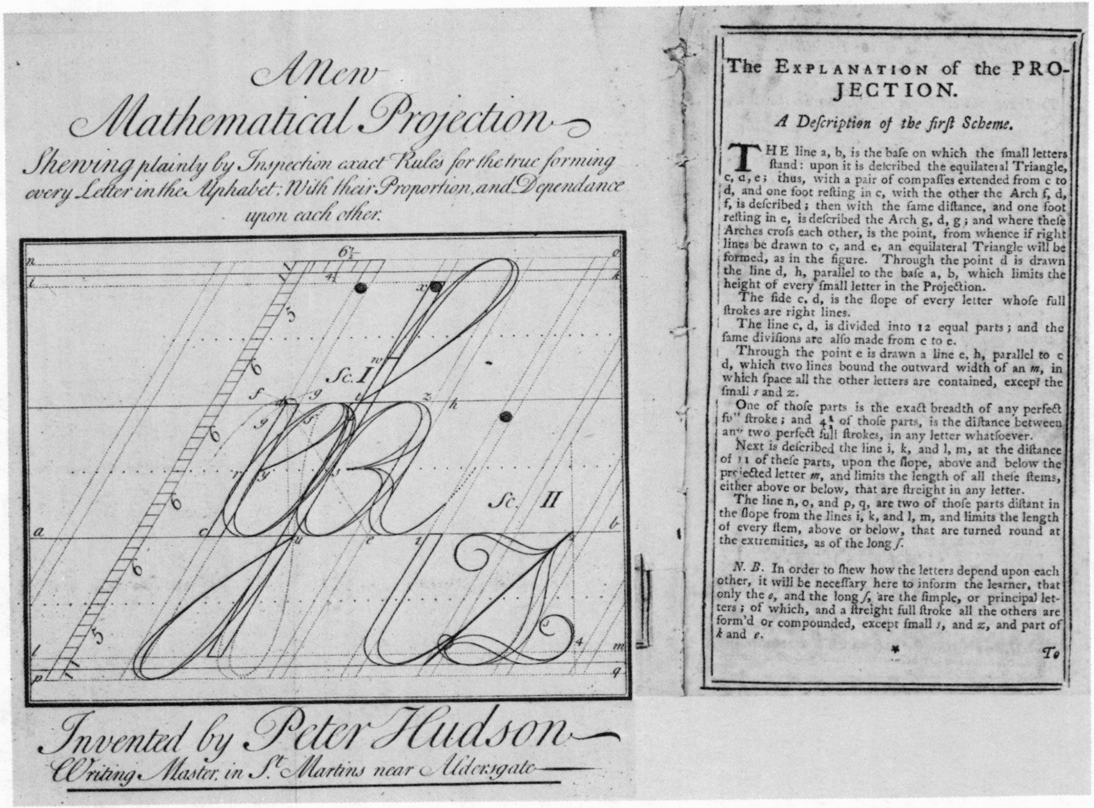


The EXPLANATION of the PROJECTION.

*A Deſcription of the firſt Scheme.*

THE line a, b, is the baſe on which the ſmall letters ſtand: upon it is deſcribed the equilateral Triangle, c, d, e; thus, with a pair of compaſſes extended from c to d, and one foot reſting in c, with the other the Arch f, d, f, is deſcribed; then with the ſame diſtance, and one foot reſting in e, is deſcribed the Arch g, d, g; and where theſe Arches croſs each other, is the point, from whence if right lines be drawn to c, and e, an equilateral Triangle will be formed, as in the figure. Through the point d is drawn the line d, h, parallel to the baſe a, b, which limits the height of every ſmall letter in the Projection.

The ſide c, d, is the ſlope of every letter whoſe full ſtrokes are right lines.

The line c, d, is divided into 12 equal parts; and the ſame diviſions are alſo made from c to e.

Through the point e is drawn a line e, h, parallel to c d, which two lines bound the outward width of an *m*, in which ſpace all the other letters are contained, except the ſmall *s* and *z*.

One of thoſe parts is the exact breadth of any perfect fu'' ſtroke; and 4½ of thoſe parts, is the diſtance between an' two perfect full ſtrokes, in any letter whatſoever.

Next is deſcribed the line i, k, and l, m, at the diſtance of 11 of theſe parts, upon the ſlope, above and below the projected letter *m*, and limits the length of all theſe ſtems, either above or below, that are ſtreight in any letter.

The line n, o, and p, q, are two of thoſe parts diſtant in the ſlope from the lines i, k, and l, m, and limits the length of every ſtem, above or below, that are turned round at the extremities, as of the long *ſ*.

*N. B.* In order to ſhew how the letters depend upon each other, it will be neceſſary here to inform the learner, that only the *o*, and the long *ſ*, are the ſimple, or principal letters; of which, and a ſtreight full ſtroke all the others are form'd or compounded, except ſmall *s*, and *z*, and part of *k* and *e*.

*

To

Figure 9. John Owen, *The Youth's Instructor* (1732), facing p. 136. Reproduced by permission of the President and Court of Governors of Sion College, London.

S. 'Tis when they are in their right Case, Gender, Number, Person, Mood, Tense, and Place.[57]

Entick acknowledges, among his "Predecessors," Vossius and the masters of Port-Royal, but his "small Grammar" is not placed before "the great Men of our Nation" and therefore need not include arguments "of little Use to Novices" (A1ᵛ). He wrote the text to enable "a very dull Boy" to write, and that is all its merit. Entick is not unaware of the principles of universal grammar as interpreted by his fellow grammarians (his text is "composed on Natural Principles"), but he does not require his scholars to learn them. Unlike the early-eighteenth-century grammarians who also distinguished between users of their books, Entick does not even provide his students an opportunity to learn the grounds of grammar.

John Henley's first effort to win the applause of London was an ambitious language project—a set of grammars for every language, dead or alive, collectively titled *The Compleat Linguist; or, An Universal Grammar to all the Considerable Tongues in Being* (1719–26). Since all the languages "contribute to give a mutual light to one another,"[58] Henley argues, all he has to do is present brief grammars for each language and the natural light will inevitably glow. He accepts the Latin model without explanation and, for each language, trusts his readers will recognize the "Nature and Terms of Grammar in general." His attempt at a polyglot grammar is perfectly congruent with the shared idea of linguistic universality in the early eighteenth century, for it assumes that what is universal is the "general System of Grammar." However, the generalization, once made, need not be repeated, and each grammar simply names the parts without giving logical definitions or philosophical explanations. In the *Introduction to an English Grammar,* for instance, Henley begins his section on nouns by stating that a "Noun is substantive or adjective" (p. 39). Universality is taken for granted, and the effect is a series of grammars without apparent conceptual claims. Grammars like Henley's become standard in the 1730s as whatever English (or England) was was thought to be "universal," that is, good enough for everyone.

Despite the title of Isaac Barker's grammar, *An English Grammar Shewing the Nature and Grounds of the English Language* (1733), there is little explicit discussion of the grounds of grammar in it. For that, Barker recommends Greenwood's *Essay.* His own sensible definitions refer to the social uses of speech. Grammar, for instance, is the "Art that teacheth whatever may be observed of those articulate Sounds, or Words in speech, whereby we communicate our Thoughts one to another."[59]

*Language and the Grammar of the Mind, 1700–1740*

The philosophical nature of language is clear—so clear that it is excluded from his grammar. This is a consistent feature of the language texts of the 1730s. William Loughton, in *A Practical Grammar of the English Tongue; or, A Rational and Easy Introduction* (1734), grants that "the End and Design of Grammar in general, is the same in all Languages."[60] But his own work better serves "the End and Design of Speech," that is, "to qualify Mankind for Society, by enabling them to communicate their Thoughts and Intentions to each other." Loughton cites Wallis but distinguishes his own debt from that of Greenwood and others, who "added many and large critical Notes which tho' of Use to Men of Learning and Judgment are no-wise necessary for the young Learner" (p. ix). The pedagogic principle implied here is as different from that of the early-eighteenth-century grammarians as theirs is from that of their seventeenth-century predecessors. Increasingly during the century, it is the social, rather than the philosophical, function of speech that introduces grammar. The new goal is to teach appropriate forms of "gentleness" rather than achieve universal "gentileness."

The page facing Loughton's title page advertises his school: "Writing, Arithmetic, And Merchant's Accounts, Taught By William Loughton, School-Master at Kensington, By Whom Youth are boarded, and fitted for Trade and Business."[61] The nature of his audience influences his decision to exclude copious rational explanations, since such notes serve "only to encrease the Bulk and Price of the Book, and in a great Measure, to prevent its being more generally purchas'd and read" (p. ix). This socioeconomic explanation does not alter the rationality of language, and its philosophical ground is still the correspondence between "the Subject of our Speech or Discourse" and "the Object of our Senses, Reflection, or Understanding" (p. 47), but the social ends of speech and the economic needs of students limit the value of philosophic arguments.

Following the first two decades of the century, there is a sense that the practice of language has been settled. The new generation of grammarians feels no need to struggle with philosophic questions, and even the battles of the recent past are forgotten. Daniel Duncan, in *A New English Grammar, Wherein the Grounds and Nature of the Eight Parts of Speech, And their Construction is explain'd* (1731), hopes that his book's "small Bulk will . . . recommend it for the Use of Children," and he cites, for those who want more discussion of "Grounds and Nature," the works of both Greenwood and Gildon, the bitter rivals of twenty years before.[62] The two antagonists are also paired by John

Collyer in *The General Principles of Grammar* (1735), perhaps the most important grammar of the decade. Collyer sums up the received opinion of "Modern Grammarians,"[63] a term that includes Lane, Johnson, Gildon, Greenwood, Wilson, and the masters of Port-Royal. This review is itself significant, for noticeably absent are the seventeenth-century English linguists in whom early eighteenth-century writers had sought support. Collyer's look backward also suggests the distinctiveness and coherence of a new tradition of English linguistics. These modern grammarians assumed that "the Essential Parts of Grammar" are "the same in all Languages" (p. vii) and that the basis of the universality is the correspondence between language and thought: "the use of Words being to express the Ideas, or Representations of Things in the Mind, and these Ideas being as various as their Objects; whether of Persons or Things, or their several Accidents, Qualities, Relations, or Connections; their Actions, or Manners of Actions, require that the Words that express them, be as different in their several manners of signifying" (p. 2). Collyer reverts to using extensive footnotes, but these merely reconcile the opinions of "our Grammarians" (p. 28) and supply his own improvements.

Collyer's assembly of orthodox opinion, like many of the other language texts of the 1720s and 1730s, has effects other than those intended. Instead of promoting, fixing, and developing the rational grammars of the earlier period, these books contribute to the division between practical and rational discussions of language. Collyer's footnotes, for example, dwell on the small points of conflicting classifications, so that instead of providing the rational grounds of speech, the notes contribute to the complexity of practical usage. Even his solutions to such problems suggest that rules are more important than reasons. He tries to settle the dispute about whether the adjective is a separate part of speech or is included with nouns by deciding that since a noun can stand by itself and an adjective cannot, the two must be separate. Since participles "in construction" (p. 32) are also adjectives, the two should be joined "under one head, as belonging to the same genus or kind of Words, notwithstanding the small difference betwixt them." Collyer's decision is not unique, but the absence of reference to mental operations and the importance of merely grammatical distinctions indicates the growing difference between Collyer's generation and Gildon's.

A final example will show not only how different the practice of language was becoming but also the direction it would take later in the century. John Milner titles his grammar *A Practical Grammar of the Latin Tongue ... The whole establish'd upon Rational Principles* (1729), and he cites on the title page and throughout his text such authorities as Vossius, Richard Johnson, and Solomon Lowe. Although a grammar of Latin, Milner's text is mainly a review of English meant to establish the principles of grammar in general. Like his fellow eighteenth-century grammarians, Milner stresses etymology and syntax, and, among the parts of speech, particles and modals. Like them as well, he defines syntax as "the right putting together of words to express our thoughts."[64] However, the explicit focus of his text is correct usage. Not only does he append a section on "Grammatical Difinitions" (p. 64), but he also begins his work by defining grammar as "a collection of Rules, for speaking and writing properly" (p. 3). The "Rational Principles" Milner advertises on his title page are undeveloped assumptions about the relationship between the system of language and the operations of the mind; as the latter drops out of the text and even out of the notes, the grammatical system takes on an independence that, during the next period of linguistic activity, results in the firm separation of rational and practical linguistics and in the freeing of practical grammar from ostensible conceptual content. The important facts about English linguistics in the first part of the eighteenth century are the thoroughness with which a distinctive linguistic epistemology comes to prevail over the study and practice of language and the ease with which it faded.

## The Grammar of Mind and New Literary Languages

At the beginning of this chapter I suggested some of the implications for the study of literary language that correspond to this epistemological reorientation, but perhaps this would be a fitter place to add to a preliminary sketch of some of the distinctive features of early-eighteenth-century literary languages. The shift in linguistic method and emphasis from lexical units to syntactic relations, from the system's taxonomy to its operations, from a locus principally *in the world* to one principally *among* ideas, is widely evident in the poetry, prose, and critical ideas of the period, but nowhere more characteristically, I think, than in the various ways in which a temporal aspect subsumes the spatial.[65] Individual schemes, particular images, and completed representations give way to arts of contrast, disruption, change, and transformation.

Throughout Swift's works, for example, the enemy is someone who completely and literally knows all, one who uses language efficiently, as if it consisted of objects, like the letters of the will on which Peter, Martin, and Jack set to work, or consisted of objective propositions such as the immoderate proposer believes. The reader's alternative to being implied and totally mirrored by the satire is to read *differently,* to recognize the mental habits that lead, miserably, to literalization. Swift's works offer us the maddening experience of translating likeness into identity, metaphor into fact, possibility into idealized actuality. His literary language, even when not antagonistically satirical, works by deidealizing, by undressing illusions. He would have us deny a self-sufficient definition of man as *animal rationale* for one that designates and values process and possibility, *animale rationis capax.*[66] For Swift, as for his striving readers, escape from the utopian evangelicalism of Gulliver is possible only by freshly valuing dispute, difference, and change. It is the critical reader of all of Gulliver's interrelated travels and not the celebrant of any one or of a climactic series who experiences the intent of the whole.

Fielding is a master among narrative's many ministers by virtue of perfecting the contrast between completed, finely imagined stories and disrupted, competing ones. Like Swift, he opens up the reading experience and invests its complexities with meaning. Remember, reader, as Fielding might say, the *difference,* in *Joseph Andrews,* between Mr. Wilson's autobiographical narrative with its perfectly pastoral climax and the violent intrusion into the scene of the local gentleman in bloody pursuit of the little pet dog. Or recall the difference, in *Tom Jones,* between the narrator's elevating introductory description of Squire Allworthy and his admission, at the sound of the breakfast bell, that we have other stylistic appetites, too, and will have to find our own way down from sublimity.[67] The reading experience, as Fielding arranges it in these quite representative moments, obliges us to stop reading in isolated or idealized units, scenes, or images or according to traditionally exclusive stylistic features and to start attending to narrative and stylistic contrasts, relations, and transformations.[68]

Fielding's favorite critical concept, the Ridiculous, is based on just such an appreciation of complex contrast and the implied obligation to read scenes and judge characters not in isolation but in relation.[69] The reader intended as the respondent to such techniques attends to several perspectives on a person or an event, and one of those perspectives, as the narrator keeps advising us, is a sense of the whole that is fully operative only on a second reading. In effect, we are directed to become conscious of ourselves as readers and aware of the significance of reading. Since, for Fielding, scenes of nature are not self-explanatory and people's motives are not self-evident, the readerly function applies the self-conscious, self-questioning disquisitions of the narrator and techniques of the narrative to itself.[70] The result is that we come to know ourselves, not principally as "wise and good" or "silly and bad," but as we are as interpreters.

This relocation of significance from scenes (or self-contained, satisfactorally completed, and idealized narratives) to the mental habits and responses of the constantly inquiring author and reader takes still another representative form in Thomson. Ralph Cohen has seen, as one of the major organizing principles of *The Seasons,* Thomson's drive to discover the means, often linguistic, to represent change, variety, and contrary aspects in order to find value in "a perspectival interpretation of human experience as well as of art."[71] One can see many of the prominent features of eighteenth-century literature interestingly brought together by a critical view that stresses the importance of contrast, temporal change, and multiple perspectives. The dominance of satire (preeminent among the arts of contrast), the widespread use of personae and epistolary competitors, the preference for characters who learn as opposed to those who know (for enquirers as opposed to systematizers,[72] Joseph Andrews as opposed to Abraham Adams), the stylistic delight (and indulgence) in complexly interrelated phrases and clauses—these are among the aspects of a literary language that shares with contemporary linguistics a theory of meaning oriented towards the relationships between mental acts.

These are suggestions that, although only literary, might overwhelm the local schoolmasters and lesser essayists who control my story, but they may also help justify the study of basic linguistics in the period as a representative and revealing expression of its intellectual life, of what it wanted to, and found it could, know. Even the deflation of linguistic intentions and performance that I traced in the texts around mid-century is matched by a diminution of poetic presumption among the poets at the same time. The confessed modesty of mid-century linguists, as we shall see more clearly in the next chapter, resembles the aggressive pathos of mid-century poets like William Collins and Thomas Gray, who seem shaken by the difference between what their poems are and what they might have been or what poetry once was. Their exquisitely developed aesthetics of failure dwells on a sense that their poetic language no longer possesses the real presence or the grammatical appropriateness that made the languages of Aeschylus or Spenser or Milton adequate to their meanings and feelings.[73] The finely tuned laments of Collins and Gray regret, most of all, distance: the distance between what the poets wrote and what they felt, between who they were and what once they had been, between what they could write and what others could once have written.[74] This diminution was not due to a change in what poets desired, but neither was the linguistic deflation; like that change, it was a matter of performance, and it was because "reasons for things" seemed beyond their practice. When we move, then, from the presumption of Greenwood or Gildon to the modesty of Loughton or Collyer, it is not a pointless descent or mere trivialization but a poignant, self-imposed dwindling of power and range. The burden of the past proves to be too much for grammarians and for poets; but trying to shed it, or share it, though it made the performances lighter, also left the performers clearly in harness.[75]

# CHAPTER 3

# Theories of Language
# and the Grammar of Sentences,
# 1740-1785

## The New Orthodoxy of Linguistics

There is more of almost everything linguistic in the second half of the
eighteenth century than in the first: more grammars and more kinds of
grammar, more theories of language, more sorts of questions asked about
language, more dictionaries, spelling books, proposals for reordering
pedagogy, and more languages taught.[1] The decline in quantity and quality
of linguistic work in the 1720s and 1730s ends around mid-century, and
a new industriousness takes over. But the tone, topics, and assumptions
of the new work are dramatically different from the ambitious, argumentative work of the seventeenth century and from the new orthodoxy
of the early eighteenth century. To most later-eighteenth-century
linguists, the ostensible categories and capacities of language seem settled;
even if they were not completely unarguable, the differences are agreeably accounted for. Differences, in fact, are at the heart of the matter.

Differences and distinctions between languages, between levels of
language learning, between kinds of linguistic inquiry are what these
linguists actively seek. While one sort of grammatical description may be
appropriate in school texts, quite another is needed for advanced
discussions; while one set of grammatical terms describes language
generally, another accounts for particular languages; while one language
has a certain set of sounds and syntactic habits, another has a distinctly
different set; while "speculative" grammar is one sort of project,
practical grammar is a completely different sort.

The essential enterprise of linguistics from the mid-eighteenth century
contradicts the basic linguistic principles found in earlier work. The older
linguistics was characterized by assumptions of the divine origin or divine
guidance of language, prospects of a renewed universal language, and
faith in the correspondence between words and the order of things (or,
later, between syntax and the ways of the mind). These earlier writers
integrated philosophical, pedagogic, and descriptive linguistics in a
synchronous system. The later linguists, whom I consider in this chapter,
propose methods of analysis that account for the differences between
existing languages, the probable diversity of the first invented languages,
the inevitable changes suffered by a living language, and the independence
and sufficiency of the system of any language.

The linguistic work of the period reflects, in one view, different
approaches to language: the separation between grammar texts and
philosophical inquiries becomes stronger, as we shall see. From another
perspective, the practical and theoretical linguists live peaceably together
because they share the contexts in which their versions of language are
presented. Both kinds of linguists socialize language, relocating its
principal context from natural or theological history (see Chapter 1) and
from the operations of the human understanding (see Chapter 2) to the
origin and progress of human societies. Both make virtues of what were
once the liabilities of any language. Variety, change, mere description of
the distinctive qualities (the "genius") of particular languages came to be
features sought out, rather than condemned or changed. What I want to
show in this chapter is, first, how the separation between levels and kinds
of linguistic activity led to mostly modest but impressively productive
work, and, second, what were the prevailing assumptions about language
near the end of the century. The cast of linguists is large, and I draw
deliberately from many because choruses are common in the period, and
the stage newly crowded.

*Theories of Language and the Grammar of Sentences, 1740-1785*

There are other types of singers, too, contributing their complimentary parts, literary figures among them as we have seen before in my brief glances at the parallel development of linguistics and literary languages. Throughout this chapter, the prominent aspects of later-eighteenth-century literature and Romanticism should be evident, and I will take just a few of the opportunities I recognize to draw out examples. Even in the quite general terms I have already used to highlight the new linguistic features of this period I think we can see some important literary shapes. We noted in the last chapter some consequences for literature when mind replaced nature as the assumed content of language; now, in this period, language increasingly assumed its own sufficiency, not theoretically independent of mind but practically divorced from logic. Two significant literary developments confirm this division between the study of language proper (linguistics) and the philosophy of mind (logic or metaphysics).

The first development is the prominence in literature of the same themes and assumptions that were coming to dominate language study, principally the social and historicist ideas and the new interest in children, primitives, Celts, Highlanders, solitary reapers and balladeers, and other exhibitors of the peculiar genius and genesis of English. This literary development echoes new methods of linguistic analysis which stressed social communication. Linguists relocated meaning from a basis in the logical relations between syntactic units to the rhetorical features of speech, and in literary texts we find an emphasis on the importance of manner of "style" rather than explicitness or precision. The new literary values include sympathy and sentiment, tone and taste—and taste not as a feature of the landscape but as a capacity for response. Jane Austen's success, for instance, in turning her readers into arch performers of her characters' finely tuned manners is a refinement of the excesses of her Gothic and sentimental predecessors. They had associated intonation, evocative gestures and settings, and certain rhythms of speech and narration with particular effects. While Austen excludes their grossness, she retains their rhetorical representation of character. We know Collins, in *Pride and Prejudice,* from the style of his first letter, as we know Bingley by his handwriting or Elizabeth by the way she plays music. The clearest images of this view of character are given by Sterne, and most vividly in the figure of Trim reading the sermon to the natural poseurs who variously attend his performance. Words, phrases, gestures, and postures in this literary language are less carriers of particular meanings than expressive possibilities. It is their "meaningfulness," more than their clear meanings, that writers were seeking.

The second general literary feature paralleling the progressive independence of language study is a sense among authors that language has been impoverished, or more extremely, that it is an enemy of poetry. The idea that language is too poor for great literature is an intensification of the feeling of poetic dimunition I associated with Gray and Collins (at the end of Chapter 2). Poets in the later-eighteenth century, for example, often defend themselves from the vanities of poetic presumption by admitting their limitations (Johnson's "Thou has convinced me, that no human being can ever be a poet"), by mocking traditional forms (Crabbe's "tinsel trappings of poetic pride"), by joking their way into seriousness (Cowper's "I sing the Sofa"), by singing past the conventional reader (Burns's "To you I sing, in simple Scottish lays"), by displacing responsibility onto a long departed, by then anachronistic bard (Macpherson's Ossian or Chatterton's Rowley), or by justifying one's shortcomings as a consequence of the diminished times (Goldsmith's "Dear charming nymph, neglected and denied").[2] The more extreme literary reaction we can see is a fight against the mere sufficiency of language by trying to force on it the content, real and mental, with which early linguists had invested it. Smart and Blake spend their vast poetic energies trying to give the literary languages real presence, but their ontological commitment to language, unlike that of poets a century and more before, goes against the linguistic conventions.[3] They are isolated speakers or, like Chatterton, antiquarian seekers, pursuing what few are willing to grant them. They test the limits of what had become intelligible. Even when a generation of strong poetic voices sounds, in the first years of the nineteenth century, it speaks often in struggle against self-contained linguistic norms. The history of change in literary languages is certainly too complex to survey easily, but it is also connected closely enough to shifts in the study and practice of language to justify our attention to the fate of these aspects of language in the later eighteenth century.

## The Practice without the Philosophy of Language

In Chapter 2, we watched as the philosophy of language was dropped from school texts; first it fell from definitions and discussions to the bottom of the page, and then it was reduced to brief references to other books or neglected altogether. The teaching of English, which not long before had been an opportunity to work toward Protestant hegemony, no longer seems, at mid-century, the focus of ambitious philosophical or theological aims. There are still important virtues claimed for teaching the language in a regular fashion, of course, but these goals are significantly different from Comenius's or Greenwood's. The new linguists, instead of accommodating the language to physical or epistemological universals, make their principal goal the description of the fullness and distinctiveness of the English language.

James Buchanan, in *An Essay towards Establishing a Standard for an Elegant and Uniform Pronunciation of the English Tongue* (1766), writes about the function of teaching grammar and pronunciation. The first beneficial consequence of teaching the language according to certain standards is that it will "attract the attention of all Europe."[4] For Buchanan, such standardized language teaching contributes to social and political ends and, more specifically, to English goals as represented by Whig policies at mid-century: a regularly taught language will lead to the reconciliation between England and Scotland and to the suppression of "provincial dialect, so unbecoming gentlemen" (p. x). These ends are already being effected, Buchanan claims, by the common use of texts that teach "a grammatical and scientific knowledge" of English. One of these is Buchanan's *The Complete English Scholar* (1753). It serves national needs by accommodating boys "who are to be put to Trades"[5] and older persons untrained in the learned languages. Latin and Greek are useless, in Buchanan's view, except in some few professions and in the church. To help guarantee that the teaching of English receive its proper emphasis, Buchanan, in *The Complete English Scholar* and in *British Grammar* (1762), employs the printer's devices so cleverly used before, but only to serve his narrower goals. Since the purpose that motivates his endeavors is the correction of contemporary faults—poor spelling, false syntax, vulgar diction—he uses his ample footnotes as a sort of teacher's manual providing masters with helpful questions and additional examples. Also, he employs italic print for rules and principles to make his texts useful to those working without a master.[6] Buchanan's work is thorough and detailed, but far removed from the theoretical assertiveness of the work of earlier linguists. In place of theory, theology, or natural philosophy, Buchanan puts a social goal—an ideal of discipline and competence.

Like Buchanan, James Gough, in *A Practical Grammar of the English*

*Tongue* (1754), separates his readers from those served by his predecessors. The grammars of Brightland and Greenwood, for instance, deserve to be studied "by all who are desirous to be . . . compleat Masters of the Language: But these seem to have been written for Men rather than Children, so that there still seemed to be room for *a practical English Grammar for the Use of Schools;* which must not be a Critical Grammar of the Language, but a Summary of the most material Rules observed by good Writers in the Construction thereof. . . ."[7] Gough writes for an expanded audience, not for "professed Scholars" or those with the "Genius and Leisure" to acquire the ancient languages, but "for the Use of Youth designed for mechanick and mercantile Arts" (p. xiii) and for women. The end of education, for Gough, reflecting somewhat acerbically on his predecessors, is "not to fill the Mouth with mysterious Sounds, but to store the Mind with useful Knowledge and Skill in those Arts and Sciences which may be serviceable in future life" (p. xii). Gough's emphasis, like Buchanan's, is not generally antagonistic to previous grammarians; it is, rather, on making English accessible and useful to its students.

In these typical grammars of mid-century, the philosophical basis of language is not so much denied or debated as ignored or put aside as inappropriate for school texts. Descriptions of the language fill the page, with distinctions between more and less important rules or between rules and examples graphically reinforced. By looking closely at what seemed to their contemporaries the best examples of a grammar text and a theoretical discourse, we will see more clearly the consequences of the consistent, but benign, separation between grammar and theory. The most cited, most praised, and most imitated grammar of mid-century was Robert Lowth's *A Short Introduction to English Grammar* (1762), and the similarly valued theory of language was James Harris's *Hermes; or, A Philosophical Inquiry Concerning Language and Universal Grammar* (1751).

For Lowth, the time had come for a new, purposefully limited grammar:

> The English Language hath been much cultivated during the last two hundred years. It hath been considerably polished and refined; it hath been greatly enlarged in extent and compass; its force and energy, its variety, richness, and elegance, have been with good success in verse and in prose, upon all subjects, and in every kind of stile: but whatever other improvements it may have received, it hath made no advances in Grammatical accuracy.[8]

*Theories of Language and the Grammar of Sentences, 1740–1785*

To justify "the necessity of the Study of Grammar in our own language, and to admonish those, who set up for Authors among us" (pp. ix–x), Lowth includes dozens of footnotes showing the errors of notable authors.[9] Such evidence ought to convince us of the importance of "Grammatical accuracy," which is the ability "to judge of every phrase and form of construction, whether it be right or not" (p. x).[10] Lowth composes his grammar with its use in mind, and this means that in his definitions "easiness and perspicuity have been sometimes preferred to logical exactness" (p. xiv). The philosophy of language will not determine whether a usage is right or not, and so must take second place to a classification and description of the language that accurately reflects the customs of the best writers. Lowth keeps "common Divisions" and "known and received Terms" in organizing the language, and he avoids discussions "which appeared to have more of subtilty than of usefulness in them." In a word, writes Lowth, his book "was calculated for the use of the learner even of the lowest class." It is not that Lowth is indifferent to or unaware of the philosophical context of grammatical inquiry; in fact, he quotes from Wilkins's *Real Character* and, more often, from Harris's *Hermes*. The focus of his grammar simply reflects the differences between the theory and the practice of grammar in the period. In theory, many issues may be pertinent, but in Lowth's grammar, words matter as words, not as things or as ideas.

Lowth defines grammar as the "Art of rightly expressing our thoughts by Words" (p. 1) and universal grammar as the explanation of "the Principles which are common to all Languages." However, universal grammar "cannot be taught abstractly; it must be done with reference to some language already known" (p. xi). To discuss the grammar of any known language requires the application of the principles of grammar "to that particular language, according to the established usage and custom of it" (p. 1). This explanatory circle that Lowth draws around himself shows precisely the necessary limits of his view of grammar. When he discusses the moods of verbs, for instance, he defines them as expressions of the primary modes of thought. However, although "in theory" the interrogative form has "as good a Title to a Mode of its own," "Practice has determined it otherwise" (p. 115) and substituted either particles or word order for distinct verb forms. Grammars, in this view, show how particular languages work when those languages consistently follow their established customs, and, as with the interrogative mood, the integrity of the theory is secondary to "grammatical accuracy." Lowth is prescriptive only with regard to his insistence on following what he determines to be established (and approved) usage, and he repeatedly acknowledges different customs among existing languages.[11]

Lowth sends those who wish to pursue the subject of philosophical language to Harris's *Hermes,* where they "will find it fully and accurately handled, with the greatest acuteness of investigation, perspicuity of explication, and elegance of method" (p. xiv). Nowhere does Lowth suggest that *Hermes* is useful or necessary to learning a language. He celebrates it, in fact, for its remoteness: "it is the most beautiful and perfect example of Analysis that has been exhibited since the days of Aristotle" (pp. xiv–xv). That compliment is not only a tribute to Harris but an indication of the division between one of the most popular grammars of a particular language and the most prominent theory of the nature of language by a contemporary Englishman. Lowth's reference to Aristotle is particularly appropriate, for Harris often fills his pages with quotations from Aristotle, Apollonius, Priscian, Scaliger, and Gaza. From these sources Harris derives his terminology, and it is on their authority that he analyzes the correlation between man's perceptions and his use of language. Indeed, Harris often seems more determined to justify his view of classical philosophy than to test his principles on languages. Although he pursues his assumption that "all Speech or Discourse is a publishing or exhibiting some part of our Soul, either a certain Perception, or a certain Volition" to an exposition of moods, his starting point is the list of moods "ranged by the old Grammarians."[12] Harris closes his inquiry by ridiculing the maxim that "*'tis Men,* and *not Books* we must study to become knowing" (p. 425). Such a notion is "the common consolation and language of Dunces."[13]

Harris idealizes his scholastic Aristoteleanism and identifies empiricism as his chief methodological and theoretical opposition.[14] He transforms existence, which he takes to be the object of his comprehensive theory, into that "*universal Genus,* to which all things of all kinds are at all times to be referr'd" (p. 88); he seeks his method in the general laws of nature, which are different from the things of man (p. 9); and he defends his enterprise by celebrating the sufficient delight of intellectual activity. The philosophical basis of language must be independent of specific languages, for its validity comes from what is universally and permanently true.[15] Since the knowledge of tenses "depends on the theory of time" (p. 99), then the "natural Number" (p. 120) of tenses should follow from an accurate expression of the theory. Though this is true, argues Harris, "it is not to be expected that the above Hypothesis should be justified through all instances in every language. It fares with Tenses, as with other Affections of Speech; be the Language upon the whole ever so perfect, much must be left, in defiance of all Analogy, to the harsh laws of mere Authority and Chance" (pp. 122–23). These "harsh laws" disappoint Harris, but they do not discourage him from pursuing the true philosophy of language. In defense of his inquiry, Harris ignores the study, teaching, or variants of particular languages. Unlike empiricism, which follows "a Labyrinth of infinite Particulars" (p. 351), Harris's idealized Aristotelianism strives for "the sublimer parts of *Science*, the Studies of *Mind, Intellection,* and *Intelligent Principles.*" The "most *excellent* and *essential*" parts of language are those that express "comprehensive *Universality*" (p. 345), and the only sciences that continue unaffected by empiricism are arithmetic and geometry.

Harris and Lowth treat different ideas of the language differently. Lowth tries to systematize the features of a particular language created by authority and chance; Harris seeks the linguistic evidence of "*the Genuine Perceptions of Pure Mind*" (p. 372). Lowth composes a grammar accessible to the poor and unlearned; Harris offers a theory attracting those who wish "to employ their liberal leisure" inspecting the "finished Models of *Grecian Literature*" rather than waste time "upon the meaner productions of the *French* and *English* Press" (p. 424). Lowth acknowledges, in passing, the epistemological context of grammatical functions; Harris seeks a philosophy of mind and language that, scorning those empirics who "view the human Soul in the light of a Crucible, where Truths are produced by a kind of logical Chemistry" (p. 405), defines words as the symbols of general ideas. That Lowth recommends Harris so positively suggests that these differences are not bases for dispute but aspects of quite separate linguistic activities.

This sense of separate audiences, assumptions, and methods had far-reaching effects on the practice of language. It provided limits beyond which grammars could not normally presume to extend and beneath which philosophers need not stoop. James Beattie, who hardly shared Harris's anti-Lockean bias, nonetheless praises Harris, in "The theory of Language" (1783), for providing discussions "not to be found in any common grammar."[16] And John Horne Tooke, to whom Harris was a principal rival, agrees with Harris that the theory of language is quite independent of pedagogy. Children, for Tooke, ought "not be disturbed or bewildered with a reason for everything: which reason they would not

understand, even if the Teacher was always able to give it."[17] Grammar
and theory develop contradictory by noninterfering linguistic responsibilities, and both exhibit a vigor and confidence in their limited goals,
uncommon since the burst of linguistic activity in the mid-seventeenth
century.

In the years after Harris and Lowth, essays on the theory and texts
summarizing the practices of language remain separate and distinct, but
the theories move away from the context-free speculations of Harris.[18]
Instead, essayists accommodate Harris's ideas to historical and sociographic contexts. The result, as we shall see, is that there continues,
throughout the century, a peaceful coexistence between practical and
theoretical linguists, although the mere tolerance Lowth shows for Harris
is replaced by approaches to language that are separate but equally sure
that language is a social activity. After we have understood the shared
concerns of different kinds of linguistics in the period, we will look, in
the rest of this chapter, at the new assumptions about language that make
all linguistic activity of the mid and late eighteenth century significantly
different from what preceded it.

Throughout this period grammarians acknowledge both a philosophical and a conventional classification, without a sense of conflict or
contradiction. Richard Wynne, in *An Universal Grammar* (1775),
organizes his work around an eight-part system, but he notes his preference for the fourfold one, which has "more propriety and simplicity."[19]
Lindley Murray, in a later, quite popular grammar reflecting many late-
century assumptions, cites Harris, Horne Tooke, and others who propose
philosophically based systems, agreeing that there are only two
"necessary" parts of speech.[20] However, he decides to use "the most
natural and intelligible distribution" of words, since adherence to "the
established terms and arrangement, produces many advantages, and
occasions no material inconvenience" (p. 56). Murray repeatedly uncovers
inconsistencies between grammatical terms and "conceptions and
volitions," which they ought to reflect, but he always and easily settles
on "established authority," since "we presume no solid objection can be
made to the use of terms, so generally approved, and so explicitly
defined" (p. 74). The grammarian's first responsibility is "to render the
knowledge of [language] easily attainable" (p. 91).

Tolerance, in this case, is a sign of indifference. Disagreements that
had once excited vigorous controversy become acceptably different
approaches to language. Oliver Goldsmith, in his preface to Charles

Wiseman's *Complete Grammar* (1764), recognizes two sorts of grammarians—one writing in obedience to a Latin model, the other denying
any "similitude whatever" between Latin and English.[21] Writing in the
voice of the author, Goldsmith chooses "to dissent from both"; yet in
describing his own method, he clearly shares the limited and utilitarian
values of mid-century grammarians:

> This Grammar will serve to shew that our language may be reduced to system,
> without the necessity of adhering so closely to the Latin as has been hitherto
> thought necessary; but, at the same time, care has been taken not to dissent so
> far from that standard language as to discard those grammatical terms borrowed
> from it, and which have acquired, by long use, a prescriptive right to be admitted
> into our own. Nothing but an excess of ridiculous affectation could induce some
> Grammarians to make use of new and barbarous terms, instead of those already
> well enough known to every novice in Grammar.... (p. 305)

A "good practical grammar" (p. 307) should be "designed not to gratify
vain speculation, but to be converted into practical utility" (p. 309).
Usefulness, as well as accessibility to youth and to foreigners, are the
crucial criteria. Subjects that might "engage the Scholar's attention" or
notes crowding the page would not only interfere with the "material
parts of the art" but would also "increase the Size, and consequently the
price," of the book. Grammars, in this view, deal with the necessary rules
of the language and enable those ignorant in the language to speak and
write in socially acceptable ways. Gone from grammars is the equal
emphasis given to the philosophy of language. Such matters may be dealt
with by other linguists, in quite distinct works, for different readers, and
in special ways.[22]

## The Modest Linguist

Gone, too, from linguistic works generally in the second half of the
eighteenth century is the ambitiousness and reforming fervor of earlier
generations. But so imposing is the native tradition of reform that many
linguists explicitly defend their decision to go along with convention and
justify their deliberately deflated intentions. Joseph Priestley, in *A
Course of Lectures on the Theory of Language, and Universal Grammar*
(1762), although eager to discover universals of language, places such
limits on his search that he completely changes the idea of universality.
Since language, for Priestley, is an invention of man and not a work or a

reflection of nature, linguists themselves must "conform to established vicious practices, if [they] would not make [them]selves justly ridiculous by [their] singularity" (p. 116).[23] This fear of seeming unusual becomes a familiar defense.[24] The linguist must accept an irregular, inconsistent language; to introduce everything lacking in a particular language would be "too great an innovation" (p. 186).[25] That would amount to making a new language, a project no one in this period proposes.

The practical linguist now felt he should have as his focus not the perfection of language but the needs of its users. Substituting arbitrary characters for some words, for instance, may be somewhat more convenient than spelling them out conventionally, but beyond that they become, in Priestley's words, "more burdensome to the memory" (p. 210). Inflections are useful, but if multiplied, the relevant rules would "bear too great a proportion to the abilities and leisure of the people who are to use" the language (p. 211). Language is not sufficiently understood to succeed in "so grand a scheme" (p. 201) as that proposed by Wallis, whose suggestions for a philosophical language were the most rational of those "who flattered themselves" with similar projects. The recently dominant drive to connect the philosophy and practice of language no longer seemed pressing or even desirable.

Even less fanciful calls for language reform are doomed according to Priestley. In his *Rudiments of English Grammar* (1761), he contrasts the modern linguists' enterprise with the goals of seventeenth-century projectors by comparing grammar with a treatise on natural philosophy: "were the language of men as uniform as the works of nature, the grammar of language would be as indisputable in its principles as the grammar of nature";[26] but such is not the case. Proposals for an academy to standardize or perfect the language are inappropriate, too, for "the best forms of speech will, in time, establish themselves by their own superior excellence; and, in all controversies, it is better to wait the decisions of Time, which are slow and sure, than to take those of Synods, which are often hasty and injudicious" (p. vii). To try to enforce linguistic change is vain; to try to inhibit it, impossible. Language, after all, shares in historical change; it is no longer a defense against it.

Robert Baker, in *Reflections on the English Language* (1770), does echo the familiar call of a century earlier for an academy, but he adds a distinctive later-eighteenth-century qualification. His academy would limit itself to promoting elegance in the language, since any "new-moulding it and altering its general Form . . . is a Thing impossible."[27]

And Abraham Tucker, in *Vocal Sounds* (1773), makes his own proposals regarding the teaching of pronunciation, assured that any desire to have them adopted quickly "would carry the air of a romantic wish rather than a serious proposal."[28] His system of rough phonetic transcription is not intended "for common use," nor does he want anyone to "alter his usual manner either of writing or speaking": "I only mean to supply him with a method whereby he might ascertain the true sound of his letters" (p. 49). Baker's academy and Tucker's new science of "philophony" are proposals that express no desire for real change. They are so qualified by the recognition of the power of custom that they can only show people how they (or approved speakers) already speak. Selected description, or "accuracy," is as much as a practical linguist can achieve.[29]

Submitting to the irregularities of language seems to these linguists simply necessary. For Robert Nares, in *Elements of Orthoepy* (1784), mutability is "too inherent in the nature of language to be removed entirely by any care."[30] This fact accounts for "the failure of the system-makers" (p. 268) whose attempts at reform were "either injudicious in themselves, or too remote from established usage." The reward for submitting patiently to linguistic irregularities is "convenience" (p. xv). Buchanan, too, in his grammar, reviews the "vain Attempts" (p. 6) of Thomas Smith, Gil, and Wilkins to reform orthography, and warns that any such proposal is doomed to failure. All that remains to the linguist is "to exhibit as plain and conclusive Rules for the Powers and Properties of the Characters we now have as the impetuous and prevailing Tide of Custom will admit." A linguist can do no more than his times will allow, for he, like the language he describes, is part of history and representative of his society.

The acknowledged source for most of these justifications of modesty in the period is Samuel Johnson, "Dictionary Johnson," of course. To Nares, Johnson is "everywhere the declared enemy of unnecessary innovation" (p. 271). The authority of Johnson's dictionary "has nearly fixed the external form of our language" (pp. 269–70) and makes Nares unwilling "to depart from the established practice, till authorized by the approbation of the public" (p. 323). John Walker, in *The Rhyming Dictionary* (1775), accounts for his resistance to reform by advising his fellow linguists to let the language "remain as it stands at present in that monument of English philology erected by Johnson."[31] Johnson's work bulks as the most thorough record of the language; it does not significantly reform or finally standardize, and these self-imposed limitations are its most oft-cited virtues. Priestley celebrates Johnson's dictionary as "a complete system of our language as now used."[32] This emphasis on the linguist as an observer of acceptable contemporary forms rather than a reformer of essential elements reflects the securely modest spirit of most later-eighteenth-century linguistic practice.

The fate of Johnson's original goals as a linguist demonstrates his own submission to a reduced achievement more in keeping with a disillusioned idea of language. Although he rarely fails to declare the vanity of his best intentions, the differences in tone and promise between his *Plan of a Dictionary* (1747) and the "Preface" to the *Dictionary* (1755) dramatize his descent from a romantic pursuit of perfection to the accurate mapping of current linguistic territory.[33] In the *Plan*, Johnson sets his promising project against the general view of the unhappy lexicographer who patiently beats "the track of the alphabet with sluggish resolution."[34] Instead, Johnson hopes "to fix the English language" (p. 11). In this, he sees himself as an explorer, as one who, though he may not "complete the conquest . . . shall at least discover the coast, civilize part of the inhabitants, and make it easy for some other adventurer to proceed farther, to reduce them wholly to subjection, and settle them under laws" (p. 33). He undertakes his romantic journey, however, fully aware of what he will not find. He does not seek innovation in orthography and dismisses those who "take pleasure in departing from custom, and . . . think alteration desirable for its own sake" (p. 10); he rejects major changes in pronunciation; and he acknowledges that any linguistic project will prove that "language is the work of man, of a being from whom permanence and stability cannot be derived" (p. 18). Yet, even with these qualifications, Johnson promises to assemble the language, "distinct in its minutest subdivisions, and resolved into its elemental principles." He rather slyly wishes that these "fundamental atoms" of speech would lead to the "primogenial and constituent parts of matter," but such is not to be expected (except by some linguists of the seventeenth century). Johnson's ambitions are clearly limited: he can provide a full, detailed survey of the language as it is, has been, and should be used. That is enough to excite his imagination and turn him into an explorer of previously unchartered territory.

As it turns out, that is also too much. By the time his project is finished (without being complete), the resolution of language into its elementary parts and principles seems impossible, and the scholar-adventurer seems like a character in a romance. In the *Plan* Johnson had preserved the methods of ambitious linguistic research while giving up the more presumptive goals of a search for elements; in the "Preface," he admits that he has so often been obliged "to sacrifice uniformity to custom"[35] that he can no more securely identify, much less fix, the elements of a living and variable language, "than a grove, in the agitation of a storm can be accurately delineated from its picture in the water" (p. 14). Throughout the "Preface," Johnson not only repeats the idea that language is man's invention, but he adds to that original limitation his sense that "the boundless chaos of a living speech" (p. 10) will always exceed the industry of any collector. Johnson, once he had decided that language, as the lexicographer approaches it, is a self-contained system, had only words to define words. And that is the limitation that bound him to a vain pursuit.

"To interpret a language by itself is very difficult" (p. 13), but that is what the lexicographer must do once he discovers that the study of language leads to nothing but itself. It is the "fate of hapless lexicography" that "nothing can be defined but by the use of words too plain to admit a definition."[36] Added to that methodological tautology are the more familiar complaints of linguists: a living language is the victim of chance, time, fashion, ignorance, and innovation. It appears so irregular, arbitrary, and almost wanton that even a persevering lexicographer's "discernment is wearied, and distinction puzzled" (p. 15). From the confidently qualified description in the *Plan,* Johnson has come to this: "it must be remembered that I am speaking of that which words are insufficient to explain" (p. 16). He looks back to his *Plan* and, comparing it with his performance, discovers that no man can ever comprehend the language. He tried to "settle the orthography" only to find it "still controvertible"; he attempted to "display the analogy, regulate the structures, and ascertain the signification," only to prove that etymology is uncertain, explanations often contracted or diffuse, and significations "distinguished rather with subtilty than skill" (p. 20). The goals of the *Plan* were illusions:

> When first I engaged in this work, I resolved to leave neither words nor things unexamined, and pleased myself with a prospect of the hours which I should revel away in feasts of literature, the obscure recesses of northern learning, which I should enter and ransack, the treasures with which I expected every search into those neglected mines to reward my labour, and the triumph with which I should display my acquisitions to mankind. When I had thus enquired into the original of words, I resolved to show likewise my attention to things;

to pierce deep into every science, to enquire the nature of every substance of which I inserted the name, to limit every idea by a definition strictly logical, and exhibit every production of art or nature in an accurate description, that my book might be in place of all other dictionaries whether appellative or technical. But these were the dreams of a poet doomed at last to wake a lexicographer. (p. 21)

Johnson, by accepting language as the invention of men and, more significantly, as the expression of their changing history and habits, surrenders the goal of fixing or even containing it all. He responds to this disillusionment with characteristically fortified despair; but as he explains his former folly, he discovers an alternative goal for linguistics. This new context for the study of language becomes the eager and conscientious pursuit of many for the rest of the century.

Johnson accounts for the necessary vanity of his former expectations by cataloging forces of linguistic change that are as inevitable "as the revolutions of the sky, or intumescence of the tide" (p. 25). Commerce, progress in the arts and sciences, division into social classes, fashion, poetry, mixed languages and translation—all these conspire to make language changeable and irregular. Such social, economic, and historical forces remain blamable as long as language is seen, ideally, as a stable, coherent system; however, those forces take on quite another character when they are considered less as the causes of redressable linguistic corruption than as the manifestations of inevitable linguistic change. In the last half of the eighteenth century, language, instead of being the lamented victim of sociographic factors themselves the results of theological error, becomes a key to understanding the nature and history of those factors. Johnson's various apologies and assertions in the *Plan* and "Preface" show his pivotal place in this shift. His important contributions to the form of the dictionary all focus on linguistic changes—in orthography, pronunciation, and meaning. Although he apologizes, throughout the "Preface" for these variations and inconsistencies, he also recognizes the service he is performing. By following accepted orthography and recording differences in pronunciation, by providing relevant etymologies, by marking the "progress" of a word's meaning, and most importantly, by contributing examples of various meanings, Johnson makes his dictionary a (partial) record of English social, political, and "intellectual history." He closes his "Preface" still confessing his demonstration of linguistic instability, yet hoping, too, that his history of changes will make the past relevant to the present, that

*Theories of Language and the Grammar of Sentences, 1740–1785*

his dictionary will "afford light to the repositories of science, and add celebrity to Bacon, to Hooker, to Milton, and to Boyle" (pp. 27–28). His diligent display of linguistic enterprise could not reveal the nature of things or the operations of the mind, but it might reveal, by its amplitude alone, a long tradition of English riches.

## Compiling the Customs of the Language

The idea that the demonstration of linguistic mutability could be a rewarding endeavor and a valuable service rather than a lamentable indictment emerges, as it does for Johnson, from efforts to organize the variables of language. Instead of precipitating out irregularities and inconsistencies in order to get at what is permanent, linguists begin to record the nature and history of the changes themselves. In this approach to language, the linguist emerges as an observer or, according to Robert Nares, a "Compiler."[37] Collecting evidence of the uses (and misuses) of language, observing the linguistic differences custom makes, and pro-moting certain prevailing forms of expression are the stated purposes of many late-century texts.

There is often a strong prescriptive attitude in these works, but only as applied to the forms established by good habits of speech. By specifying and assembling the rules, Nares seeks to correct the corruption and to resist the innovations of the spoken language. The rules derive from "frequency of occurrence; that being called regular which appears to be most usual ... practical convenience being rather the object of this Work, than speculative acuteness of distinction."[38] Evidence, not speculation, is also the claim with which Lowth credits himself when he devotes his footnotes to lengthy lists of errors by prominent writers. Mere collecting seems, to the new linguists, an activity that justifies itself. The projects of linguists a century before had made methods of ordering essential to their purposes. There is little intentional significance in open-ended word lists or in Nares's justification for including material in his book: some matters may appear "not strictly belonging to the subject, but such as, having been collected, it seemed better to add than to suppress" (p. xviii). Since there is no longer a dominant model (of things or mental operations) external to language that a practical linguist had to confirm, there is no end to collecting—none but the collector's fatigue or inadequacy, according to Johnson.[39] Practical linguistics do not have to prove anything about existence or thought, for completeness becomes the chief justification.

Several reasons are given for detailing particular language customs. Principally, custom determines linguistic development and performance. John Fell, in his *Essay Towards an English Grammar* (1784), wants to correct, improve, and preserve the language, but his goal is not simply accuracy. Rather, he wishes to preserve variety and avoid reducing composition "to an insipid uniformity."[40] An academy for legislating the language would sacrifice what is living in language and would cramp English freedom.[41] What were linguistic defects two generations before— change and variation—are now virtues worth recording. For Fell, the proper role of the grammarian is

> to teach the grammar of the *English* tongue; not by arbitrary and capricious rules, and much less by such as are taken from the customs of other languages, but by a methodical collection of observations, comprising all those current phrases and forms of speech, which are to be found in our best and most approved writers and speakers. It is certainly the business of a grammarian to find out, and not to make, the laws of a language. In this work the Author does not assume the character of a legislator, but appears as a faithful compiler of the scattered laws. He does not presume to regulate the customs and fashions of our speech, but only notes and collects them. (p. xii)

Fell is only as independent as his socially determined compilation of the "best and most approved" language allows. Like Lowth, he legislates what he considers to be an accurate description of "proper" speech. In choosing the language to be compiled he and Lowth illustrate two ideas: that they, unlike former linguists, do not mean to change the language or invent a new one, but only to represent contemporary English as a full and various language; and that its fullness and variety are best represented in approved speakers and writers. Both ideas indicate the degree to which language is considered principally in a social rather than a philosophical context in the period.

Fell subscribes to conventional grammatical categories drawn from the "customs of other languages" in spite of his intentions to describe English independently. He allows the public to choose terms and systems for themselves, defending his own choice on the basis of custom and convenience. For Fell, linguistic goals are determined in part by the needs of the audience. William Kenrick, in *A Rhetorical Grammar of the English Language* (1784), recognizes the defects of the language; but since this is the language people must use, he does not make the correction of its defects the job of "those who would investigate, or describe its present state."[42] Describing the habits of contemporary speech in conventional ways becomes a goal linguists stop apologizing for.

In fact, Nares makes a virtue of describing a language that must, according to his own assumptions, change: "The whole Book, if it performs what its Compiler intends, will offer a clear and intelligible view of the externals of the English language, as they stand at present: and, should it exist for any length of time, will be a monument of the pronunciation which prevailed in England towards the end of the eighteenth century" (pp. xviii–xix). This is a remarkable statement, not only for its winning way of recommending a self-imposed limitation but also for its acceptance of change.[43] In this representative practical work of the late eighteenth century, the linguist is no longer dealing with what is original or immutable but is representing, even requiring, change and variety; he substitutes descriptions of historical episodes for the synchronous schemes, ontological or epistemological, of his predecessors.

Priestley, in his first linguistic work, *The Rudiments of English Grammar,* is equally aware of the altered role of the grammarian. His work describes "only the present state of our language," which "admits of no standard but that of custom" (p. iv). The power and inherent mutability of this "all-governing custom" (p. vii) are what make the idea of an academy inimical and foolish. For Priestley, as for Nares, one must conform to contemporary conventions destined to change. Linguists, therefore, by accurately recording local habits also compose historical documents.[44] V. J. Peyton, in *The History of the English Language* (1771), argues that the inconsistencies and inconstancies of the language, which once were liabilities linguists felt charged with correcting, had become virtues. English, especially, benefits from having been influenced by diverse languages throughout the history of the island: "like bees, we gather the honey of their good properties and leave the dregs to themselves."[45] This combination of praise for the language's distinctive assembly of parts and national pride is typical of linguistics in the period.

## Studying the Functions, Not the Parts, of Language

This new role for the practical English linguist means that certain aspects of his preparation, once regarded as necessary, are no longer required, at least in principle. If the linguist is chiefly a compiler of contemporary (and approved) customs, then knowledge of other languages, even classical learning, is unimportant. Such learning, indeed, may interfere with the effectiveness of teaching by introducing irrelevant analogies. Daniel Fenning, in his quite popular *New Grammar* (1771), argues forcefully that one can be a "complete master of the English tonge without troubling himself with any other language whatever."[46]

Fenning criticizes both Lowth and Priestley for introducing too much learning into their texts, although Priestley, in his *Lectures,* had refrained from multiplying distinctions and rules since these would soon exceed the "abilities and leisure of the people" (p. 211) using the language. Most linguists and schoolmasters continued to receive the same sort of training they had traditionally received, but there emerges a striking sense that knowledge of the classical languages does not give one a better command of English. Robert Baker, in his *Reflections,* even makes a virtue of his ignorance of Latin and Greek. Why "should this incapacitate a Man for writing his Mother-tongue with Propriety?" (p. ii). More conservatively, James Buchanan announces that his countrymen have already derived all that is valuable from the dead languages and that it is time to tap the distinctive riches of contemporary English.[47]

Knowledge of arcane languages is not only viewed as inappropriate to the teaching and learning of English, but for many, it is also irrelevant to general discussions of language. By forcefully declaring their disinterest in such topics as Egyptian hieroglyphics and Chinese ideograms, linguists of the later eighteenth century advertise their difference from their predecessors. Linguists once proved their seriousness by relating their investigations to the oldest and most object-based sign system; these later workers often declare their sensibleness by distinguishing their compilations from peculiar foreign and antique systems. According to Anselm Bayly, in *An Introduction to Languages* (1758), Egyptian hieroglyphics cannot be considered as a language because they do not consist of letters, words, and syllables. With revealing logic, Bayly insists that hieroglyphics "come under the Denomination of representative Symbols [rather] than any Species of Writing; because they denote not single Letters and Words, but Things themselves and Sentences, as among the Chinese."[48] The emblematic or symbolic relation between signs and things which, with equal clarity, had struck seventeenth-century linguists as the obvious (and desired) nature of language, appears to Bayly self-evidently to disqualify hieroglyphics from consideration as a language at all. Hieroglyphics seem to several later linguists, such as

Bayly, like a remote, exotic means of hiding religious mysteries from the people. For James Parsons, in *Remains of Japhet* (1767), the origin of language must be sought in the history of letters, not in hieroglyphical systems. The latter hide; the former communicate, and communication is the first principle of language.[49]

The once formidable example of Egyptian and Chinese hieroglyphics gets even harsher treatment from James Beattie and Lord Monboddo. Their shared premise is that language consists of artificial signs "employed universally for the purpose of communicating thought."[50] These invented signs are so convenient that they supersede natural signs. Since none can use an artificial sign system, like language, except those who have been taught to use it, such a system will encourage efficiency of communication. Hieroglyphics, according to Beattie, must have been inefficient: "They took up a great deal of room; could hardly be connected so as to form a sentence; were made slowly, and with difficulty; and, when made, were no better than riddles" (p. 311). Beattie also doubts that picture writing is the most ancient form of writing, since it is "so laborious, so liable to be misunderstood, expressive of so few ideas, and in general so inconvenient" (p. 312). These are convincing arguments only if one gives priority to social communication above all language uses. Anyone desiring a return to a sign-object system, writes Beattie, invites regression to the level of the Chinese, whom he calls "ignorant and narrow minded" (p. 121), inverting the characterization of a century before. In the second volume of his *Origin and Progress of Language* (1774), Monboddo mocks the Chinese system as being nearly barbaric since its characters are "no other than natural representations of things," much abridged.[51] The Chinese, he declares, were so ignorant in philosophy that they were not capable of inventing a language and probably relied on Egyptian signs. And those represent no more progress in the art of language "than to shorten . . . their barbarous cries" (p. 439). The modern linguist, according to Monboddo, should be demonstrating the progress achieved by man's artful languages. He should, like Lowth, preserve the gains that mark man's emergence from the barbarity of natural languages. Human speech, in this view, is a social art, an art of inference and inflection, which functions perfectly when it conveys someone's intentions to someone else.

Monboddo turns from this attack on hieroglyphics to a more generous attempt to salvage the reputation of a "little known" (p. 486) linguistic work of the previous century—Wilkins's *Real Character*. He regards

Wilkins as an antique figure whose linguistic work was like his project to teach man to fly–"though not so romantic" (p. 442). Although Monboddo gives Wilkins credit for ordering his material well, he dismisses the intention behind the method. Wilkins's work proves, almost in spite of itself, that every language is artificial, though it fails, as Monboddo says it must, to discover a source in natural philosophy. Still, Wilkins is one of the few seventeenth-century language writers who is remembered at all. Even Horne Tooke, who, in *The Diversions of Purley* (1798), reveals a more informed sense of the past than most of his fellow linguists, cites Wilkins as an insightful but slightly amusing predecessor. Tooke repeats Wilkins's illustration of the prepositions (fig. 5) and characterizes it as an "ingenious attempt" (p. 429). Wilkins erred by "confining his attention to ideas (in which he was followed by Mr. Locke)" and by overlooking "the etymology of words." Renewed fascination with etymology is another characteristic of later-eighteenth-century linguistics;[52] but in the context in which we have been discussing the practice of language here, it may also be seen as an aspect of the turning of the study of language on itself.

The second major shift in English linguistics in the years I am considering is the confinement of words to other words. At one time regarded as the signs of things themselves and later as the key to mental operations, words now become items in a self-contained, independent human invention. What the new linguist discovers by studying language is not the order or nature of things or the methods of thinking but the specific structure of a language and the status (and stature) of the society that has developed its linguistic habits in a particular manner. To William Kenrick, John Wallis's speculations on the relationship between sounds and the shapes of letters "may be a subject worthy the curiosity and investigation of a philosopher; but [the] distinction, difference and separation [of letters and sounds] form the great object of the practical linguist."[53] It is not what may be originally, generally, but remotely true that interests the "modern" linguist, but what is specifically and distinctively descriptive of a particular language.

## Practical Linguistics: Self-contained and Self-justifying

Although much of the inventiveness and suggestiveness of the early decades of English linguistics is absent from successors in the later eighteenth century, ample recompense comes in the form of more modest goals diligently pursued. Among grammarians there is a widely shared sense that the time has come for a summary of the art. Several writers note the abundance of grammars, the absolute quantity of linguistic work. James Gough looks back as far as Brightland and Greenwood and decides that what is needed is "a Summary of the most material Rules observed by good Writers."[54]

A still more modest note is frequently struck. Ralph Harrison, in *Institutes of English Grammar* (1777), for instance, acknowledges the "numerous publications on this subject" (p. v) and announces that "little originality is to be expected in a work of this nature" (p. iv). Less is expected, and less is found. Lindley Murray traces the distinctive logic of most of the period's grammarians as he considers the number and variety of English grammars: "little can be expected from a new compilation, besides a careful selection of the most useful matter, and some degree of improvement in the mode of adopting it to the understanding, and the gradual progress of learners" (p. v). Murray draws on Harris, Johnson, Lowth, Priestley, Beattie, Thomas Sheridan, and John Walker and extracts whatever of theirs is "easy, intelligible, and comprehensive" (p. vi). That is, he chooses material suited chiefly to the users of the language.

This restricted role for grammars needs no apology. Self-imposed limitations are, for George Neville Ussher, a sign of privilege. A century before, the language "was thought incapable of grammatical accuracy," but this view has been corrected by the many "who have investigated its nature, remarked its peculiar idioms, and reduced it to grammatical precision."[55] Definitions of grammar record this significant shift in the grammarians' approach to language. Since the forms of the language seem as settled as they are likely to become, grammars ought to collect the prevailing rules governing usage. There is little seeking after first principles or basic elements in the manner of seventeenth-century linguists; rather, there is what Daniel Farro offers, in *The Royal Universal British Grammar* (1754), "the System of a regular Digestion of Rules and Observations, which properly and absolutely appertain to each Part of a Language or Speech as is intended to be taught."[56] Grammar, writes Priestley in his *Rudiments,* is "the art of using words properly" (p. 1). Priestley deliberately emphasizes "using"; but in making "words" the entities that grammar describes, he is also declaring a conscious choice common in the period. James Buchanan defines grammar as "the Art of expressing the Relation of Words in Construction, with due Quantity in Speaking, and Orthography in Writing," and, in a footnote to this definition, goes back to Richard Johnson to take issue with the latter's "art of expressing the relation of things."[57] For Buchanan, as for most of his contemporaries, Johnson "should have said of Words, not Things, as Grammar treats of Words and not of Things." Words matter—their relation to one another, their history, their variety—and the matter they make is language itself.

This turning of language study on itself does not mean abandoning the idea of universal grammar. But it does result in a radical redefinition of universality. The term *universal* appears frequently in texts of the later eighteenth century, but linguists take care to distinguish its use from past emphases. Their goal, usually, is to apply the term to their descriptions of the language itself rather than to speculative systems, whether created or rediscovered, arbitrary or essential. What emerges as universal are the traditional categories of the parts of speech. Priestley, whose *Lectures* is the most substantial survey of the idea of language universals in the period, restricts universality to functions exhibited by most languages. Since languages did not generate spontaneously and were not made by philosophers, "but suggested by the necessities of beings in their first uncultivated state" (p. 113), one could not expect their rules and laws to be "either perfectly natural or consistent." What is left for universal grammar is "such a description of any particular mode of speech as [would] agree with the general practice of those who used it, without taking notice of those deviations which fall within the province of particular Grammarians" (p. 114). Universals represent a level of generalization that is irrelevent to those who study particular languages. Even the quality of mind needed for insight into universals— "not taking notice"—indicates Priestley's opinion of this familiar-sounding linguistic goal.

Most grammarians state their interest in universals in a way that justifies their descriptive summaries of English. Lowth, as we have seen, insists that universal grammar "cannot be taught abstractly: it must be done with reference to some language already known" (p. xi). If universal grammar "explains the Principles which are common to all languages," then English grammar "applies those common principles to that particular language, according to the established usage and custom of it" (p. 1).[58] That is to say (and it is what Lowth does) that the syntax he adopts shows how English fits the general scheme of language or, more accurately, how English distinctively accommodates to that scheme.[59] Daniel Farro carries the redefinition of universals to the final consequence of the idea that one's language is a version of a general system. If all languages share "the same substantial Notion of Beings, Actions, and Passions" (p. xv), then English is as "universal" as any, and a valid purpose of vernacular grammar, his *Royal Universal British Grammar* particularly, is to render English grammar "universal" by spreading its influence.[60]

Grammarians in this period, in effect, radically limit the methods and goals of language study and then claim universality for these deliberately restricted descriptions. Most often, they settle on the principle of analogy as the key to linguistic universals, but take as analogous functions the conventional distribution of words into parts of speech. James Elphinston, in *The Principles of the English Language Digested* (1765), accepts Johnson's *Dictionary* as his model of completeness and sets out to show "the same general plan of Nature" as the basis for English, French, and the learned languages.[61] The natural plan he offers actually "digests" these various languages; it shows "a demonstrative analogy, respective and relative," of them all. Yet, the general plan does not obscure the distinctiveness of each. All the languages are "reduced to one general, yet each to its separate system." The element of universality in this presentation belongs more to the grammarian than to the language. He describes languages in the same way, but the consistency of his method points out the differences between them.[62]

## Language, Thought, and Style

When grammarians of the later eighteenth century defend the idea of universality, they often do so only briefly and casually. As we have seen, some leave the subject to philosophers, as Lowth does to Harris. But it is clear that their basic premise is that the common aspects of language are found in meanings and usage, not in the relation between sounds or shapes of letters and things or ideas. The theorists, too, except for some self-consciously exotic projectors, agree that the forms of language develop from patterns of thinking. This is James Beattie's working principle when he suggests a universal grammar, and this is the context in which he dismisses hieroglyphics, natural signs, and the Chinese. Parts of speech are universal, he writes, because they express "certain modes of human thought."[63] Beattie follows Harris in accounting for the parts of speech, gender, moods, and tenses, and he notes his reliance on Gildon and Brightland as well. In seeking these universals, however, Beattie uses a method increasingly common in most linguistic works of the period: in examining words philosophically, one must ignore their derivative forms and inflexions. This is a version of Priestley's "not taking notice" of distinguishing elements when seeking common factors.[64] For Beattie and Priestley, the discovery of universal elements is not an end in itself as it is for Harris. They are more interested in characterizing the different forms and combinations of these general functions. Their goal is not Comenius's one world or Greenwood's one mind, but enough methodological consistency to note clearly different linguistic practices.

What happens to the study of language in the period is an odd combination of early-eighteenth-century linguistic ideas and mid-seventeenth-century methods. Essayists like Priestley and Beattie take over the vocabulary of linguists in the early part of the century—the shared premise being the relation between language and mind. However the linguists do not discuss the operations of language in terms of the operations of the mind; that is, they drop the logical analysis of syntax. Instead, they revive the seventeenth-century technique of associating linguistic features with a parallel scheme. Their scheme, however, is not the order of things predicated by seventeenth-century linguists, but another aspect of language—manners of speaking. They discuss the relation between mind and language rather than language and nature and do that in stylistic rather than in logical terms.

Once syntactic features become the distinctive aspects of speech in this new way, then mental habits can easily be characterized by stylistic traits. Style, a century before, was the pattern of language appropriate to the subject of the discourse, a definition consistent with a view of language that stressed the correlation between language and things. Now, style is the pattern of language manifesting the speaker's attitude toward or understanding of his subject.[65] This definition is consistent only with an approach to language that emphasizes the relationship between language and its users. The tendency to itemize linguistic differences, which we have already noted, also reappears here in a striking way, as language becomes an expression of mental styles. The universal classifications of speech are mostly assumed; what is pursued are the distinctive forms occupying those classes. Language users are distinguished, then, by their choices from among established usages. For

*Theories of Language and the Grammar of Sentences, 1740–1785*

Priestley, what is universal in language is almost beyond study and certainly irrelevant to the practical linguist. The "correspondence between every person's thoughts and language is perhaps more strict, and universal, than is generally imagined" since we cannot think (even meditate) without words. It follows, for Priestley, that someone who expresses himself in a confusing way is confused: "Everything therefore, that is maimed, distorted, or redundant in a person's style, must proceed from the same kind and degree of imperfection in his ideas" (pp. 47–48). However, the correlation between thought and style is not limited to faults. Just as each person has some physical peculiarity, so "hath every man a peculiar manner of conceiving things, and expressing his thoughts" (p. 57). Priestley uses the assumption that thinking is a linguistic activity to get to the rhetorical variations that mark different expressions of thought.[66]

Linguists in the first part of the century, following the model of the Port-Royal grammarians, had sought in the convolutions of syntax a philosophical basis for thought. Lindley Murray, summarizing much of the work done in the second half of the century, passes over the assumption that words are signs of ideas and moves, typically, to the rhetorical basis of communication: "it is evident that in proportion to our knowledge of the nature and properties of words, of their relation to each other, and of their established connexion with the ideas to which they are applied, will be the certainty and ease, with which we transfuse our sentiments into the minds of others."[67]

In having all philosophical assumptions point to the rhetorical psychology of that last clause, Murray effectively captures the disposition of later-eighteenth-century English linguistics. The two fondest principles become the relationship between thought and style and the evaluation of that relationship in terms of the effectiveness of communication.[68]

These two assumptions also help characterize the fashions of literature in the period. I referred briefly, at the beginning of this chapter, to a rhetorical method of characterization that presents characters in terms of their manners of speaking, acting, style of play, or handwriting. These are characters, for instance, who are not generally reported as simply "saying" or "replying" but who are portrayed as speaking in a particular way, as, among hundreds of possible examples, at the meeting between Morano and Montoni in Ann Radcliffe's *The Mysteries of Udolpho* (1794): "'Was it for this' . . . said Montoni, in a cool sarcastic tone of voice. . . . 'Who talks of treachery?' said Morano, in a tone of unrestrained vehemence." The principle aim of this sort of emphasis on a character's tone (or style of gesturing or dressing) is to involve the reader's affect by connecting the thought and expression of the character with the effect of the style on the reader.

The most popular forms of literature in the period compete, in fact, for the intensity of readers' responses. Gothic and sentimental novels; the poetry of obscurity, sublimity, and melancholy; the psychological aesthetics of involvement, experience, and excess vie for the emotional commitment of their audience. The reader of much late-eighteenth-century literature is not intended, as was the reader earlier in the century, to negotiate his way through a cleverly interrelated logical (or satirically illogical) process, but to respond to a series of charged expressive scenes or to identify (with) several distinctly affected characters. Readers are now given a space in literary texts—in the blanks left by Sterne or in the corner chair drawn up for us by Austen—in order to locate their response in the rhetorical scenes prepared with their attitudes, more than their judgments, in mind. Or, better, with their judgment guided by their responses rather than by their knowledge.


## The Arts of Reading and Hearing

A distinctive manifestation of these new linguistic emphases appears in books devoted to the "art of reading," that is, not the art of merely understanding what one reads, but the art of conveying one's understanding through oral delivery. At issue is Murray's goal, "the certainty and ease with which we transfuse our sentiments into the minds of others." John Rice, in *An Introduction to the Art of Reading* (1765), thinks it remarkable that so few have treated this art—the art "of intelligibly and emphatically repeating or rehearsing what is written in any Language."[69] Rice, describing his intention, elevates his standard of pronunciation to the status of what his contemporaries accept as a universal language. The "Art of Pronunciation in general" disallows "Patavinity or Provinciality of Dialect, which is merely local and transient, interfering with an Art, established on the fundamental Principles of all Language." Rice wants recitation to evoke the relationship between thought and speech; but since his is a system of pronunciation more than an analysis of logic, oral emphasis replaces syntax as the linguistic key. This is a notion of universality, then, based on the

competence of the speaker rather than on qualities embedded in the
language. But, as important to Rice as this plan is training students to
acquire a style of "expressing themselves on any Subject with Ease, and
in their own Way" (p. 11). Like many of his contemporaries, he
combines a descriptive method for which he claims universal appropriateness with a desire to account for, and encourage, individual expressions.
Individuals, like nations, had a "genius" evident in their use of distinctive
linguistic features.

In the earlier linguistic practices we have seen, the universal elements
in the system were both the means of analysis and, combined in their
ideal form (or forms), the language of individual speakers. Now, although
the relationship between speech and thought is assumed to be universally
necessary, the goal of analysts and speakers alike is to discover the bases
for separate styles. Not only has the idea of language universals changed,
but so has the relationship between what is thought to be generally true
and how individuals learn to read and write and speak. John Walker, in
*A Rhetorical Grammar* (1785), recommends making "pronunciation an
exact picture of the words."[70] What he means by this is neither the
seventeenth-century notion of object-words nor the earlier-eighteenth-
century idea of the logic of syntax, but the arrangement of voice
inflexions and pauses so as to express each sentence with appropriate
"passion or emotion" (p. 93). The "mind" that is expressed by vocal
tones giving evidence of passion or emotion and the "mind" evident in
syntactic logic are obviously two quite different ideas. The first, and the
dominant idea in the period we are discussing, defines the linguistic
expression of mental activity in a social, specifically rhetorical context
stressing communication of intention through oral/aural signals associated
with feelings or intentions.[71]

James Buchanan, in his *Grammar,* approaches grammar in just this
way. Grammar derives from discourse, therefore a grammarian's treatment of the written language should resemble a fair presentation of the
spoken:

> As in Speech or Discourse there are several Motions made by different Parts of
> the Body . . . in order to excite Attention and transmit a more clear and perfect
> Idea to the Hearer, of the Meaning and Intention of the Speaker: So Writing
> being the very Image of Speech, there are several Points or Marks made use of
> in it, not only to mark the Distance of Time in Reading, and to prevent any
> Obscurity or Confusion in the Sense; but also, that the various Affections and

> Emotions of the Soul, described by the Writer, may be more clearly distinguished and comprehended by the Reader.[72]

We can trace the history of English linguistics in this statement. Buchanan recalls punctuation marks first defined casually as temporal pauses, then those points as markers of syntactic (or sense) units, and finally elaborates his own emphasis on them as substitutes for vocal gestures clueing the reader to the true intentions, that is, the "Affections and Emotions" of the writer.[73] If one could read the written language with proper accent and "quantity," one could "hold the Passions captive, and surprize the Soul itself in its inmost Recesses" (p. 65). Such a correspondence between intentions (or emotions) and language leads to new linguistic descriptions, in which "different Passions of the Mind are to be expressed by a different Tone of Voice" (p. 67). Buchanan's work is representative of his contemporaries' efforts to make general vocal sounds the basis for communication. It is this desire and ability to communicate vocally if not verbally that is the only true language universal, as even the Shandy brothers discover at moments when intonation or whistling mean more than words.

Sounds, in fact, become the objects of new and widespread interest. By shifting the basis of universality and of communication from the elements of a physical or logical language system to the signals of the writer-speaker, linguists make the study of language a function of psychology and a means of access to individual intentions. Linguists argue that intentions are exhibited less by features of the language than by techniques of oral delivery, by the effects of pitch patterns and intonation, for instance. John Herries presents his *Elements of Speech* (1773) as an "enquiry into the human voice," describing the voice as the means of a speaker's expression in the same manner as colors are to a painter, or instruments to musicians.[74] Sounds, not words, are the principal tools of communication because through them we recognize "the powers of the Living Voice" (p. 32). Sounds, not words, give "spirit and variety . . . energy and gracefulness" to speech, and the simple sounds Herries records and arranges are "universally the same" (p. 92).[75] Pronouncing and hearing these sounds effectively leads us into the passion or sentiment of every speech—a crucial recognition, since the goal of speech, according to Herries, is to affect the passions. Herries writes excitedly at the end of his lengthy treatise about sounds

*Theories of Language and the Grammar of Sentences, 1740–1785*

expressing sense, not when words are considered as pictures of thought but when speech is "animated by the tones of nature" (p. 244). He finally points to "an infinite variety of vocal tones, corresponding to every impression of the imagination and the senses. This is the universal, untaught language of nature" (p. 247).

For William Kenrick, too, there must be "rules for the utterance of speech in general, independent of particular languages."[76] These rules have euphony as a natural motivation. Kenrick writes that too much attention has been given to the question of "the natural order or succession of words in discourse" (p. 28). Since languages "were not originally formed on philosophical principles" (pp. 28–29), the order of words has nothing to do with the order of ideas in the mind. Rather, languages, according to the different construction and genius of each, develop toward a euphonic idiomatic expression. As Anselm Bayly maintains in *A Plain and Complete Grammar* (1772), not only is language "a thing which changes, and is acquired," but "the ear will overrule judgment and theory."[77]

Thomas Sheridan develops similar ideas in his *Rhetorical Grammar* (1781) by distinguishing between the language of ideas, which expresses thoughts by means of words, and the language of emotion, which expresses internal feelings. The latter language seems, to Sheridan, to be the more important, since "the communication of these internal feelings was a matter of much more consequence in our social intercourse, than the mere conveying of ideas."[78] Sheridan's vocabulary is strikingly like that used by seventeenth-century linguists, except that it is applied not to words as "real" objects but to feelings as expressed tones:

> ... The Author of our being did not leave the invention of this language [of emotion]... to man; but stamped it himself upon our nature, in the same manner as he has done with regard to the rest of the animal world, who all express their various feelings by various tones. Only ours, from the superior rank that we hold, is infinitely more comprehensive; as there is not an act of the mind, an exertion of the fancy, or emotion of the heart, which have not annexed to them their peculiar tone and notes of the voice, by which they are to be expressed; and which, when properly used, excite in the minds of others, tuned invariably by the hand of nature in unison to those notes, analogous emotions. Whenever therefore man interferes, by substituting any other notes in the room of those which nature has annexed to the acts and feelings of the mind, so far the language of emotions is corrupted, and fails of its end. For

> the chords of the human heart, thus tuned in unison to the natural notes only,
> will never vibrate in correspondence to those of the artificial kind. (pp. 100–101)

These natural tones constitute a true "universal language, equally used by
all the different nations of the world, and equally understood and felt by
all" (p. 120). Sheridan's proposal is an extreme statement of what most
of his contemporaries assume—that what speech universally does is communicate and what it chiefly communicates are feelings and intentions.

In the literary languages of the period, too, new value is given
feelings, intentions, and responses. Words, as I have already suggested,
come to function less referentially or logically and more affectively. The
shift from the complex and argumentative to the uncomplicated and
evocative is evident in many popular forms, but none more revealingly
than in the poetic use of popular song measures. In the spirit of
Sheridan's call for an analysis of language "annexed to the acts and
feelings of the mind," poets like Chatterton and Burns seek rhythms and
tunes that will "vibrate" with their intended moods. As Bertrand
Bronson has so expertly shown, the relationship between literature and
music early in the century "relied ... upon using the accepted modes of
expression with deepened awareness, refined sensitivity, and precision,"
while later in the century the relationship exhibits the evolution of "a
common and universal language ... not by the cerebration of an aristocra-
tic tradition, but by the gradual and unconscious sifting out of the graces
and subtleties" of the people's tunes.[79] These later poets rely on their
talent for striking respondent chords and count on readers who will give
the right vibrations. When Cowper writes, mournfully, that he "knew at
least one hare that had a friend," the simple pathos needs the support of
readers who share the poet's chief comfort when confronting the
"diversity of tongues" that followed Babel.[80] Although people were
scattered then, "Ample was the Boon" God gave shepherds, and it is
still their retirement, isolation, and natural tunefulness that makes the
poet feel intermittently connected to nature. Cowper hears a primitive
harmony repairing Babel, and this is a distinctively late-eighteenth-
century version of the proposals made by the tower-fixers of a century
before. Cowper's ear, if we are to hear with it, needs readers uncritical
enough to respond to the still, sad music it listens for beyond the din.
And the ear which hears beyond chatter belongs, erratically, to individuals who may convey but cannot tell what they hear.

Rhetorical Phonetics

The remarkably widespread and intensive interest in sounds maintained by linguists of the period goes well beyond the elocutionary movement, although the figures associated with it—mainly Sheridan and Walker—are particularly important to the general trend.[81] The rules of grammar, pedagogy, methods and order of study, and theory are commonly based on preliminary remarks about sounds and often associated with discussions of basic sounds, emphasis, pause, modulation, articulation, accent, pronunciation, quantity, and tone. Sounds, in fact, reappear in linguistic texts as the first elements of speech: not, however, as vowels and consonants constituting the units of meaning as once they were in seventeenth-century proposals but as the sources of communicating attitudes of speakers. This is as much a rhetorical as an articulatory phonetics. In all of Buchanan's texts, he gives "first Consideration" to "the various Forms, Powers and Sounds of Letters, and their different Combinations in the Production of Syllables."[82] This is the "Foundation of the whole." In his *Complete English Scholar,* he recommends "that excellent and rational Method of teaching to read by the Powers of the Sounds" (p. ii), and in his *Essay Towards Establishing a Standard for . . . Pronunciation,* he promotes a standard as the goal of a "grammatical and scientific knowledge" (p. x) of English. The consistency of Buchanan's approach to grammar, pedagogy, and pronunciation shows clearly the impact of the idea that communicable sounds constitute the foundation of the language.

Frequent efforts are made in this period to determine the basic or "simple" sounds and to associate these firmly with letters. Anselm Bayly, in his *Introduction to Languages,* opposes those who teach reading by alphabets and spelling books since in these texts letters do not correspond to sounds. Students would be able to read "rationally . . . were they taught by an Alphabet of simple and familiar Sounds" (Part 2, p. 15). These simple sounds are universal in all languages and form the only part of language that is natural, since they are formed by the organs of speech. They should be taught orally, not visually, since letters do not invariably have the sounds shown in traditional spelling books (as, "c see"). Children (and foreigners) taught visually "learn to read as they speak, mechanically, by Dint of Memory. . . . Whereas they might be able to read, and that rationally, . . . were they taught by an Alphabet here proposed of simple and similar Sounds."[83] Bayly argues most forcefully for this method of teaching the "elements of the English language" (Part 1, p. iii) in a book the title of which connects grammar to the aural foundation of language and shows how far we are from the primarily visual, taxonomic grammars of a century before: *The English Accidence, Teaching by an Easy Method the Pronunciation of English and the Parts of Speech* (1771).

This new scientific study of the language begins with sounds and uses comprehensive phonological descriptions as the secure basis for a thorough-going linguistics, reaching to grammar, rhetoric, and criticism. By starting with sounds defined in physical terms, linguists like John Elphinston can make English, "its whole Analogy independent in itself, and its very Sounds, as much objects of demonstration as the theorems of Mathematics."[84]

Elphinston, like his contemporaries, first elaborately ascertains the sounds of the language and then demonstrates the "manner of painting them" (p. 1). The aural elements of language rationally presented and studied offer the best means of teaching, too. Goldsmith, in his preface to Wiseman's *Grammar,* firmly maintains that it is "absolutely necessary for the young scholar to begin with pronunciation, on which, in a great measure, depends all [the] harmony and force" of language.[85]

Sounds, unlike the meaning of words or the complexities of syntax, are to these grammarians describable and limited. Sounds seem a fit scientific base for whatever variations occur at other levels of the language to Solomon Lowe, who, in his *Critical Spelling-Book* (1755), criticizes those books that list words of various sounds and the same letters instead of sorting words according to accent and sound. He distinguishes his own efforts from those of Dyche and Dilworth by concentrating on pronunciations that come "nearest to the sound" of words.[86] Bayly wants children first taught the alphabet of real sounds and afterward the common alphabet represented in most spelling books.

Bayly admits, in *Accidence,* that he must define and describe the "primitive sounds."[87] His phonological descriptions of the sound represented by *n,* for instance, as being produced by the "tongue placed softly, and not quite flat to the roof of the mouth, and forcing the sound through the nostrils" (p. 4), are detailed but facile, really summaries of the more thorough investigations of sounds common in the period. Herries's *Elements of Speech,* as we have noted before, is an "enquiry into the human voice," and Benjamin Martin's *Institutions of Language* (1748) consists of a *Physico-Grammatical Essay on the Propriety and*

*Rationale of the English Tongue.* In one section, Martin discusses each letter in terms of the physiology of its pronunciation. At the end of this section he proudly labels it the "philosophy of letters and language."[88] William Kenrick, too, claims as the chief distinction of his *New Dictionary* (1773) his inclusion of instructions for pronunciation.[89] Instead of the usual method of enumerating the literal elements of language to show how these are pronounced, Kenrick recommends describing oral elements to show how they are formed by the organs of speech. He then goes through each sound, giving a physical description; this section is called "The Alphabet of Speech." The practical linguist in this period presents language as a social activity—language as it is spoken and heard during oral communication.

Herries includes a printed plan "to exhibit at one view, the number, formation, qualities, and arrangement of the simple Articulate Sounds"[90] (see fig. 10). By reducing speaking to a "mechanical art" (p. 63), Herries believes he can propose a method for teaching the deaf to speak. However, his method is quite different from that of Wallis and Holder and is based on equally distinctive assumptions. Instead of assuming rational and visually reinforced relations between sounds and things, Herries relies on "simple and mechanical principles" (p. 70), chiefly vibrations felt in the throat on emission of sounds. Such an empirical basis serves Rice, too, in the *Art of Reading.* He contrasts "the mechanical Theory of Speech, as founded on actual Observation, and the Principles and Experiments of natural Philosophy" and the "practices of the Ancients or Opinions of classical Authority.[91] His phonological descriptions are modeled on terms derived from physics;[92] but whatever the source of the descriptions, they are so common by the last quarter of the century that Abraham Tucker, in *Vocal Sounds* (1773), refers to a new science of "philophony," then only half formed "in the nursery of grammarians."[93]

In determining the simple, natural, or primitive sounds, these linguists rarely propose a philosophical basis or seek authority other than "common" usage. Lowe recommends the pronunciation of words "as commonly spoken by the better sort of people at London" (p. 12). Robert Nares, in his more substantial *Elements of Orthoepy,* openly admits that in drawing up his rules, he always attended to "frequency of occurrence."[94] Throughout this work, Nares takes habits of pronunciation "as they are found in common practice, and in the simplest form" (p. 2). The standardization Nares hopes for is no more than rules adequate to

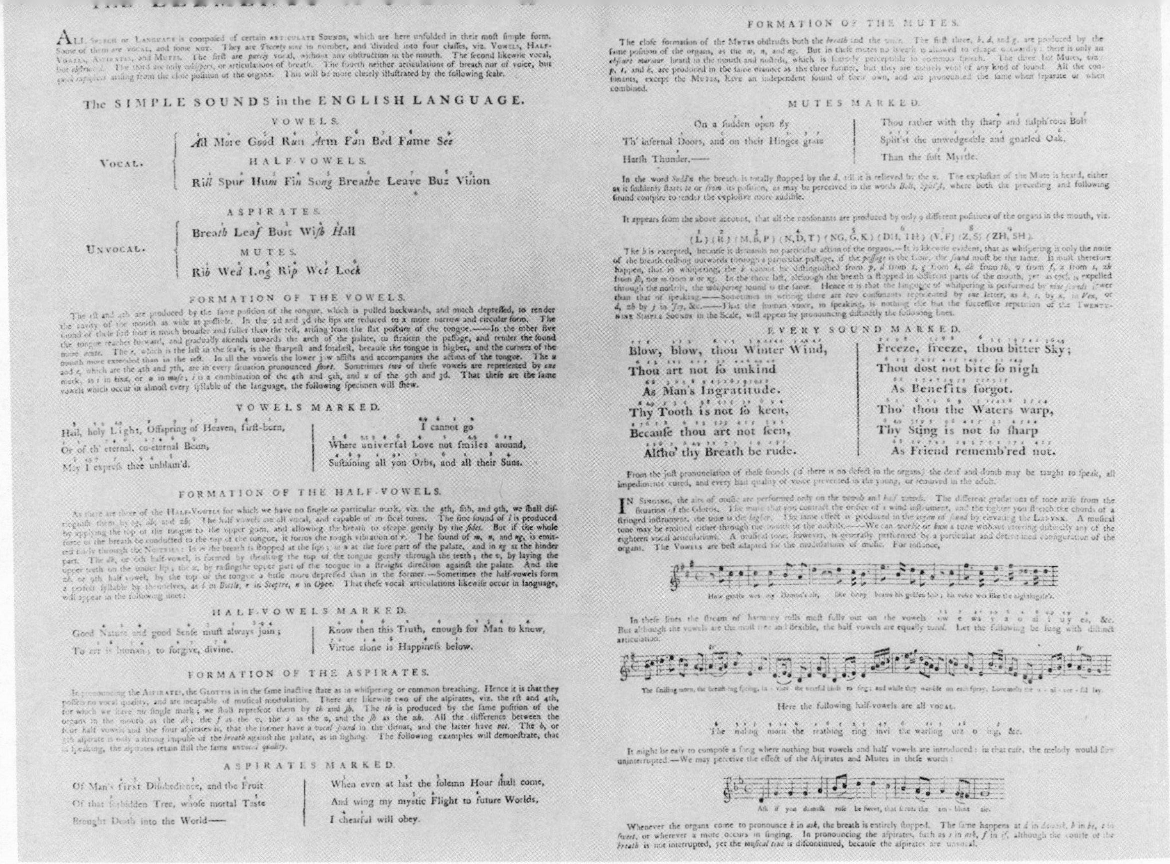

Figure 10. John Herries, *The Elements of Speech* (1773), facing p. 25. Reproduced by permission of the Houghton Library, Harvard University.

the language as it is (well) spoken. When Robert Baker, in *Reflections upon Learning,* echoes the call for an academy to settle the English language, he reveals how radically different such proposals are in 1770 compared with similar-sounding projects of previous generations. Baker offers the nation's theaters as ready-made "academies" since actors, who already speak well and, most usefully, know accurate stresses, could be instructors.[95] This notion of an academy combines the new emphasis on pronunciation with the pervasive assumption that language is, chiefly, a means of oral communication.

Once again Thomas Sheridan states the new attitudes most decisively. In one of his early publications, *A Dissertation on the Causes of the Difficulties, which occur, in learning the English Tongue* (1761), he claims that the chief fault with English is the traditional emphasis on orthography at the expense of orthoepy. His own mission is "to restore the first, and noblest part of grammar, to its just rank and power . . . to make the spoken language, as it ought to be, the archetype; of which, the written language should be considered only as the type."[96] He criticizes linguists who insist on preserving the inconsistencies of the written language as "sticklers for derivation" (p. 14) who have "a partial and mistaken view of the end and use of written language" (p. 15). Sheridan sides with the "partisans of pronunciation" and promises a rhetorical grammar and a pronouncing dictionary that will determine the number of simple sounds in language generally and in English particularly, the number of diphthongs and syllables, and the "use of our accent, that grand master-key to the pronunciation of our tongue" (p. 31). He delivers these, with his *Rhetorical Grammar of the English Language, Calculated solely for the Purposes of Teaching Propriety of Pronunciation, and Justness of Delivery, in that Tongue, By the Organs of Speech* (1780) as an introduction to his *Complete Dictionary of the English Language, Both with regard to Sound and Meaning.* This remarkable reliance on sound as the principal source of the study and practice of language depends, in turn, on the "undisputable truth, that the sounds which are most easily uttered by the organs of speech, are most pleasing to the organs of hearing" (p. 35).[97] The pleasures of communication, that is, justify the study of sounds, and the sounds studied are those "used by people of the best taste at court." These three assumptions—the priority, theoretically, of tonal and accentual communication in the origins of speech; methodologically, of sounds; and socially, of court pronunciation—summarize the methods of practical English linguists in the later eighteenth century.[98]

In the prominent theories of language, too, versions of these same principles prevail. Adam Smith, for instance, in his essay "Considerations Concerning the First Formation of Languages" (1761), traces the development of language from vocal variations and additions "introduced chiefly for the sake of a certain similarity of sound, of a certain species of rhyme, which is naturally so very agreeable to the human ear."[99] Euphony, here, not ideas of natural or achievable universality, motivates the development of language. Most grammar rules, according to Smith, result from the "Love of analogy and similarity of sound" (p. 312). For Monboddo, as well, a philosophical view of grammar that assumes that whatever is expressed by a word "is either substance, accident, or an energy of the mind of the speaker" must account for the origins of speech, not in the nature of things, but in the pleasure of sounds.[100] The roots of classical Greek, Monboddo's example of a perfected language, were chosen principally "on account of their sweet and flowing sound" (2:219). And the men who formed and improved the Greek language must have "thoroughly studied, and minutely dissected, the operation of the several organs of articulation" (2:235). English linguists in the later eighteenth century assume that similar studies of sounds are necessary to any accurate description of improvable English.

Monboddo develops his premises into an argument about discourse when he defines "the natural order of words in a sentence" as the agreement between oral emphasis and the sequence of words; the right sequence occurs when whatever is "principal in the mind of the speaker, and which, if he pronounce properly, he would lay an emphasis upon, should be first in the composition" (2:348). A proper study of the composition of language would be divided into sections on articulation, accent, and quantity and would try to make language "pleasant and flowing" (2:373). These methods and goals are, in fact, common in the practical language texts of the period.

## Sense, Sounds, and Musical Notations

The importance of sounds to language study can also be seen in the widespread interest of linguists in music during the late eighteenth century, especially in the relationship between musical notation and instructions for pronunciation. Joshua Steele's *An Essay Towards Establishing the Melody and Measure of Speech* (1775) is the most detailed effort to provide notations for spoken sounds and to organize these on the model of a musical scale (see figs. 10 and 11).[101] But the works of John Mason were more influential.[102] His *Essay on Elocution or, Pronunciation* (1748) and *Essay on the Power and Harmony of Prosaic Numbers* (1749) both connect "the Art of managing and governing the Voice" with the chief end of discourse, that is, to instruct and affect those who hear. Herries, too, deals with speech defects by comparing the voice to a musical instrument, and Sheridan writes approvingly and enviously of musical notation as a model for graphically specifying sounds.[103] All these linguists share the idea of the speaking voice as a musical instrument conveying meaning through the manner, as well as the matter, of expression. "Vocal sounds," writes John Walker, are a "species of chromatic music."[104]

Sheridan's efforts to reduce the "pronunciation of each word to a certainty by fixed and visible marks," as in music, resemble several attempts during the period to find adequate phonetic symbols.[105] The revealing difference between these efforts to represent pronunciation graphically and the spelling reforms proposed earlier is that the newer systems assume the "sense" of sounds has more to do with sensibility than with sensory knowledge. William Kenrick adds a rhetorical grammar to his *Dictionary* (1773) in which the *Elements of Speech in general and those of the English Tongue in particular are analyzed; and the Rudiments of Articulation, Pronunciation, and Prosody intelligibly displayed.* He proposes reforms in printing "in which the word is literally presented in its due proportion of number and character to the eye."[106] Although he approves Sheridan's proposal for using certain typographical marks, he substitutes directions of his own. Kenrick has accents printed over radical words, syllables separated with numerals placed over each denoting the exact quality of sounds according to a table provided, and consonants distinguished by Roman or italic type as they are hard or soft, audible or mute. However, he objects to making orthography reflect orthoepy by declaring that attempts "to convey sounds merely by letters, and teaching the pronunciation of words by a different mode of spelling" (p. ii) are absurd. His solution is phonetic spelling, not phonetic writing, and he uses it as a descriptive tool, not to make a theoretical point.[107] Kenrick actually elaborates the method proposed in Buchanan's *Essay*. Buchanan,

ſhall be nearly divided under the ſeveral degrees of emphaſis of
heavy (∆), light (∴), and lighteſt (..); as thus,

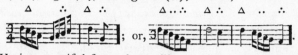

Having premiſed ſo much, I will now give a general precept
and example in the following ſentence:

Every | ſentence | in our | language, | whether | proſe or | verſe,
∆ ∴ | ∆ ∴ | ∆ ∴ | ∆ ∴ | ∆ ∴ | ∆ ∴ | ∆ ∴

r r | has a | rhythmus | r r | pe | culiar | to it | ſelf; | r r
∆ ∴ ∆ ∴ | ∆ ∴ | ∆ ∴ ∆ | ∴ | ∆ ∴ | ∆ ∴ | ∆ ∴ | ∆ ∴

That is, in the | language of | modern mu | ſicians, | it is
∆ .. ∴ | ∆ .. ∴ | ∆ .. ∴ | ∆ ∴ | ∆ ∴

either in | common time | or | triple time; | vi | delicet,
∆ .. ∴ | ∆ .. ∴ | ∆ ∴ | ∆ .. ∴ | ∆ ∴ | ∆ ∴

minuet time, | or | jigg time, | or | mixed.
∆ .. ∴ | ∆ ∴ | ∆ ∴ | ∆ ∴ | ∆ ∴

To the firſt member of the above ſentence (which I have
written in common time, as marked by $\frac{2}{4}$), I have noted the
*accents*, the *quantity* and *cadence*; to the latter member, which
is in triple meaſure, I have only marked *quantity* and *cadence*,
together with the proper *reſts* or *pauſes* throughout the whole. I
have

Figure 11. Joshua Steele, *An Essay towards Establishing the Melody and
Measure of Speech* (1775), p. 28. Reproduced by permission of the
Bancroft Library, University of California, Berkeley.

wanting to mark long and short sounds and syllables, supplies his words in two columns, one recording the "true orthography" and the other "the true pronunciation."[108] Students should learn both "erectness' and "eerektniss," but they should always use the first form in writing.

John Walker, in *Rhetorical Grammar* (1785), recommends marks for pronunciation as a teaching device. Students should read aloud while the teacher puts marks on the page, particularly under mispronunciations. This method "will direct the eye, and the attention, so much to it, as soon to remove the defect."[109] Walker prefers notations that convey "the several forces of speaking sounds" (p. 111), first suggesting underlining and then adding hyphens between accented and unaccented words: "With-honest *scorn* the-first-fam'd-Cato-view'd." Printing sentences in these distinct "portions" reveals their "accentual impulses" (p. 114). Sheridan's system too, uses four different marks to note pauses that "answer the same end that shades do pictures; by the proper use of which, the objects stand out distinctly to the eye.[110] Along with the other marks, Sheridan proposes to note accent, syllabification, and length, and the resulting mode of printing contributes to the larger end Walker has in mind—to show how one could speak in such a way as to suit one's voice to the "intention or sentiment" (p. 177) of each statement. For both Walker and Sheridan, and for others, these suggestions for printing are not meant to alter spelling or provide a "real" picture of the human voice, but to influence the way words are spoken in society, to ensure that speech reflects intention and stimulates the proper affect.

Proposals for significant spelling reform are unusual in the period. Predictably, they seem inconsistent with contemporary views. Thomas Spence, in the *Grand Repository of the English Language* (1775), taking Sheridan's remarks more literally and more thoroughly than their author intended, ambitiously proposes a new alphabet of forty letters constituting a "natural or philosophic orthography."[111] Later, Noah Webster, after some reluctance, supports slightly less radical reforms, but, as with Spence, these unusual language proposals are made in a context of revolutionary political ideas.[112] The prevailing linguistic orthodoxy conserves socially accepted speech.

What interests the linguists of the period is the ability to communicate through speech (hence the emphasis on sounds) and the social context of speaking. One of the native forms of the period, as we have noted, is the essay on how to read aloud, and another is the rhetorical grammar. We have already drawn from the contributions to this second type by Kenrick, Sheridan, and Walker. Walker thinks of his work as a supplement to that of Lowth, as a grammar of elocution that will adapt pauses, tones, and variations of voice to conventional grammar. Similarly, Johnson's successors defend their dictionaries by claiming the valuable addition of more sophisticated notations of sounds and pronunciation. The rhetorical grammar is a grammar of communication, of speaking, defined by Walker as "an adaptation of the voice to the structure and import of a sentence."[113] To everything else in grammar must be added directions that will make the intentions of speakers evident to hearers. Walker even proposes a "Rhetorical Punctuation" (p. 38) to supplement Lowth's grammatical punctuation. Walker cites Harris as often as Lowth does, and he agrees with both of them that the forms of language reveal habits of thinking; but his chief interest is in the vocal performance of these intentions. The rhetorical dimension of language is added to all sorts of language texts. Kenrick adds a rhetorical grammar to his dictionary, and Rice proposes one to follow his *Art of Reading*. Rice promises, in fact, both a rhetorical grammar and a rhetorical dictionary that will reconcile orthography and orthoepy, not by reducing one to the other, but by applying general written types to the modes of articulation in English.

Another revealing habit of language texts in the period is their inclusion of a brief section proving the importance of emphasis by showing how the shifting of emphasis from one word to another in a sentence also changes the meaning. It is a strikingly new idea, but one consistent with the new linguistic assumptions. Several linguists give prominence in this way to the importance of the voice. Herries, in his detailed study of the mechanics of speaking, shows how meaning changes according to "the mode of utterance," by which he means stress; William Cockin, in *The Art of Delivering Written Language* (1775), includes the same demonstration and refines a distinction between the natural emphasis of sense and an artificial emphasis of force—a distinction Cockin thinks ought to be marked by printers; and James Beattie, in his "Theory of Language," demonstrates, by means of the same proof, the importance of emphasis and accent to communication.[114] These men share a conception of language in terms of speakers and listeners and a commitment to the priority of the oral over the visual. In these studies speech is first of all a social act manifesting itself rhetorically.

## Language as Social Communication

As new and as widespread as interest in the meaningfulness of emphasis are additions to the definitions of language that place particular stress on communication. Language is an event requiring at least two people, and a mode of communication including not only the words but their expression orally in particular situations. When Herries gives his physical descriptions of speech, for instance, he does so in terms of audibility. Unlike earlier studies of sounds, which tried to isolate distinctive properties of sounds, Herries's work displays a continuing concern for how sounds are heard. Sounds voiced derive from sounds heard. For Herries, as for his contemporaries, sounds make sense not when words are considered as pictures of thought but when speech is "animated by the tones of nature."[115] Even syntax, in Monboddo's view, represents thought for the sake of hearers. To make a sentence, "the words that compose it must be some way or another connected together, so that the mind of the hearer may perceive their relation."[116] Horne Tooke objects to divisions of language based on differences of things, or ideas, or operations of the mind; rather, he thinks, words should be divided according to their manner of signification, that is, either as words necessary for communication or as abbreviations. There are, for Tooke, no operations of the mind, but only operations of language. When one considers ideas, things, or the mind, one is really dealing with nouns. To account for the other part of speech, the verb, one must consider "the necessary use of it in communication."[117]

In the definitions of language given in textbooks, there is the same emphasis on speech as a social action. George Brown, in *The New English Letter-Writer* (1779), defines grammar as "the art of one human creature speaking to another, so as to be understood."[118] For Daniel Fenning (1771), grammar is the "Art of communicating our thoughts in the plainest and most intelligible manner," and, for Daniel Farro (1754), words are "the Medium by which we convey all our Ideas, and Notions of Things in Communication and Conversation one with another."[119] The ability of men to understand one another, not the power of language to represent things or ideas, is the gift of language. Joseph Priestley declares communication to be God's gift, one made appropriate to each kind of society. This view takes care of the universality of language, since communicating is the same need everywhere; and it acknowledges the diversity of languages, since the ability is

differently manifested in each society. This analysis also permits Priestley
to describe societies, and classes within a society, in terms of their manner
of communicating: "The power of communication being, exactly pro-
portioned to our social connections, must be nearly of the same extent
with the furniture of the mind."[120] The new linguistic perspective on man
puts interpersonal communication at the beginning of social development
and distinguishes among societies according to their modes of communication.

   Communication to these linguists is a human need that not only
begins spontaneously and develops variously but functions by conveying
feelings and affections as much as ideas. In uncovering these assumptions,
we come around, again, to the stress on sounds, on meaning as accent
and emphasis, on the linguistic expression of mind in terms of style, on
reading as oral interpretation, and on understanding as responsiveness.
John Mason, in his *Essay on Elocution, or, Pronunciation* (1748), defines
"good Pronunciation" as that which makes ideas "seem to come from
the Heart" and excites "the Attention and Affections of them that
hear."[121] To read well means to enter the spirit of the writer and affect
the hearers with "the same Ideas as he intended to convey [and] the
same Passions he really felt" (p. 20). Mason's key to this performance of
critical understanding is, simply, conversation, in which "all is free,
natural and easy" (p. 30). This advice and this goal are common in the
period. Rice, for instance, defines the art of reading as the ability to
convey "to the Hearer the whole Meaning of the Writer" and "recommends encouraging students to recite as they converse.[122] This ideal of
communication through conversation is usually described in the terms
each linguist proposes as the best means of learning and using the
language. Thomas Sheridan argues for an extreme version of the idea
that we should read as we speak. He suggests observing the illiterate man
who "without rule or thought," exhibits the ideas that proceed through
the mind "exactly as they pass."[123] Speech, according to Sheridan,
properly expresses ideas considered as the evidence of emotions, and in
the illiterate man, emotions are naturally manifested "by suitable tones,
looks, and gestures" (p. 107). Sheridan studies sounds to discover the
basis for an expressive view of language: of language as oral communication; communication as a means of expressing ideas; and ideas as the
sources and objects of affect and intentions (not of logic).

   As we have seen in this section, the practical linguists in the period
find a new mission after the neutralization of the philosophical context

of language. In their short, rule-summarizing grammars, their arts of
reading and inquiries into the human voice, their rhetorical grammars,
and their proposals for pronunciation and practiced conversation, they
become industrious compilers of the linguistic habits of a community of
speakers and compliant recorders of the historical situation of contemporary English.

## New Versions of the Origins and History of Language

The basic language texts we have been surveying in this chapter are
organized and oriented to stress communication. In language theories,
too, there is a comparable socialization, which takes place after Harris.
The questions that appear with startling frequency in general discussions
deal with the origins of language,[124] classifications of societies according
to linguistic habits, and history; and the newly emphasized methods of
linguistic analysis include studying the language of children and
"primitives," stressing the distinctive genius of each language, and using
etymology to gather sociographic and historical knowledge. Neither the
questions nor the methods are unprecedented; in fact, both recall some
of the plans and practices of linguists a century and more before. But the
context is completely different, and it is the relationships among ideas
that determine the distinctive shapes of intelligibility at a given time.

Interest in the origin of languages fascinates these linguists in ways
that recall the frequent evocations of the Word in the seventeenth
century. References to Babel occur almost as prominently; however,
whatever happened then is no longer considered as the end (or the ideal)
of linguistics, but as its beginning. Even those seventeenth-century
linguists who moved away from the idea of divine origin and asserted the
human invention of speech were governed, in their projects, by the
possibility of an ideal language meeting the theological implications of
those seeking Adamic knowledge. Most later linguists explicitly reject
the idea of divine origin and largely ignore the idea of divine governance
over language. They reorient themselves away from the theological,
social, and literary assumptions of earlier work.

Instead of giving the history of English in order to trace its lineage
to the first tongue, later eighteenth-century linguists use the history to
show how (and why) the language has changed.[125] From a careful observation of the "defects, superfluities, and imperfections" of all alphabets,

including the Hebrew, Priestley concludes that there could not have
been a "divine alphabet."[126] Instead, "the first attempts towards speech
must have been automatic sounds, excited by particular circumstances"
(p. 237). Priestley, in a note at this point, acknowledges the tradition of
divine origin but clearly indicates his preference for a social and historical
explanation: "Notwithstanding the powers of speech might have been
communicated, in a considerable degree, to the first parents of the
human race; yet, since it is natural to suppose it would be only sufficient
for the purposes of their own condition, we may perhaps conceive more
justly of the manner in which language was improved, by supposing
mankind to have begun from so small a beginning" (pp. 237–38).
Beginning with imitative sounds, man slowly progressed from an
instinctive need to communicate about local realities. What is original
(and universal) is the need to communicate, and languages are differentiated by historical and local variations between groups of language users.
According to Priestley, the linguist ought to investigate the history rather
than speculate about the premise. Monboddo sketches a similar program.
He begins with sounds as they were developed by primitive man to
communicate impressions. The "faculty of speech," writes Monboddo,
"is not the gift of nature to man, but, like many others, is acquired by
him."[127] The process of acquiring speech begins with imitative sounds
and progresses according to principles of euphony. By relating the
progress of languages to aural factors, Monboddo shows what practical
and theoretical linguists share, at least in terms of how they discuss
language, if not in what they say.

The methods of seventeenth-century linguists were connected, of
course, with the goals of their study—the divine origin of speech or the
divine order of things was proof to them of the possibility of rediscovered
or reinvented linguistic brotherhood. A century later, both the practice
and the ideas of language are different. For William Kenrick, the "means
of communicating human knowledge is, like that of knowledge itself, the
work of ages";[128] that is to say, the linguist studies the changes in
language over time, and he demonstrates what it is possible to know at a
certain time. Kenrick perfectly expresses the difference between his own
and earlier ideas about the origins of language in the introduction to his
rhetorical grammar: "Speech, say the Divines, is the gift of God. It
undoubtedly is so; as he hath given mankind the faculties and talents of
attaining it: but a philosopher, employed in the investigation of second
causes, who would trace the rise and progress of human attainments,

should consider it is an art, which has gradually improved, from the rudest efforts of simple nature, to its present degree of artificial perfection" (p. 1). Theologians must be content with a universal, divinely granted disposition to speak, since any serious study of speech must be a history and a demonstration of a human art.[129]

The history of language seems to these new linguists to be also a record of the progress of societies; Priestley accounts for differences between languages in this way. Since language develops in societies, its nature inevitably reflects not only the stage any society has reached in its development but also the particular way in which the language was formed. The "method of learning and using a language that is formed must be analogous to the method of its formation at first,"[130] and this sociohistorical explanation permits Priestley both to account for the regular progress of languages and to describe social differences in linguistic terms. Languages, like all other human arts, "have a kind of *regular growth, improvement,* and *declension*" (p. 169), and Priestley uses the history of the Roman language to prove his theory of linguistic-political rise and fall.[131] Even his definition of the perfection of a language reinforces the social context of his analysis. A language has reached its perfection "when the people that speak it have occasion to make the greatest use of it; which will be when their power and influence abroad, and when their arts, sciences, and liberty at home are at the greatest height" (p. 177). English has reached such perfection, given the evidence of and in Johnson's *Dictionary;* but even as he says this, Priestley recalls the authority of custom, which will inevitably change the language. Johnson's work, admits Priestley, is only a record of "our language as now used" (p. 186). Linguistic perfection, for Priestley, is a sign of political and cultural dominance; it has little to do with the synchronic ideals of his predecessors. It is one stage in a regular pattern of linguistic change that can, at any time, be described in terms of the relationship between linguistic, political, economic, and social factors. Contemporary Italian, for instance, is the result of invasions from the north, which entirely changed one language to "another of a quite different genius and constitution, with different laws of the modifications of words, and a different syntax" (p. 222). When one studies language, then, one is studying a system that signifies the history and current cultural status of a society. Syntax, like every linguistic feature, is vulnerable to historical changes.

Without society, there would be no language. Several theorists argue that a preexisting society is the necessary condition for the development of a language. Monboddo makes this assumption his fondest principle; and Anselm Bayly argues that since only the "Powers," not the "Application and Exercise" of speech,[132] are innate, children who were not part of human society "would have no language" (p. 25). Language, to James Beattie, is also a form of social contract: "To speak as others speak is one of those tacit obligations, annexed to the condition of living in society, which we are bound in conscience to fulfil, though we have never ratified them by any express promise; because, if they were disregarded, society would be impossible, and human happiness at an end."[133] Beattie is one of the few linguists at this time who still subscribes to the notion of the divine origin of speech; but whenever he writes about language as it is known, he supplies the sort of sociological perspective indicated by his reference to "tacit obligations."

Evidence that the history of societies is expressed by the history of languages comes from both particular societies and from the history of the individual. Benjamin Martin provides an argument of the first type in his *Institutions.* He intends his method to show how a particular linguistic function is treated in different languages over a period of time and thus to reveal "the genius and rationale" of modern English.[134] In attempting this, Martin relies on the "mother tongues" of English; by this he does not mean original speech, but those languages that, historically, have had the greatest influence on English.

The history of the individual also proves to these linguists that language is developmental; the child is "discovered" linguistically, as well as in other ways, in the later eighteenth century. Priestley, for example, supports his argument that early man could have invented speech gradually as he made more and more vocal distinctions by referring to the way children vocalize when they acquire a language.[135] Monboddo refers to children even more frequently to substantiate his claims about the origins of language. Indeed, Monboddo groups children, savages, and the deaf together as proof of the lengthy and difficult development of the language arts. Since there is a "necessary connection betwixt thinking and speaking," we can find in children, the deaf, and in primitive languages (which represent man's "state of infancy") the first stages of the "progress of the human mind."[136] Such linguistic progress, of a society or of an individual, takes time, of course, and this sense of slow development, along with the rejection of (or indifference to) the divine origin of language, contributes to the notion that the history of language corresponds to the origins and progress of human societies. Bayly stresses the difficulty and length of time it takes children to acquire a language,[137] for instance, and Monboddo traces the slow progress of language from its primitive beginnings. Monboddo cites "evidence" from transcriptions of various "savage" nations to support his theory of the "natural progress of the human mind, with which language always keeps pace."[138] It is in this seeking for the remote beginnings of a slow developmental history that Monboddo scavenges for exotic predecessors to man, including his notorious orangoutangs.

Other linguists make history serve different purposes, but what they share is the idea that in the history of languages is history itself. John Williams, in *Thoughts on the Origin and on the Most Rational and Natural Method of Teaching the Languages* (1783), recommends learning languages in the order of their historical dominance. This method "seems to be the most natural . . . because in this order, these languages have prevailed in the world."[139] Learning languages in this order forces the student to relive all of human history to the present, that is, to English and to England. For Priestley, too, the growth of language parallels the perfection of the arts. Improvements in language correspond to the figure a nation makes in arms and politics.[140] For Sheridan, the goal of perfecting the pronunciation of English is something the English need "as subjects of one king" and as a restoration "to their birthright."[141] Some, like James Parsons, in *Remains of Japhet* (1767), believe that the history of languages is the key to the history of the people, and the variety of languages evidence of the progress of societies; others, like Adam Smith, think that the development of the human mind manifests itself in the growth and variety of parts of speech in different languages. For all the linguists, history, change, and progress are the methods and the goals of linguistic study.

This discovery of history takes many well-known shapes in the period and contributes a distinctive sense of the past to ideas of biography, the shape of the novel, the practice of politics, and to every human institution and science.[142] The new historicist sensibility is clearly evident in the literary prominence and popularity of discovered or invented examples of England's linguistic past, the "ruins" of the native language. Chatterton's Rowley, Macpherson's Ossian, Gray's bards all indicate an interest, often antiquarian, in what once were the ways of speaking. Gone is Dryden's fear that in a few years his language might well be as remote to Englishmen as Chaucer's was to Spenser or Spenser's to his own. In place

of the idea of linguistic stasis that underlies Dryden's fear is the fascination of linguistic change and the imitation, collection, and translation of
antique forms from England and beyond. The possibility of runic poetry
and prophetic bards becomes a source of national pride as what might be
called a literary relativism comes to match the linguistic relativism so
often discussed at the time.

Like the linguists, the poets pay special attention to the distinctiveness of their own speech. By discovering the changes evident in the
history of literary languages, poets at last gain confidence in their own
speech. Like the linguists, they come to feel that their language has its
own describable features and that it is part of history.[143] One poetic
consequence of this double awareness, at and beyond the century's end,
is a poetry that takes the evidence of literary and linguistic history and
rediscovers and redefines its resources in its own way, as, say, Keats does
upon reading Chapman's Homer or Shelley does upon remaking old
myths.[144] Whereas Gray and Collins hear a language they could not
imitate, Keats and Shelley imagine a language that their poems could, at
least, intimate.

## The Diversity of Languages and Speakers

The new language theorists highlight historical and sociological contexts
compatible with the emphasis on sounds and communication in the
practical texts; and they thrive on the diversity of tongues just as the
practical linguists stress and encourage richness and variety of styles and
oral delivery. Language differences are as essential to the ideas of
multiple origin, local development, irregular progress, and sociopolitical
changes as they are to the importance of emphasis, mood, or variety of
styles. Discussions of the distinctive genius of each language take on a
new importance in all kinds of linguistic work. Priestley surveys a number
of languages to show which of their features are "peculiarly suited to the
manners and occasions of the people that use them."[145] Priestley not
only accounts for natural diversity of languages, but he attributes
political and pedagogic virtues to this diversity. Since "the diversity of
languages and diversity of government" contribute to one another, the
variations of speech have tended to check the propagation of vice and
false religion" (p. 292); and the study of different languages frees the
mind "from many prejudices and errors," since people who know only

one language "are perpetually confounding the ideas of words with the idea of things; which the comparison of languages, and frequent rendering from one into another, helps to make us distinguish" (p. 293). So far is Priestley from the ideas and methods of seventeenth-century seekers after a universal language and brotherhood, and so important to him is the comparison of divergent languages, that "the nature and rationale of language" should not have been understood had there actually been a universal language.

The very hypothesis of a universal language must divert linguistics from its proper study—the variety and differences of languages. Priestley wants to understand the "subject of language in general"—quite a different matter from trying to comprehend language itself, as if it were a single reality without significantly different modes. Only "comparison of the properties of different languages actually subsisting" (p. 296) will lead to a metalinguistic description of individual and ever-changing languages. This new study of language will not itself be a language, as the universal language projectors had claimed theirs to be, but a commentary on man's desire to communicate.

Practical and theoretical linguists place similar stress on the distinctive qualities of particular languages. Learning another language does not mean simply filling in a standard (or innovative) system with new words, but, according to Benjamin Martin, it means putting the proper words together "as is agreeable to custom and use of that tongue."[146] This is a demanding requirement since "every language has a Syntax peculiar to itself." Bayly admits a similar and strong condition to his discussion of a universal grammar. Since every language has its peculiarities, one language expresses those of another not "by what is called a literal translation, but by its own modes of speech."[147] Buchanan is another linguist who orients his search for the general properties of language to the isolation and preservation of the distinctive features of different languages. Although in his *Essay* his goal is stated to be "one language and one speech," he means nothing more by this than the exclusion of local dialects from elegant speech.[148] Pronunciation is "a proper utterance of articulate sounds, according to the idiom of any language," and the pronunciation of English "can be represented only by the particular sounds we give our letters" (p. xiii).[149] It sounds as if he is trying for more, but all his assumptions allow him is a socially preferred form of what will always sound distinctively English.

If there are linguistic features as common as the consistency and

coherence of human nature, writes Buchanan in his *British Grammar,*
there are also peculiarities in each language as significant as divergent
religions or governments. And "to the Causes of Diversity may be added
the distinguishing Character and Genius of every Nation."[150] These
linguistic differences become essential qualities of a language; they are
not only objects of study but sources of pride as well. Literary languages
become similarly distinctive, as each poet not only advertises his compatibility with the special features and history of English but also
dramatizes the particular qualities of his own language.

These differences seem as evident and representative as similarities
once seemed to earlier linguists. John Fell proposes avoiding "an insipid
uniformity" of style by surveying the diverse customs of "approved"
speakers and writers.[151] Rice even objects to references to a "natural
order" of words, since there are only "habitual" orders customary in
each language.[152] Each language, writes Rice, has its "idiomatical Order"
(p. 266). In recommending a style of oral delivery, Rice, like his fellow
elocutionists, recommends an apparent conversational manner that
nicely imitates the familiar tones of conventional, but courtly, speech.
The idea of imitating ease and carefully representing natural responses
is more prominent as a critical premise in the works of the associationist
rhetoricians, like Blair and Campbell.

## Etymology and the Sociography of Language

Linguists come to believe that the best means of discovering the distinctive genius of a language, of representing the origins and history of
the society it expresses, and of justifying pride in the heritage of English is
etymological investigation. Traditionally a part of language study,
etymology becomes a specialist's tool toward the end of the eighteenth
century, a tool as crucial to the general study of languages as it is
frequently irrelevant to the practice of any particular language. Sections
on etymology are dramatically reduced in size and importance in school
texts and dropped completely from rhetorical grammars, books on the
art of reading, and studies of sounds. Tucker, in *Vocal Sounds,* argues
strenuously for concentrating on the "component sounds of our
syllables."[153] This will improve spelling, and although it may sacrifice
etymological evidence, the loss will hardly be important since etymology
is "a matter of no concern to the generality" (p. 22). Even V. J. Peyton,

in his *History of the English Language,* answers arguments that altering spelling would sacrifice evidence of origins by declaring etymology to be "a matter of curiosity that concerns the learned only."[154] Peyton's remarks are surprising because he seeks to deduce the language from its origin "by investigating who were the primitive inhabitants of the country, whose language one would trace, what tongue they spoke, and whence they came" (p. 3). Peyton, like his contemporary practical linguists, believes that since English is as excellent as it can be and England as superior as it deserves to be, the time is right for making language acquisition easier.

Practical linguists distinguish between a language that is easily acquired and that reflects current usage and one that rigorously preserves signs of its origin. They choose to promote ease and currency at the expense of etymological evidence. This self-imposed narrowing of the function of practical linguistics not only reinforces its difference from theoretical studies but also guarantees that these basic texts will inevitably have to be replaced. These works of practical linguistics become the accurate but temporary descriptions of custom that the theoreticians use as evidence of changes in the language over time. Grammar has come to be merely a preliminary and partial aspect of linguistics; it is the source *in* history available to those contemplating linguistics *as* history. Both practical and theoretical linguists view language as a social activity in time; but while the former describe it as it is (at its best), the latter account for the particular development of its distinctive qualities.

In most sophisticated studies of the language at the time, etymology is prominent as the means of discovering the origins and progress of the English people.[155] John Free, in *An Essay towards a History of the English Tongue* (1749), trusts that the rise and progress of the English language parallels the rise and progress of the English nation and that etymology will show the language to be closer to Saxon than to French. Free's *Essay,* then, is a contribution to the conflict between Hanoverian and Jacobite and a valuable compilation of learned opinion on the languages spoken during the history of Britain. Benjamin Martin, like Free, uses etymological investigations to describe the language and narrate the history of its use. These linguists do not use the information they derive as a rationale for standardizing or radically altering the language. Martin devotes his studies of Saxon to the discovery of the "original and genius of our tongue," and "more than a just account of the original, progress, and present state of our tongue, I know nothing that can be done."[156] All proposals for "fixing a standard to the purity and perfection of any language" are "utterly vain and impertinent." Such projects pass away with the general deflation of intentions; but in choosing to document "the original, progress, and present state of our tongue," linguists eagerly and industriously take on the responsibility of historical and comparative studies.

John Williams collects several of the assumptions and practices of the period in his *Thoughts*. He writes as a schoolmaster interested in methods of teaching and in public service. He promotes Latin as a universal tongue not because of any virtue inherent in the language nor because of any special priority but because it is the most widely known language. He hopes to make language acquisition more efficient and to have works of science, especially, quickly and generally available (in Latin). Williams also believes, as we have seen, that learning the languages in the order in which they were politically and culturally dominant is the most rational and natural method. It is through variations in words, that is, through etymology, that Williams finds the relations between languages, and these relations reveal to him the progress and order of man's knowledge. This connection between history and language leads Williams to define the principal project of historical linguistics in the next century:

> To illustrate my meaning, I beg leave to consider language as a wide-spreading oak, having many branches, and these branches bearing many others. If I were desirous of examining any of these branches, in order to see their composition, and texture, I should not lay hold of any one branch to get up to the top of the tree. Common sense would direct me first to examine the trunk, to observe its construction and appearance, then, as I advanced, I should more easily perceive the connection and dependence of every branch with and upon the others; and of the whole with and upon the trunk and roots.[157]

Languages, for Williams, are distinctively "textured" versions of a general human habit that can be described only in terms of the relations between these versions. Williams does not discuss languages as more or less ideal but summarizes the common characters of diverse expressions. His "trunk" is the unspoken, hypothesized language necessary to the support of actually existing languages. The trunk also represents the track of history, since Williams combines the historicist assumptions of the new linguists with their habit of generalizing language into a hypothetical disposition preexisting or necessarily implied by actual languages. These sorts of approaches to language form the native context in which William Jones works later in the century.[158]

Monboddo, after dismissing the idea of an original, universal language, proceeds to generalize about a variety of primitive languages in order to define the original, universal conditions necessary to each of the multiple inventions of speech. These prerequisites define why and how languages were made. Monboddo thinks that the best method for discovering these origins and the radical words of individual languages is through etymology. He complains that the "matter of etymology" is the chief defect of the modern languages, especially English, but he also sees improvement in etymology as the most effective means of showing "the great art that appears in the structure of a regular language."[159] The study of language, then, must depend on the close study of particular languages. All the evidence needed is in words, the true (that is, historical) nature of which is revealed by etymology.

It is Horne Tooke who most effectively, and most aggressively, turns to etymology as the key to the history of man as a speaking animal. Tooke develops ideas drawn from continental, chiefly French, sources, and also reinforces the tendencies of the native linguistics, which began to appear during the later eighteenth century.[160] To Tooke, the practical grammarians have properly narrowed their interests to supervising conventional rules, while the theorists—Locke, Harris, Monboddo, and Beattie—have asked some of the right questions (the historical ones) and have used some of the right techniques (especially etymology). They have, however, included too much philosophical speculation in what ought to be an independent science. In his early *Letter to John Dunning* (1778), Tooke objects to linguists who give different names to the same word if it had more than one syntactic function. He insists that such appearances of fluctuation as abbreviated construction or difference in position are accidents obscuring the consistent significance of words. The true significance "must be sought ... by the help of the particular etymology of each respective language."[161] Unlike Locke, Harris, and the other "mystifiers" of language who, he feels, were hopelessly caught in difficulties they created by philosophising syntax, Tooke seeks good reasons for the changes in the form and place of words. A good reason for Tooke is "a probable or anatomical reason for those not arbitrary operations" (p. 12). Tooke, like Williams, accounts for linguistic diversity and mutability by assuming that the true study of language investigates the rules of change.

This linguistics does not itself create a language, but, in Priestley's terms, it is a study of language that accounts for the origin and progress of human speech. Tooke no more wants to be like the inventive etymologists of a century before than he wants to be like Locke and Harris since, for him, words are no more the signs of ideas than they are of things. He resolves not to force derivations from "Greek or Hebrew, or some imaginary primaeval tongue" (p. 698). His etymological investigations stop whenever he gets to the "evident meaning and origin" of a word in the particular language he is studying. Words change their ostensible form and function when, as a result of "frequent, long-continued, and perpetual use," abbreviations or refinements are introduced.[162] The number, form, and place of these altered words say a great deal about the origins, developments, and habits of a people; and in this way Tooke offers his own version of the proposition that linguistics is a historical and social study.

Even the ostensibly stranger linguistic works of the period display the governing assumptions we have been tracing in this chapter. In the language proposals of Rowland Jones, L. D. Nelme, John Cleland, and Thomas Browne, we hear strong echoes of seventeenth-century projects but revised to reflect the prevailing concern for questions about the origin and historical development of human societies. Nelme, for instance, contributes *An Essay Towards an Investigation of the Origin and Elements of Language and Letters; that is, Sounds and Symbols: Wherein is Considered Their Analogy, and Power to Express the Radical Ideas on which the Primitive Language Appears to have been formed* (1772). He properly considers his predecessors to be Descartes, Kircher, Becher, Wilkins, and Leibniz, men whose linguistic works had only infrequently been referred to, and then often dismissively, in the later eighteenth century. Nelme's first principle is that words and things "mutually illumine, declare, explain, and lead to each other," and he claims that letters are the "Symbols of Things."[163] To get to these significant elements, Nelme proposes a new method, "De-composition, i.e., reducing words to their first principles . . . thereby bringing to light the power of each letter, or Symbol" (p. ii). The form of the Letter *c* is the "symbol of a receptacle, or a ca-pacious body: thence ca-t, an open mouthed creature" (p. 8), and Nelme proceeds in like fashion through the alphabet. He even proposes a more radical analysis than this one, one that would account for the letter-symbols according to a binary system generated from *l*, the symbol of altitude, and *o*, signifying capacity for

reception. Nelme speculates that his book will be the means of "bringing
about an universal character and language" (p. x). What is immediately
noticeable about Nelme's work is its peculiarity for its time; it is, as
Nelme himself suggests, a return to the goals that had motivated seventeenth-century linguists. However, when Nelme reports on the origin of
his idea, he describes a situation quite consistent with contemporary
linguistics. He recalls imagining himself among the first inhabitants of
England, trying to ascertain "the power of Sounds to express Ideas"
(p. vi). He suddenly realized these sounds seemed Saxon; and, years later,
when presented with a Saxon-English dictionary, he was confirmed in his
earlier apotheosis of the historical imagination. The combination, in this
story, of the importance of sounds, the interest in origins, the sense of
social development, and the implied value of etymology evoke the
distinctive context of later-eighteenth-century linguistics.

John Cleland also makes his claims for the "harmony of words and
things" depend on conjectures about "those antient times" in which "the
universal elementary language of Europe" flourished.[164] Even that qualification—"of Europe"—suggests a historical and comparative consciousness
unexpressed a hundred years earlier. In *The Way to Things by Words, and
To Words by Things* (1766), Cleland sees his responsibilities as "illustrating dark passages in history . . . disembroiling the chaos of antient
mythology . . . discovering the elementary foundations of our own living
language" (p. iii). He uses, that is, etymology to explore the history of
early England through its language. Etymology gives current words "a
new air and life . . . you find every word strongly stamped with nature;
full of energy, meaning, character, painting, and poetry" (p. 23); it
discovers the "atoms" (p. 71) of Celtic, the "primordial language" (p. 76).
Much of this sounds like the language proposals of a century earlier
except that, as with Nelme, the original language sought has a specific,
local history and, moreover, a social history directly relevant to the living
language spoken in England.

Rowland Jones is the most prolific and demanding of the linguists
who promote Celtic as the original, rational language of the island and as
the means whereby the strengths and origins of English society and the
English language can be discovered. In the title of the first of his many
futile publications, *The Origin of Language and Nations, Hieroglyfically,
Etymologically, and Topografically Defined and Fixed* (1764), Jones
exhibits the combination of linguistics and social history common to the
period and the recasting of older goals (hieroglyphic language) into newer

methods (etymology). Jones's purpose is first of all historical—to restore and fix "the ancient language, origin, and antiquities of the Celtic nations."[165] The book concludes with an "Historical Lexicon," which cites topographical names to prove the Celtic origin of British places.

Jones realizes that he is a rebel linguist.[166] His general purpose is to refute the view of Locke and his followers that there is no natural connection between words and things. All his publications describe sounds as letters, as if they were "engraved on the bark of the tree of knowledge," but by the time of *Io-Triads . . . The Origin, Nature, and Connection of the Sacred Symbols, Sounds, Words, and Ideas and Things* (1773), he feels he has wasted his efforts and suffered neglect by "scholastic traders . . . disingenuous party-politicians, and the still more illiberal biblio-pagans."[167] He advertises himself as someone providing a "primitive universal grammar" like Wilkins's *Real Character*, only improved. Jones reprints a version of Wilkins's illustration for prepositions (fig. 5) as unacknowledged tribute to Wilkins and promotes his own rediscovery of the natural hieroglyphics of English as in the tradition of, but superior to, Wilkins's "arbitrary real characters." These features of his work make him unintelligible to his contemporaries, although the sociographic and historical context he gives his inventions indicates what he shares with them. To Horne Tooke, however, Jones's work is not worth serious consideration, because his "method of referring words *immediately* to God as their framer is a short cut to escape inquiry and explanation."[168]

Tooke has two reasons, really, for dismissing Jones, and these constitute the primary values for the laboring linguists of the period. First, language study requires microscopic work among the details of words, for there is no "short-cut" explanation uniting language to natural history or philosophy. From Johnson through Tooke, linguists claim credit chiefly for compiling their material in order to explain, not excuse or avoid, changes in the language. Second, the relationship between words and their significations is thoroughly *mediated* by social factors and historical development, each of which makes the job of compiling more difficult.

Near the end of the century, language is thought of and taught as a social and historical subject. The linguists, both theoretical and practical, understand language to be the means of communicating the intentions and feelings of speakers to hearers. The psychological needs and purposes of the participants in these various social dramas are determined, in large measure, by their local environment and by the status of their society. In ways we have not, perhaps, appreciated before, the study and practice of language passes from being a justification of the order of things or the ways of the mind to being a record of the habits and history of a man speaking to men.

# NOTES

## Introduction

1. R. S. Crane, in *Critical and Historical Principles of Literary History* (Chicago, 1971), has some quite sensible things to say about varieties of literary and intellectual history. He sees directly to the assumptions of dialectic and narrative histories, and he opposes to them an historical sense of individual works that are not "simply causes, consequences, or signs of other things" (p. 48). He assumes—wrongly, I think—that the history of literary forms that he suggests refers to facts, not ideas. For Crane, "forms" are the "universal elements and principles contained" (p. 50) in the arts, they are "species... inductively known, and differentiated, more or less sharply, in terms of their peculiar artistic elements and principles of construction" (p. 15). Although he rightly criticizes other historians for reading texts as allegories of their general idea, Crane, by assuming the universality of forms, also reduces history to an explanation of his premises.

2. Claude Lévi-Strauss, *Tristes Tropiques,* trans. John Weightman and Doreen Weightman (New York, 1975), p. 333.

3. Richard Foster Jones, *Ancients and Moderns: A Study of the Rise of the Scientific Movement in Seventeenth-Century England,* 2d ed. (St. Louis, 1961), p. vii.

4. The books that most effectively imitate the explanatory range and methodological limitations of Jones's work are those by Marjorie Hope Nicolson, especially *The Breaking of the Circle: Studies in the Effect of the "New Science" on Seventeenth-Century Poetry,* rev. ed. (New York, 1960); *Newton Demands the Muse: Newton's Opticks and the Eighteenth-Century Poets* (Princeton, 1946); and *Mountain Gloom and Mountain Glory: The Development of the Aesthetics of the Infinite* (New York, 1963). Ernest Tuveson, in a review of the last book mentioned (*Journal of Aesthetics and Art Criticism* 19 [1960]; 108-9), summarizes the goals of this kind of intellectual history. Nicolson, he writes, is "studying the origins of Romanticism," which is "the end product" of "a kind of matrix of Romanticism, which was no accident

but indeed a truly inevitable result of the history of European culture since the Renaissance" (p. 108). In this view of history everything either fits the goals set by the historian or is characterized by its not fitting. In either case, the significance of a work, author, or idea is determined by an external rule. See also Ernest Lee Tuveson, *Millenium and Utopia: A Study in the Background of the Idea of Progress* (New York, 1964), and *The Imagination as a Means of Grace: Locke and the Aesthetics of Romanticism* (Berkeley, 1960); and William Powell Jones, *The Rhetoric of Science: A Study of Scientific Ideas and Imagery in Eighteenth-Century English Poetry* (Berkeley, 1966).

5.  Richard Foster Jones, *The Triumph of the English Language: A Survey of Opinions concerning the Vernacular from the Introduction of Printing to the Restoration* (Stanford, 1953); Hans Aarsleff, *The Study of Language in England, 1780–1860* (Princeton, 1967); Stephen Land, *From Signs to Propositions: The Concept of Form in Eighteenth-Century Semantic Theory* (London, 1974).

6.  Thomas S. Kuhn, *The Structure of Scientific Revolutions* (Chicago, 1964).

7.  I use the concept of the "episteme" in discussing Foucault because it is a ready means of characterizing his work. Although Foucault features the term, and the concept, in *The Order of Things: An Archaeology of the Human Sciences* (New York, 1970), he shows in *The Archaeology of Knowledge* (trans A. M. Sheridan Smith [New York, 1972]) that it derives from a method of historical analysis that typifies the limitations of modern discourse and therefore biases our representations of the past (see pp. 191–95).

8.  The works of Thomas Kuhn and Michel Foucault have been cleverly brought together in a brilliant interpretation of Foucault's work by Edward Said, "An Ethics of Language," *Diacritics* 4 (1974): 28–39.

9.  Kuhn, *The Structure of Scientific Revolutions*, p. 7.

10.  For example, Tuveson, *Millenium and Utopia,* suggests that the value of his book is its explanation of continuity, its innovative organization of scattered traditions to prove that the present is the goal of the past. The idea of progress, he writes, "has been of the most vital importance in forwarding the emergence of a 'modern' viewpoint. In the authors studied—who represent the barest sampling of the movement as a whole—we see how a dogma of progress, shedding its ecclesiastical trappings, nevertheless retained a smuggled Providence; we see also how it was that a faith in absolute values, fixed once and for all, could find a harmonious relationship with a relativism. We see how 'primitivism' and progress, ideas apparently so contradictory, could fit together in a new theology. Above all, we see the origin of the faith in History, History the magical: that basic faith of the modern world" (p. 201). As with the best intellectual historians in this tradition, Tuveson makes good his promise. He finds progress continuously, even when disguised in borrowed trappings, or when counterindicated by other beliefs, or when stood on its head. And he proves we are not alone, that we are what history intended.

11.  I borrow the terms *linguistic characterizations* and *linguistic explanations* from John Searle, *Speech Acts: An Essay in the Philosophy of Language* (Cambridge, 1970). Searle, in his account of language, distinguishes between (1) talking, (2) characterizing talk, and (3) explaining talk (p. 15). For Searle, the middle term is the most important; indeed, controversies over characterization prompted him to his "discussion of their epistemological status." Just so, it is through changes in the description of objects that Kuhn finds the key to paradigm distinctions and Foucault the touchstone of epistemic changes. Explanations reinforce descriptions, and justify

them. This idea of philosophical priorities describes the error of conventional intellectual historians who read merely for summarizable ideas; and it supports Kuhn and Foucault as they seek out discrete habits of perception.

12. Kuhn, *The Structure of Scientific Revolutions,* p. 108.

13. Foucault, *The Archaeology of Knowledge,* p. 108.

14. Michel Foucault, *The Order of Things: An Archaeology of the Human Sciences* (New York, 1970).

15. *The Archaeology of Knowledge,* p. 227.

16. Ian Michael, *English Grammatical Categories and the Tradition to 1800* (Cambridge, 1970). Michael's work is ample and helpfully organized, but it can be usefully supplemented by Ivan Poldauf, *On the History of Some Problems of English Grammar before 1800* (Prague, 1948), and Emma Vorlat, *Progress in English Grammar, 1585-1735,* 4 vols. (Louvain, 1963).

17. E. J. Dobson, *English Pronunciation, 1500-1700,* 2d ed. (Oxford, 1968).

18. Wilbur Samuel Howell, *Logic and Rhetoric in England: 1500-1700* (Princeton, 1956), and *Eighteenth-Century British Logic and Rhetoric* (Princeton, 1971).

19. There have been several studies of the universal language inventors. Michael's *English Grammatical Categories* provides the clearest survey, but it should be reinforced by the more detailed accounts of the careers of these men in Barbara Shapiro, *John Wilkins, 1614-1672: An Intellectual Biography* (Berkeley, 1969), and George H. Turnbull, *Hartlib, Dury, and Comenius* (Liverpool, 1947), pp. 370-97; Jonathan Cohen, "On the Project of a Universal Character," *Mind* 63 (1954): 49-63; and Benjamin DeMott, "A Study of Constructed Languages in England with Special Reference to Their Relations with Science and Attitudes toward Literary Style, 1605-1686" (Ph.D. diss., Harvard University, 1953). Vivian Salmon, *The Works of Francis Lodwick: A study of His Writings in the Intellectual Context of the Seventeenth Century* (London, 1972), has surveyed the material in its intellectual context, as have Paolo Rossi, *Clavis universalis arti mnemoniche e logica combinatoria da Lullo a Leibniz* (Milan, 1960), and L. Couturat, *La logique de Leibniz* (Paris, 1901).

20. See, preeminently, the essays of Morris Croll, collected by J. Max Patrick et al., eds., *Style, Rhetoric, and Rhythm* (Princeton, 1966), and George Williamson, *Senecan Amble* (Chicago, 1966).

21. The chief of the science seekers, is, of course, Richard Foster Jones. In addition to *Ancients and Moderns,* see the collections of Jones's essays in *The Triumph of the English Language* and *The Seventeenth Century* (Stanford, 1956). Also see note 4 above.

22. See Robert Adolph, *The Rise of Modern Prose Style* (Cambridge, Mass., 1968), and an important review of Adolph's work by Jackson Cope, "Modes of Modernity in Seventeenth-Century Prose," *MLQ* 31 (1970): 92-111. Cope discusses Adolph's claim to offer "the isolation and description of the normal literary style of the day" (Adolph, p. 4): Adolph "is in fact only defining the modern in terms of 'normality,' a concept superimposed upon history by the investigator's chosen method" (p. 96). Cope contrasts Adolph's "methodologically induced leveling" (p. 98) and a study, like Joan Webber's *The Eloquent "I": Style and Self in Seventeenth-Century Prose* (Madison, 1968), in which norms are thought of "as means for the critic's discovery of uniqueness and for the author's establishment of an individual voice" (p. 105). Stanley Fish, in the epilogue, "The Plain-Style Question," to *Self-*

*Consuming Artifacts: The Experience of Seventeenth-Century Literature* (Berkeley, 1972), pp. 374–82, makes a similar point while reviewing the works of Croll, Jones, and Adolph. Croll and Jones suffer from their desire to establish two camps and to bring all writers (many against their words) into one tent or the other. Adolph "solves the problem of seventeenth-century style by generalizing it out of existence and in the process the dimensions of any number of writers are flattened out" (p. 377). Fish offers "an opposition of epistemologies" (p. 378) in place of "a political, social, or religious opposition" (p. 377). Although his suggestion "is at best partial and at worst distorting," it properly puts the problem. Fish has brilliant insights into differences— between Donne and Browne, between Bacon's *Advancement of Learning* and his *Essays;* his is "an explanation that does not explain away" (p. 379)—not, perhaps, until he dichotomizes all reading experiences as either "self-satisfying" or "self-consuming." But the "epistemological shift" (p. 380) Fish observes in the second half of the century supports the assumptions about language that came to prevail during that time.

23. I also use the term *linguists* throughout this book to refer to all writers of language texts and theories. I do so first because linguistics is a term covering all varieties of language study, and second, because it suggests the conceptual interests of all the writers I consider.

24. James Knowlson's otherwise interesting and useful book, *Universal Language Schemes in England and France, 1600–1800* (Toronto, 1975), is marred, I think, by such a purposeful pursuit of a continuous "theme" that he gives too much space to speculating about lines of influence, as if such were necessary to stitch his chapters together.

25. One important exception to this general failure to make significant use of school texts is the example proposed by E. H. Gombrich, *Art and Illusion: A Study in the Psychology of Pictorial Representation* (Princeton, 1961), especially pp. 146–78.

26. George Snyders, *La pedagogie en France aux XVII$^e$ et XVIII$^e$ siècles* (Paris, 1965), p. 1. Some of Walter J. Ong's work has also explored the relationships between pedagogy, thought, and literature; see, especially, "Latin Language Study as a Renaissance Puberty Rite," and "Ramus Classroom Procedure and the Nature of Reality," both of which are reprinted in his *Rhetoric, Romance, and Technology: Studies in the Interaction of Expression and Culture* (Ithaca, 1971), pp. 113–41, 142–64.

27. Jean-Claude Chevalier, *Histoire de la syntaxe: Naissance de la notion de complément dans la grammaire française (1530-1750)* (Geneva, 1968), p. 9.

28. Chevalier's attempt to correct Snyders's sweeping historical view is particularly important (*Histoire de la syntaxe,* pp. 371–412). For his modifications of Foucault's characterizations, see pp. 497–506.

29. In *The Imagination as a Means of Grace,* Ernest Tuveson usefully stresses the force of Locke's epistemology, but he misinterprets what that epistemology is. Tuveson's reading of Locke's *Essay* selects those elements, primarily words, most amenable to Tuveson's principal argument—the development of the aesthetics of eighteenth-century romanticism. In an article summarizing the Lockean sections of the book, *"An Essay on Man* and 'The Way of Ideas,' " *ELH* 26 (1956): 368-86, Tuveson characterizes Locke's "revolution in epistemology" (p. 368) in terms of its emphasis on sense perception and vision. These two factors, as I indicate in my first chapter, are the basic elements of the epistemology of mid-seventeenth-century

linguists; they do not constitute an adequate basis for the study of Locke. What distinguishes Locke from his contemporaries is his addition of rules of relation to our perceptions (which are *not* merely visual images). These rules, for Locke, are equally applicable to the mind and to language: man proposes what his mind disposes. Tuveson, wanting to save Locke for the nineteenth century, misreads Locke on sense impression: "Locke considers all ideas as composed of and never transcending sense impression" (p. 372). Locke, writes Tuveson, has "complete confidence in impressions" and "seeks to eliminate 'ratiocination' altogether." In arguing thus, Tuveson ignores the discussion of real and nominal essences, misses Locke's doubts about the reliability of our perceptions, and neglects the basic goal of the *Essay*—to study man's understanding, that is, the emergence of knowledge from ideas and words. Tuveson transfers his interpretation of Locke to Pope's *Essay on Man* and decides that Pope's poem "constantly emphasizes, not intellectualizing, but simply visualizing in wider and wider perspectives" (p. 380). But many of the things Pope invites us to "see" cannot be seen in the sense Tuveson claims he derives from Locke: "See, thro' this air, this ocean, and this earth, / All matter quick, and bursting into birth" (I, pp. 233–34); or "Look round our World, behold the chain of Love . . . See plastic Nature working to this end, / The single atoms each to other tend" (III, pp. 8, 10–11). Sight for Pope is more a mental activity than a physical one; and his, too, is a work about understanding. After a harsh review of this article by Robert Marsh (*PQ* 39 [1960]; 349–51), Tuveson defended his views in "An *Essay on Man* and 'The Way of Ideas': Some Further Remarks" *PQ* 40 [1961] : 262–69). Tuveson insists on his own misreading of Locke as a sensationalist and makes Pope sound even more like a seventeenth-century natural historian: Pope's "aim" was "to make the intellectual world seem clearly visible, like those objects which we most fully apprehend in the world around us" (p. 268). See Chapter 2, note 15.

30. Kuhn, *The Structure of Scientific Revolutions,* p. 108.

31. See Donald Ault, *Visionary Physics: Blake's Response to Newton* (Chicago, 1974), pp. 4–17. Ault draws attention to the two poles of Newton's dialectical system: "the mathematical and the atomic . . . form only one pole"; the other is "the shadowy process of integration" (p. 7).

32. See the concluding section to Chapter 1, below.

# Chapter 1

1. Although Beck's *The Universal Character* (London, 1657) was read by both John Wilkins and George Dalgarno well before 1657 (see note 9 below), there is no other evidence of Beck's meeting or corresponding with any of the groups interested in language. During his years at St. John's College, Oxford, from 1638 to 1642, the notable Oxford intellectuals of mid-century had not yet taken their positions: John Wilkins was traveling with the Palatine, Charles Lewis; while Seth Ward and John Wallis were at Cambridge.

2. Of the two prominent study groups meeting in mid-century one gathered around Samuel Hartlib and the other around John Wilkins and John Wallis. The question of the development of the Royal Society out of one or the other group or out of some combination of members from each has troubled historians since John Wallis's own account in *Defence of the Royal Society* (London, 1678). Margery Purver (*The Royal Society: Concept and Creation* [Cambridge, Mass., 1967] doubts

Wallis's version; but Barbara Shapiro (*John Wilkins, 1614–1672: An Intellectual Biography* [Berkeley, 1969]) supports Wallis's sense of the society's eclectic beginnings. See also G. H. Turnbull, *Hartlib, Dury, and Comenius* (Liverpool, 1947); his "Samuel Hartlib's Influence on the Early History of the Royal Society," *Notes and Records of the Royal Society* 1 (1953): 101–30; and Charles Webster, "The Origins of the Royal Society," *History of Science* 6 (1967): 106–28. Benjamin DeMott stresses the shared interests of the Hartlib and Wilkins groups in "Comenius and the Real Character in England," *PMLA* 70 (1955): 1068–81, and in "The Sources and Development of John Wilkins' Philosophical Language," *JEGP* 57 (1958): 1–13.

3. Beck, *The Universal Character*, A6$^r$.

4. A French version of Beck's work, *Le caractere universel* (London, 1657), published in the same year as the English text, includes a frontispiece showing a meeting of deputies from the four corners of the world—Europe, Asia, Africa, and America.

5. Ricci's journals have been translated by Louis J. Gallagher, S.J.: *China in the Sixteenth Century: The Journals of Matthew Ricci, 1583–1610* (New York, 1953). See also D. C. Allen, "The Predecessors of Champollion," *Proceedings of the American Philosophical Society* 104 (1960): 527–47; and, on Ricci, his followers, and their impact on the universal language projectors, see Madeleine V. David, *Le débat sur les écritures et l'hiéroglyphie aux XVII$^e$ et XVIII$^e$ siècles* (Paris, 1965), especially pp. 31–42.

6. Francis Bacon, *The Advancement of Learning,* ed. G. W. Kitchin (London, 1915), p. 138. See Paolo Rossi, *Francis Bacon: From Magic to Science,* trans. Sacha Rabinovitch (Chicago, 1968), pp. 152–85; and David, *Le débat sur les écritures,* pp. 37–40.

7. John Wilkins, *An Essay towards a Real Character, And a Philosophical Language* (London, 1668), p. 13.

8. Comenius's influence on English education and language study is reviewed by G. H. Turnbull and Benjamin DeMott (see note 2 above). See also R. F. Young, *Comenius in England* (Oxford, 1932), and Charles Webster, *Samuel Hartlib and the Advancement of Learning* (Cambridge, 1970). Useful summaries of Comenius's work are offered by John Edward Sadler, *J. A. Comenius and the Concept of Universal Education* (London, 1966), and by Hans Aarsleff in his entry, "Comenius," in the *Dictionary of Scientific Biography,* vol. 3, ed. Charles Coulston Gillispie (New York, 1971).

9. Wilkins distinguishes his "Philosophical" character from the numbers used by "Mr. Beck of Ipswich" (*Real Character,* p. 452). Wilkins associates Beck's numerical universality with subsequent works by John Becher (*Character, Pro Notitia Linguarum Universali* [Frankfort, 1661]) and Athanasius Kircher (*Novum inventum Linguarum omnium ad unam reductarum* [Rome, 1660]. For Dalgarno's opinion of Beck, see Vivian Salmon, *The Works of Francis Lodwick: A Study of His Writings in the Intellectual Context of the Seventeenth Century* (London, 1972), p.18.

10. For the history of Lily's grammar in the schools and the mounting challenge to it in the seventeenth century, see Foster Watson, *The English Grammar Schools to 1660: Their Curriculum and Practice* (Cambridge, 1908), and Vivian Salmon, "Joseph Webbe: Some Seventeenth Century Views on Language-teaching and the Nature of Meaning," *Bibliothèque d'humanisme et renaissance* 23 (1961): 324–40.

11. There are noticeable distinctions among the varieties of universal language systems and the schemes for teaching languages in the seventeenth century, but I am passing by some of these mostly superficial discords in order to get to what I think

are the most important features of all linguistic work of the period. Wilkins and Dalgarno, like Locke after them, distinguish between systems in which symbols naturally reflect existence and those, like theirs, in which the symbols are as arbitrary as words (see note 9 above). In their work, Vivian Salmon and R. F. Jones stress these differences in order to argue the distinctiveness of all activities associated with the new science. For them, the systems that propose an essential, original correspondence between words and things are only erratic symptoms of certain mystical strains in the seventeenth century. James Knowlson, *Universal Language Schemes in England and France, 1600–1800* (Toronto, 1975), reviews this vexed question—are the two kinds of systems, the essential and the arbitrary, connected or sharply separated?—but does not resolve it (pp. 86–88). Madeleine David, in *Le débat sur les écritures,* tries another discrimination—between poeticizing emblem seekers and projectors of universal language schemes—but, although this is suggestive, it does not hold, especially for figures like Comenius. It is also true, as David observes, that everyone in the period was significantly motivated by a "préjugé théologique." My view is that there are more than two categories among the vital and interrelated linguistic practices, that competitiveness characterizes all of the linguistic workers from the planters to the gleaners, and that there are basic strategies common to all their linguistic taxonomies. The strategies I stress in this chapter are systematization, sequentiality, division into elements, and visualization. I agree, for instance, with the suggestions of Frances Yates (*The Art of Memory* [Chicago, 1966]) regarding the resemblances between Bruno's and Lull's techniques for memory, which presumed to arrange the symbols of the memory system to correspond, essentially, with reality, and Ramus's significantly nonmagical and emphatically arbitrary system (pp. 232–37); but my emphasis differs from Yates's own microanalysis of the quite different traditions and motives behind Bruno and Ramus. On the question of difference and resemblance in intellectual history, see Foucault's discussion of different thresholds of intelligibility, in *The Archaeology of Knowledge,* trans. A. M. Sheridan Smith (New York, 1972), pp. 186–95.

12. Jean-Claude Chevalier, in *Histoire de la syntaxe* (Geneva, 1968), stresses, throughout his discussion of the late Latin and early French grammatical traditions, the central importance of organizing according to assumed laws of symmetry and hierarchy (see, for instance, pp. 130–32, 391–96, and passim).

13. I associate this "visualization" of language with the tendencies Forrest G. Robinson has assembled in his book, *The Shape of Things Known: Sidney's Apology in Its Philosophic Tradition* (Cambridge, Mass., 1972). Robinson's phrase is the "tradition of visual epistemology" (see particularly pp. 6–9). And see, in the text, my own brief discussion of literary languages in the period (and note 65).

14. All of the linguists I discuss in this chapter are interested in the correspondence between the elements of language and the order of things. Some, like Comenius, are attracted to the recovery or reinvention of Adamic speech, in which words contain the essence of the things they name; others, like Wilkins and Beck, accept the arbitrariness of words and invented symbols but work to make the presentation of linguistic elements correspond to the composition of the world. The antagonisms between these two tendencies have been noted by historians (see note 11), but the linguists of the period share a taxonomic methodology and a theory of correspondence between linguistic features and the nature of things, whether "nature" refer to the essence, the composition, or the order of things.

15. To find the "contributions" of the members of the Hartlib circle, the

Wilkins group, or the Royal Society committee assigned to improve Wilkins's *Essay,* one must look carefully through correspondence and unpublished notes (see especially Vivian Salmon, "John Wilkins' *Essay* (1668)," *Historiographia Linguistica* 1 [1974] : 147–63; and Knowlson, *Universal Language Schemes).* But the way in which their representative assumptions about language got into practice was principally through the works of schoolmasters like Cave Beck. This is a practical fact of the period reinforcing the generally applicable principle that it is in school texts that we find the best evidence not only for the importance and spread of ideas at a particular time (see Introduction, notes 25–26) but also for the accommodation of particular ideas to the core of intelligibility.

16. John Amos Comenius, *Orbis Sensualium Pictus,* trans. Charles Hoole (London, 1659), A6$^{r}$.

17. Hoole also published, years after its composition, his *New Discovery of the Old Art of Teaching Schoole* (London, 1660), and it is as the author of this that he serves so prominently as the representative pedagogue of the seventeenth century for John Muldar, *The Temple of the Mind* (New York, 1969), pp. 18–25.

18. Watson, *The English Grammar Schools to 1660,* commenting on the effect of using Lily's grammar, notes that the "idea of the sentence as a unit was impossible when the grammar had first settled in the child's mind the mysteries of the accidence of the single words" (p. 284). This suggestion about the relationship between pedagogic methods and patterns of thought is well worth pursuing. To date, even the best works on the history of pedagogy have stressed student schedules and teacher attitudes rather than the conceptual impact of different kinds of texts. See, however, the work of Chevalier, *Histoire de la syntaxe,* pp. 371–412, 600–649. Chevalier, by paying close attention to the methods of some popular mid-eighteenth-century French texts, corrects the otherwise suggestive overviews of George Snyders, *La pedagogie en France aux XVII$^{e}$ et XVIII$^{e}$ siècles* (Paris, 1965), pp. 356–81; and Philippe Ariès, *Centuries of Childhood: A Social History of Family Life,* trans. Robert Baldick (New York, 1962), pp. 286–314.

19. John Bird, *Grounds for Grammar* (Oxford, 1639), A3$^{v}$.

20. See Vivian Salmon, "Joseph Webbe," and also "Problems of Language Teaching: A Discussion among Hartlib's Friends," *MLR* 59 (1964): 13–24.

21. Hezekiah Woodward, *Light to Grammar and all other Arts and Sciences. With a Gate to Sciences opened by a Natural Key* (London, 1641), p. 2.

22. Hezekiah Woodward, *A Child's Patrimony* (London, 1640), p. 98.

23. John Twells, *Grammatica Reformata* (London, 1683), writes a history of grammar which, however imprecise, offers an indication of the seventeenth-century grammarians' sense of their historical role. Twells claims that there were no new grammars between 1551 and 1636 (this is only mildly inaccurate), but "since then New Grammars have been ever and anon coming forth ('tis to be concluded somewhat is amiss in the Old, why else should the learned Authors of them spend their pains in the compositions of New?)" (p. 18).

24. Ian Michael, *English Grammatical Categories and the Tradition to 1800* (Cambridge, 1970), considers the inconsistencies and instabilities of the grammars as handicaps, whereas they should rather be thought of as pointing forcefully (if not always in the same direction) to the relationship between language and mind. Thomas Baker, *Reflections upon Learning* (London, 1700), observes many of the same qualities as Michael—the cumbersomeness of the dictionaries and the failure of academies—and accounts for them, not by ignoring the question of intention, but by

comparing the goals of competing linguistic systems. For Baker the inconsistencies are morally significant. Chevalier, *Histoire de la syntaxe,* reviews in great detail the comparable strains and strife among French text writers and convincingly diagnoses the furious activity of those who complain about the rule (and rules) of grammar by producing their own. He calls it a clear case of "sadisme professoral" (p. 373).

25. The earliest English grammars I have seen that set out to model their method on nature and in print are Alexander Gil's *Logonomia Anglica* (London, 1619) and Joseph Webbe's *An Appeale to Truth* (London, 1622). Chevalier, *Histoire de la syntaxe,* has amply and accurately reviewed the Latin traditions of the fourteenth through the sixteenth centuries, and his study is equally applicable to England (see, particularly, pp. 15–132, 173–307).

26. Joseph Aickin, *English Grammar* (London, 1693), p. 66. The continuing freshness of the Comenian alternative to Lily is also suggested by John Locke's *Some Thoughts concerning Education* (London, 1693), in which Locke objects to rule-based grammars and supports texts that associate words with things.

27. The reliance of grammarians on visual schemes that can only be made with the help of printers is a dramatic effect of what Walter J. Ong has described, in a number of suggestive books and articles, as the aural-to-visual shift, which marks the transition from the ancient world to the Renaissance. See, too, note 13 above. Ong's most important work documenting this development remains his *Ramus, Method, and the Decay of Dialogue* (Cambridge, Mass., 1958). Ong has commented briefly on the effect of the new typographical culture on seventeenth-century schools in "System, Space, and Intellect in Renaissance Symbolism," *Bibliothèque d'humanisme et renaissance* 18 (1956), reprinted in *The Barbarian Within* (New York, 1962), pp. 68–87; and on typographical schemes in "From Allegory to Diagram in the Renaissance Mind," *Journal of Aesthetics and Art Criticism* 17 (1959): 423–40. In the latter, Ong writes that "tabular arrangement, which we take entirely for granted today (a column of first, second, and third persons singular paired off against a column of first, second, and third persons plural) establishes itself as a regular phenomenon only slowly, coming into use in typographical practice together with centered headings, regular paragraphing, tables of contents, and other spatial displays of words which became commonplace only gradually . . . " (p. 432). Also see Chevalier, *Histoire de la syntaxe,* on the use of tables in early French grammars (pp. 76–78). Ong gives the right emphasis in his works to the influence of typographical techniques on thought. One point evident from my study of the history of language theories is that the effect of visual schemes has often been other than what the authors intended, because the schemes make, as it were, suggestions of their own. Thus, the taxonomies dear to the methods of seventeenth-century linguists showed the need for principles that would relate parts as well as define or place them. In effect, what happened during the century is that taxonomies, once used principally for enumerating, come to be used to analyze the functions of the system itself. Ong passes by this shift, seeing instead a continuous and consistent spread of the typographical, spatial, and geometric. This absolutist view blurs the significant redirection I stress at the end of this chapter. The restrictiveness of Ong's view can be estimated by his determination to turn Swift into a stubborn, and unhappy, physicophilosophical writer: "Swift on the Mind: Satire in a Closed Field," reprinted in *Rhetoric, Romance, and Technology: Studies in the Interaction of Expression and Culture* (Ithaca, 1971), pp. 190–212.

28. *The Compendious School-Master* (London, 1688), A6$^{\text{r.}}$ Earlier syllabic

wordbooks include George Robertson, *Learning's Foundation Firmly Laid* (London, 1651); J. Brooksbank, *An English Monosyllabary* (London, 1651), and *An English Syllabary* (London, 1654); and Thomas Lye, *Reading and Spelling Made Easie wherein All the Words of our English Bible are set down in an Alphabetical order and divided into their distinct Syllabls* (London, 1673).

29. The alphabet itself was recognized as a conceptual tool in the seventeenth century, and this is another reason why the distinction between universal languages based on "philosophical" characters and those using numerical-alphabetical lists is more important to historians who wish to discover the pedigrees or descendants of particular ideas than to those, like myself, who inquire into the practice of ideas at a particular time. See notes 11 and 14 above. Thomas Urquhart, in his *Logopandecteision* (London, 1653), traces variations in living languages to the absence of an alphabetical consistency he plans to correct, as a "Grammatical Arithmetician" (p. 13), by a "Trissotetrial trigonometry, for facility of calculation by representatives of letters and syllables" (p. 15). Words "may be increased by addition of letters and syllables; so of numbers is there a progress *in infinitum*" (p. 21), and this is Urquhart's authority for giving each letter its meaning. Lines from a prefatory poem to Thomas Blount's *Glossographia; or, A Dictionary Interpreting all . . . Hard Words* (London, 1656) suggest the importance of the alphabet:

> Our Tongue, grown Labyrinth and Monster too.
> Confusion, in this Book, in Order's set,
> An Heap is form'd into an Alphabet:
> Old Babels ruins this in part repairs
> And in an handsom Work the rubbish rears. . . .(A8[r])

30. Louis Gerard de Cordemoy, in *A Philosophicall Discourse concerning Speech* (London, 1668), begins his Cartesian analysis with a physical description of vocalization to prove that words give the "signs of our thoughts" (p. 2). The significance of words depends on the agitation of air on the ear (pp. 55–56), and signifying depends on "the disposition of the Wind-pipe" (p. 44). Henry Rose's *A Philosophicall Essay for the Reunion of the Languages* (Oxford, 1675), a translation of Pierre Besnier, *La réunion des langues* (Paris, 1674), also argues that the first step toward a universally accepted language would be to study the vocal organs to find the "precise number of all the simple sounds" (p. 46). An analysis of the original corporeal nature of all words would lead to an original language, "Naked and intirely dispoil'd of all that trompery that disguis'd" it (p. 60). Rose indicates the importance of the project by trusting that the projector will "receive the same favour that persons . . . granted Copernicus" (p. 79). Also, Matthew Hale, in *The Primitive Origination of Mankind* (London, 1677), argues that Chinese characters represent original speech since they were monosyllables fitted to "the apertures and lips" (p. 162). Other works claiming correspondence between sounds and meaning include Urquhart, *Logopandecteision* (1653); Seth Ward, *Vindicae Academiarum* (Oxford, 1654); and the work of Cyprian Kinner (see DeMott, "The Sources and Development of John Wilkins' Philosophical Language.")

31. Edward Somerset, *A Century of the Names and Scantlings of Such Inventions as at present I can call to mind to have tried and perfected* (London, 1663), A3[v].

32. The relationship between taxonomies, by being isomorphic, committed linguistics to ontological claims.

33. See Dobson, *English Pronunciation 1500–1700,* 2d ed. (Oxford, 1968), pp. 46–88.

34. Elisha Coles, *The Compleat English Schoolmaster* (London, 1674), B2ʳ.

35. Elisha Coles, *Syncrisis; or, The Most Natural and Easie Method of Learning Latin* (London, 1675), A2ʳ. Probably preceding Coles's use of the term *syncrisis* is Mark Lewis's *An Essay to Facilitate the Education of Youth, by bringing down the Rudiments of Grammar to the Sense of Seeing* (London, 1674). Lewis's work also derives, as he admits in *An Apologie for a Grammar* (London, 1671), from Ramus and Comenius (see note 46). A. B., *A Model for a School for the better Education of Youth* (London, 1671), reinforces this connection by citing Lewis and Comenius as his sources.

36. Christopher Cooper, *The English Teacher* (London, 1687), A3ʳ.

37. The conventional categories of historical linguists give misleadingly narrow senses of such works as Cooper's. Ian Michael draws exclusively from the section on etymology in the 1685 *Grammatica,* lamenting that there "is very little grammatical material" in *The English Teacher* (*English Grammatical Categories,* p. 556), whereas Dobson draws almost entirely from the sections on phonology. Dobson simply acknowledges that the section on accidence and syntax is "not of direct concern" (*English Pronunciation,* p. 299).

38. The trend in seventeenth-century pedagogy was to design the educational system to reflect the students' developmental interests and needs. See, most interestingly, Locke, *Some Thoughts concerning Education,* and, for a summary of the French evidence, Chevalier, *Histoire de la syntaxe,* pp. 371–72.

39. Timothie Bright, *Characterie* (London, 1588). See E. H. Butler, *The Story of British Shorthand* (London, 1951), pp. 9–18. David, *Le débat sur les écritures,* glances perceptively at the connections between universal language schemes, shorthand systems, and the discovery of Chinese characters (pp. 35–36). See, too, note 48.

40. John Willis, *The Art of Stenographie; or, Short Writing by Spelling Characterie* (London, 1602; 14th ed., 1648).

41. R. C. Alston, *A Bibliography of the English Language,* vol. 8, *Treatises on Shorthand* (Leeds, 1966), lists twenty-eight separate titles before 1659. Alston includes many facsimile pages that show the persistent, often peculiar, effort of shorthand inventors to provide helpful and ingenious visualizations of their systems.

42. John Willis, *The Art of Memory* (London, 1621), p. 12. Willis defines his symbolic characters as those that "hath some agreement with the signification of the word" (1628 ed., B5ʳ). See Salmon, *The Works of Francis Lodwick,* pp. 114–16, 144–46.

43. Interest in the art of memory among seventeenth-century linguists is surveyed by Salmon, *The Works of Francis Lodwick,* pp. 110–14, and, more extensively, by Paolo Rossi, *Clavis universalis arti mnemoniche e logica combinatoria da Lullo a Leibniz* (Milan, 1960). Frances Yates, *The Art of Memory,* discusses Willis's work briefly (pp. 324–26), but the connection between the development of linguistic schemes and the fate of memory systems in the seventeenth century has not been fully explored. Since both interests deal with the relationship of the mind to the world, it would be interesting to compare what scholars have suggested about the theater of the mind and the efforts of linguists interested in building minds with linguistic tools. See also Yates's *Theatre of the World* (Chicago, 1969).

44. Samuel Botley, *Maximo in Minimo: or, Mr. Jeremiah Rich's Pen's Dexterity Compleated* (London, 1674), B2ʳ.

45. Theophilus Metcalfe, *Short Writing* (London, 1645), pp. 4–5.

46. [Francis Lodwick], *A Common Writing* (London, 1646), A2ʳ.

47. John Lowthorp, ed., *The Philosophical Transactions and Collections, to the End of the Year MDCC,* 3 vols. 5th ed. (London, 1749), 3:378. The combination of interests in a universal language and in shorthand systems is common in the period. The obvious case is Wilkins, but see also William Petty, *The Advice of W. P. to Samuel Hartlib* (London, 1647). Petty summarizes the Comenius-like goals of the Hartlib group by associating the advancement of learning, an art of double writing, and the reformation of style. He emphasizes in this tract suggestions for educating children to "not onely . . . write according to our Common Way, but also to Write Swiftly and in Reall Characters" (p. 5).

48. George Dalgarno, *Didascalocaphus* (Oxford, 1680), A2ᵛ. See J. R. Knowlson, "The Idea of Gesture as a Universal Language in the XVIIth and XVIIIth Centuries," *Journal of the History of Ideas* 26 (1965): 495–508, for a summary of methods of teaching the deaf and dumb.

49. George Dalgarno, *Works* (Edinburgh, 1834), p. 164. On Dalgarno's *Ars Signorum* and its relation to shorthand systems, see Vivian Salmon, "The Evolution of Dalgarno's 'Ars Signorum,'" in *Studies in Language and Literature in Honor of Margaret Schlauch,* ed. Mieczyslaw Brahmer et al. (Warsaw, 1966), pp. 353–71.

50. The literal and physical connection between characters and meaning occurs commonly in discussion of real character and, as with Dalgarno, in commentaries on Hebrew, Chinese, and Egyptian characters. The most impressive commentary on Egyptian characters is Athanasius Kircher's *Oedipus Aegyptiacus* (Rome, 1652), the context of which is established by D. C. Allen, "Some Theories of the Growth and Origin of Language in Milton's Age," *PQ* 28 (1949): 5–16; and David, *Le débat sur les écritures,* pp. 43–56. An example more in keeping with the level of works discussed in this paper is John Webster's *Academiarum Examen* (London, 1653). Webster proposes relating "Hieroglyphical, Emblematical, Symbolical and Cryptographical learning" (p. 24) to grammar. His evidence that such a means exists to repair "the ruines of Babell, and . . . Cure . . . the confusion of tongues" (p. 25) comes from dactology ("the ability of the deaf and dumb to communicate by signs"), Chinese characters, and the natural language of Boehme.

51. William Holder, *The Elements of Speech: An Essay of Inquiry into the Natural Production of Letters* (London, 1669), p. 15.

52. The mid-century debate between John Webster and Seth Ward over the integrity of the academy shows the variety of impulses that led to quite compatible linguistic approaches. Webster's objections to the philosophical indifference of the universities and Ward's ill-humored defense of experimental science, although mutually antagonistic, exhibit similarly grounded theories of language and meaning. Both men agree that a clear and distinct linguistics would fully represent the God-given order of nature, though for one the representation would be essential and, for the other, arbitrary (see notes 11 and 14 above). For a view that emphasizes the contrasting origins of the two positions, see Allen G. Debus, *Science and Education in the Seventeenth Century: The Webster-Ward Debate* (New York, 1970).

53. John Amos Comenius, *The Way of Light,* trans. E. T. Campagnac (London, 1938), p. 8.

54. John Amos Comenius, *A Patterne of Universal Knowledge* (Notthampton, 1651), p. 4. Henry Edmundson, *Lingua Linguarum* (London, 1658), recommends

Comenius's classification of things into "Philosophicall Heads," as does James Howell in *Lexicon Tetraglotton* (London, 1660).

55. Jan A. Comenius, *The Gate of Tongues Unlocked and Opened,* trans. Th. Horn (London, 1633), A3$^v$. See also Wye Saltonstall, *Clavis ad Portam* (Oxford, 1634). Saltonstall's key is an alphabetized list of words with page references to Comenius's *Porta Linguarium* (London, 1631).

56. John Amos Comenius, *Orbis Sensualium Pictus,* A3$^v$. David, *Le débat sur les écritures,* specifically relates Comenius's work to the genre of hieroglyphic Bibles that began to appear on the continent at mid-century (p. 20).

57. James Bowen, "Introduction," to his edition of the *Orbis Sensualium Pictus* (Sydney, 1967). Bowen notes ten editions in the decade after its first appearance (in 1658) and claims that the *Orbis* was the first illustrated school text. The best and fullest bibliography of Comenius's many works (and of secondary works) appears in Klaus Schaller, *Die Pädagogik des Johann Amos Comenius und die Anfänge des pädagogischen Realismus im 17. Jahrhundert* (Heidelberg, 1962), pp. 482–520.

58. Alsted's works include a discussion of language in his *Encyclopaedia* (Herborn, 1630) and a contribution to the proof that Adam spoke Hebrew: *Pentateuchus Mosaica et Pleias Apostolica* (Herborn, 1631).

59. Boehme's contributions to the common idea of Adamic naming include his *Signatura Rerum* (London, 1651). On the relation of Alsted and Boehme to the arts of memory and the schemes for universal language and brotherhood, see Rossi, *Clavis Universalis,* pp. 41–80.

60. This is the exclusive thesis pursued by R. F. Jones, in *The Triumph of the English Language* (Stanford, 1953) and in *The Seventeenth Century* (Stanford, 1956); but, see Introduction, note 4.

61. See note 15 above.

62. Knowlson, *Universal Language Schemes,* discusses this problem among competing historians of ideas (pp. 86–95) and usefully justifies his own more widely cast interests.

63. Webster frequently invokes the spirit of Bacon in *Academiarum Examen* (London, 1654). With Bacon, Webster hopes to overcome the schoolmen, "and for the *arcana et magnalia naturae,* aimed at by Sir Francis Bacon, they might be brought to some reasonable perfection, if the waies and means that he hath prescribed, were diligently observed, and pursued; and if these poor lines of mine contained but any treasure comparable to any of their rich mines, I should set an higher Character of esteem upon them, than now I ought, or they any way merit" (B2$^r$).

64. Ward, in *Vindiciae Academiarum* (Oxford, 1654), leaves his abuse of Webster when it comes to the latter's "smatterings" about a universal character and offers, quite straightforwardly, the development of his own interests in the subject (pp. 20–22) and concludes, mildly, that his opponent ought to "acknowledge that these things are considered in the Universities" (p. 22).

65. This is Frances Yates's argument in *The Art of Memory,* pp. 260–78, 355–74.

66. Rosemond Tuve, *Elizabethan and Metaphysical Imagery* (Chicago, 1947), pp. 390–91. Tuve's book remains the closest study of the linguistic sources of the metaphysical poets' uses of imagery, but still more of the philosophical context is presented by Forrest Robinson in *The Shape of Things Known.* Robinson offers an extended and provocative historical discussion of the "tradition of visual episte-

mology" (pp. 11-96), and, while summarizing his findings, he connects some of the techniques for representing language and some of the distinctive features of literary language in the same period: "The printing press and its immediate effects, along with the increased quantification of logic and the growing emphasis on simplicity and visual presentation in the teaching profession, radically altered the nature of words themselves. In a very real sense, words functioned more and more as images. Stretched evenly on a page they became the well-ordered objects of sight. Meanings could be pinned down, and terms were made to stand for concepts in a way impossible before the invention of printing" (p. 96). See, too, Joseph H. Summers, "The Poem as Hieroglyph," in *George Herbert: His Religion and Art* (Cambridge, Mass., 1954), pp. 123-46, for a discussion, in an emblematic frame, of Herbert's significantly shaped poems; John Muldar, *The Temple of the Mind,* for some general resemblances between seventeenth-century education texts and techniques and some features of prose and poetic style; and, Walter Ong, "Oral Residue in Tudor Prose Style," in *Rhetoric, Romance, and Technology,* pp. 23-47, for some connections between changes in poetic language and developments toward a fully typographical culture. Also see Chapter 2, note 15.

67. John Dryden, "Absalom and Achitophel," in James Kinsley, ed., *The Poems and Fables of John Dryden* (London, 1962), p. 190. References to the text will appear by line references to this edition.

68. John Dryden, "To the Right Honourable Roger, Earl of Orrery" (prefixed to *The Rival Ladies* [1664]), in James Kinsley and George Parfitt, eds., *John Dryden: Selected Criticism* (Oxford, 1970), p. 5.

69. Robert Hume, in *Dryden's Criticism* (Ithaca, 1970), has given the best sense yet of his subject's desire to combine accuracy and clarity of poetic expression with an insistent moral intent engaged in the service of his audience.

70. I take the word *drift* from Dryden's *Essay of Dramatic Poesy,* where it serves important literal and symbolic functions. In that work, Dryden places his debaters on a barge that takes the tide down the Thames as leisurely but as purposefully as he composes "the drift of the ensuing discourse" (Kinsley and Parfitt, eds., *Selected Criticism,* p. 19).

71. Stephen Land, *From Signs to Propositions: The Concept of Form in Eighteenth-Century Semantic Theory* (London, 1974), makes some excellent observations on Dryden's *Essay* and the debate, between Crites and Neander, about literary languages and ideas of meaning (pp. 31-35). Land concludes: "Dryden holds that the meaning of the sign need not consist solely in its relation to a referent—although such a relation is essential—but may involve something more than is contained in the referent. This means that the symbol may have cognitive content beyond that of the mere perception of the object it refers to or represents" (p. 35). This is right and suggests the cognitive content Dryden attributes to his rhymed units as opposed to what he saw as the clever but obscure symbolic and lexical representationalism of his poetic predecessors. Land, however, puts Dryden at an opposite corner from Wilkins and Locke and regards his *Essay* as participating, uniquely it seems, in a "Platonic tradition." This separation of Dryden's view of literary language from contemporary theories and practices is, I think, an error.

72. On the basis of the researches being done in the history of linguistics and in the theoretical relationships between linguistics and literature, a closer and fuller discussion of the changes in literary language from this perspective is also called for. I expect to contribute to it.

73. Chevalier, *Histoire de la syntaxe,* most ably presents the developing interest

in syntax throughout the period I am discussing. See, especially, his emphasis on the changes in ideas of syntax associated with Port-Royal (p. 484 and passim).

74.  See note 27 above.

75.  The different audience intended by Donne's poetic language and Dryden's matches the difference between the ideas of the student implied by early- and late-seventeenth-century grammars. In the earlier period, there is a uniform rite of sophistication that readers and students pass through or fail; in the later period, there is an adaptable pedagogy fitting preconceptions about different groups of users and a sense, on the poet's part, of involving a larger and more diverse audience. Among the later poets and pedagogues, too, there is an admitted responsibility to bring readers and students along more slowly. Grammar books, like the language they treat, become products vying for consumers by appealing to a widespread sense of what is generally appropriate for making one's way in society.

76.  Robert Plot, *The Natural History of Oxfordshire* (Oxford, 1676), refers to the development of a universal language system out of Dalgarno's work with short-hand characters. Dalgarno tried to add syntax to a catalog of words signifying basic things and ideas (that is, lexical "radicals") "by expressing the auxiliary Particles of the English language, by distinct points and places about the radical or integral words, after the manner that 'tis done by prefixes and suffixes in the Hebrew" (p. 282).

77.  John Wallis, *Grammatica Linguae Anglicanae* (Oxford, 1653), p. 68.

78.  See Ian Michael, *English Grammatical Categories,* on the question "Has English Any Syntax?" pp. 467–89. Michael's historical survey of the question misses the growing interest of linguists in relations between parts of speech and the significant increase in sophistication regarding syntax following the popularity of the Port-Royal logic, grammar, and rhetoric. See Chevalier, *Histoire de la syntaxe,* on the limitation of syntax, in this early period, to the summaries of relations between the tables of the parts of speech (pp. 130–31). According to Chevalier, early French grammarians discovered a new subject: "essaient de dresser une ébauche d'inventaire; ceci répond à l'état d'esprit d'un époque, la Renaissance, qui découvre le monde et en dress le catalogue" (p. 130).

79.  Similarly, the growing reliance on rhymed couplets in the poetry of the period stresses the relationship between syntactic units in the couplet. There is an increasing sophistication in the manipulation of the couplet parts, reaching its finest tone in Pope. See, for the early history of the couplet, Ruth Wallerstein, "The Development of the Rhetoric and Metre of the Heroic Couplet Especially in 1625–1645," *PMLA* 50 (1935): 166–209. Hugh Kenner, in "Pope's Reasonable Rhymes," *ELH* 41 (1974): 74–88, writes suggestively about Pope's rhymes and Wilkins's orders of words. However, Kenner looks exclusively at Wilkins's isomorphic lexical and natural taxonomies and their relationship to Pope's witty opposition of rhymed words. This emphasis misses Wilkins's responsibility for syntax (see my discussion below) and Pope's elaborate manipulation of the syntactic units created by rhyme.

80.  Bassett Jones, *Herm'aelogium; or, An Essay at the Rationality of the Art of Speaking* (London, 1659), A3$^r$.

81.  Lewis, *An Essay to Facilitate the Education of Youth,* p. 16. See Michael, *English Grammatical Categories,* on Lewis's work generally and especially for his surprise at Lewis's interest in syntax (pp. 474–75).

82.  Mark Lewis, *Vestibulum Technicum; or, An Artificial Vestibulum* (London, 1675), A1$^r$. Lewis took his title from Comenius's *Vestibulum Linguarium* (London,

1667). Lewis repeatedly cites Comenius and Ramus; the latter reference is suggestive, for it is Ramus's logic that is a likely starting point for the interest in the visual representability of language, logic, and meaning. See, of course, Ong, *Ramus, Method, and the Decay of Dialogue* (and notes 27 above). For an excellent discussion of Ramus's work on language see Chevalier, *Histoire de la syntaxe,* pp. 247–307. Chevalier takes care to characterize Ramus's views on syntax as being essentially linear, dependent on the paradigmatic tables of the parts of speech, and hence significantly different from the revolution in syntax wrought by the Port-Royal (p. 261). Chevalier's review of the predecessors of the Port-Royal is generally pertinent here (pp. 311–412).

83. Lewis, *An Essay to Facilitate,* p. 13.

84. For example, see *Vestibulum,* A4$^v$, and *An Essay to Facilitate,* p. 12.

85. The significant distinction between the words and images in emblem books and the words and images illustrating grammars, phonologies, shorthand systems, and the like is that in the former, the two are equivalent significations while in the latter, the two are parts of a system in which the relationships between units are frequently more crucial than the units themselves. See Rosemary Freeman, *English Emblem Books* (London, 1948), and Ong, "From Allegory to Diagram in the Renaissance Mind."

86. On Lewis's inconsistencies see Michael, *English Grammatical Categories,* pp. 158–59, 281–82.

87. For suggestive, if rapid, surveys of punctuation theory see Walter J. Ong, "Historical Backgrounds of Elizabethan and Jacobean Punctuation Theory," *PMLA* 49 (1944): 349–60; and Mindele Treip, *Milton's Punctuation and Changing English Usage, 1582–1676* (London, 1970), especially pp. 14–53.

88. Mark Lewis, *Plain and short rules for pointing periods* (London, 1675), p. 2.

89. Mark Lewis, *Grammaticae Puerilis* (London, 1670), A1$^v$. In referring to this book, Michael, *English Grammatical Categories,* suggests Lewis's debt to Port-Royal theory (p. 464; also p. 213).

90. I have discussed an aspect of the literary debate above with regard to Dryden's "Absalom and Achitophel," and Michael McKeon has drawn together some closely related political and religious versions in his excellent discussion of Dryden's *Annus Mirabilis: Politics and Poetry in Restoration England* (Cambridge, Mass., 1975). See, especially, his documentation of the interpretive methods behind different brands of eschatological prophecy in the 1660s (pp. 190–266). McKeon justifies the cumbersomeness of his organization by pointing, justly, to the awkward problematic he is trying to explore: specifically, the relationship between allegory and history in the poem and in the period. The importance of this uneasy and uneven alliance be.ween, effectively, a literalist hermeneutic and an historicist one is more engagingly suggested by its prominence in Defoe's *A Journal of the History of the Plague Year* (1722). In that account of the public trials of 1665/6 (and 1722), H. F., the narrator, seeks a secure interpretation of events that is not, on the one hand, only literally and mysteriously emblematic or, on the other, a merely local eruption of natural history. Students of Restoration and eighteenth-century literature and politics might look to the linguistic history I am outlining for a useful glass in which to see this crucial problematic.

91. Samuel Shaw, *Words Made Visible* (London, 1679), A1$^v$. Shaw also wrote *Grammatica Anglo-Romana; or, A Syncritical Grammar* (London, 1687).

92. This is Wilkins's admission: "It were exceeding desirable that the Names of

things might consist of such Sounds, as should bear in them some Analogy to their Natures; and the Figure or character of these Names should bear some proper resemblance to those Sounds, that men might easily guess at the sense or meaning of any name or word, upon the first hearing or sight of it. But how this can be done in all the particular species of things, I understand not; and therefore shall take it for granted, that this Character must be by Institution" (p. 386). Land, *From Signs to Propositions,* is determined to read Wilkins as someone who holds a thoroughly "naive" theory of language as simply an aggregate of discrete signs. Wilkins, in Land's estimation, is principally a natural philosopher and "only secondarily" a linguist (p. 3). Land thereby misses the significance and intensity of the trials Wilkins's crucial linguistic intentions encounter.

93. For the sparse history of the fate of Wilkins's *Essay* see Knowlson, *Universal Language Schemes,* pp. 102–7, supplemented by Salmon, "John Wilkins' Essay."

94. Thomas Baker, *Reflections upon Learning,* takes pains to cite one philosopher against another to prove "the Weakness of the Humane Understanding" (p. 1), if only because of these disagreements. When he gets to Wilkins, he notes that the philosophical language "being design'd not to express Words by Things, we must first be agreed about the Nature of Things" (p. 18). And such agreement, writes Baker, is unlikely: "when Bishop Wilkins first undertook this Design, Substances and Accidents were a receiv'd Division, and accordingly in ranking things, and reducing them to Heads . . . he proceeds according to the Order they stand in, of Substance and Accidents, in the Scale of Predicaments; but were he to begin now, and would suit his Design to the Philosophy in Vogue, he must draw a new Scheme, and instead of Accidents must take in Modes . . ." (pp. 18–19).

95. For the context in which the syntactic revolution of Port-Royal occurred see Chevalier, *Histoire de la syntaxe,* pp. 311–412.

96. Antoine Arnauld and Pierre Nicole, *La logique ou l'art de penser,* ed. Pierre Claire and François Girbal (Paris, 1965), p. 37.

97. See Wilbur Samuel Howell, *Logic and Rhetoric in England, 1500–1700* (Princeton, 1956), pp. 342–63. The most suggestive study of Port-Royal linguistics is Noam Chomsky's *Cartesian Linguistics: A Chapter in the History of Rationalist Thought* (New York, 1966), especially pp. 33–59. Chomsky's major interest is "the development of ideas that have reemerged . . . in current work" (p. 2), not "with the transmission of certain ideas and doctrines" (p. 76). But his emphasis on the habit of arguing "from the structure of mental processes to the structure of language" (p. 31) among the grammarians he discusses exactly captures what their actual effect was on late-seventeenth-and early-eighteenth-century English linguists. Although Chomsky admits that he wants "to characterize a constellation of ideas and interests" (p. 75) rather than provide a complete historical study, he has been criticized for not doing what he did not intend to do. Vivian Salmon, in a review article in the *Journal of Linguistics* 5 (1969): 165–87, charges Chomsky with failure "to take into account the whole intellectual context" (p. 167). Ms. Salmon supplies much of that relevant context, and her review is an important essay in its own right. However, in seeking bits of resemblance between the Port-Royal grammar and earlier linguistic works (including Bassett Jones's *Herm'aelogium*), Salmon misses the importance of the clarity, integrity, and popularity of the former. In a much harsher review of *Cartesian Linguistics,* Hans Aarsleff, "The History of Linguistics and Professor Chomsky," *Language* 46 (1970): 570–85, calls "Chomsky's version of the history of linguistic . . . fundamentally false" (p. 571). Aarsleff adds more piecemeal precedents

to Salmon's list but has little to say about English linguistics. See, as well, Robin Lakoff's review of Herbert Brekle's critical edition of the *Grammaire générale et raisonnée,* 2 vols. (Stuttgart, 1966) in *Language* 45 (1969): 343–64; and Gilbert Harman's review of Chomsky, *Language and Mind* (New York, 1972), in *Language* 49 (1973): 453–64. Harman's comments correct Aarsleff's hostility (especially pp. 454–56). Chevalier, *Histoire de la syntaxe,* provides the fullest analysis of the linguistic work of the Port-Royal (pp. 483–539), and he also redresses, historically, Chomsky's transformational slant on it by stressing as its most important contribution the identification of the sentence as dependent on the priority of logical relations over static forms (pp. 490–91).

98. With "accessory ideas" as part of the act of communication, the Port-Royal analysis of language becomes a study of human behavior, integrating psychology and linguistics. See Jan Miel, "Pascal, Port-Royal, and Cartesian Linguistics," *Journal of the History of Ideas* 30 (1960): 261–71.

99. See Chomsky, *Cartesian Linguistics,* pp. 33–39, on the Port-Royal analysis of deep and surface structures. According to Chevalier, *Histoire de la syntaxe,* the grammarian, in the Port-Royal works, "considère la langue, non comme un agrégat, un processus d'association, mais comme une organisation, comme une création" (p. 505).

100. Seven editions of the *L'art de penser* were published in England before 1700—four in Latin and three in English (1685, 1693, 1696). Howell, *Logic and Rhetoric,* cites an eighth, in French, but this is shown to be a French edition by Brekle in his edition of *La logique ou l'art de penser* (Stuttgart, 1968), p. 27.

101. Claude Lancelot and Antoine Arnauld, *Grammaire générale et raisonée* (Paris, 1660), p. 26.

102. This is how Lancelot and Arnauld justify their emphasis on judgment: "D'où l'on voit que la troisième operation de l'esprit [raisonner] n'est qu'une extension de la seconde [juger]. Et ainsi il suffira pour nostre sujet de considerer les deux premières [concevoir et juger] ou ce qui est enfermé de la première dans la seconde. Car les hommes ne parlent gueres pour exprimer simplement ce qu'ils conçoivent; mais c'est presque toujours pour exprimer les jugemens qu'ils sont des choses qu'ils conçoivent" (p. 28).

103. The full text of the *Essay* was issued nine times in the twenty years after 1690 and twice in an abridgment. On the impact of Locke's *Essay,* see John W. Yolton, *John Locke and the Way of Ideas* (Oxford, 1956).

104. See Hans Aarsleff, "Leibniz on Locke on Language," *American Philosophical Quarterly* 1 (1964); 165–88. Aarsleff, in this substantial essay, effectively distinguishes between Leibniz's attraction to the search for a natural language and Locke's "emphatic rejection of the viability of a philosophical language" (p. 168). Aarsleff cites a number of points at which Locke responds to contemporary discussions of a natural language. More importantly, Aarsleff characterizes the *Essay* as a "discussion of the ways in which knowledge may be obtained and secured" (p. 175) rather than as a metaphysical treatise. Aarsleff only hints at Locke's familiarity with Port-Royal (p. 168), but W. Van Leyden, *Seventeenth-Century Metaphysics* (London, 1968), suggests that the Port-Royal logic is Locke's source for the distinction between real and nominal essences (p. 48). Locke's relation to the Port-Royal school is also noted by John W. Yolton, "Locke and the Seventeenth-Century Logic of Ideas," *Journal of the History of Ideas* 16 (1955): 431–52, especially 445–46.

105.  John Locke, *An Essay concerning Human Understanding,* ed. Alexander Campbell Fraser, 2 vols. (New York, 1959), 1:535 (2. 33. 19). See also Locke, 3. 9. 21.

106.  Land, *From Signs to Propositions,* forcefully argues that Locke's theory of language is entirely unlike the Port-Royal ideas with which I have associated it. For Land, it seems that Locke, like Wilkins, Hobbes, and the Royal Society generally, explained "meaning entirely in terms of the representational relation between individual signs and their referents" (p. 30). Locke's brief remarks about particles, which I discuss below, seem to Land to be as "loose and unadventurous" (p. 3) as Wilkins's. Land applies what I think is a misreading of Locke to a misrepresentation of early-eighteenth-century literature as essentially naively pictorial (pp. 21–30).

107.  Aarsleff, "Locke on Leibniz on Language," discusses the historical context of Locke's reference to Adamic language (pp. 179–83).

108.  In *Some Thoughts concerning Education,* Locke argues against teaching any language by a Lilylike grammar and recommends, instead, visual grammars and practical conversation.

109.  For studies that stress Locke's relationship to seventeenth-century science, see Maurice Mandelbaum, *Philosophy, Science, and Sense Perception* (Baltimore, 1964), especially pp. 93–103. Although John W. Yolton, *Locke and the Compass of Human Understanding* (Cambridge, 1970), elaborates on the connections between Locke's philosophy and the principles of other Royal Society members, he concludes his impressive study with a chapter on "Signs and Signification," which clarifies Locke's own idea of the "grammar of our thought" (p. 220). This grammar can be learned only *after* one has acquired concepts: "The way of ideas was Locke's attempt at uncovering at least part of the epistemic structure of thought, especially of our thought about the physical world. The epistemology of thought is like the grammar of language in that both reveal the structures implicit in the use of words and ideas."

## Chapter 2

1.  The lack of bold and elaborate universal language schemes and the absence of a dominant figure in the early eighteenth century are responsible, in part, for the striking indifference of historians and critics to the ideas of language in the period. In surveying universal grammars, for instance, it is conventional to jump from John Wilkins (1668) to James Harris (1751) with little or no mention of the linguistic work in between. Ian Michael, in *English Grammatical Categories and the Tradition to 1800* (Cambridge, 1970), briefly refers to a couple of grammarians (A. Lane and Charles Gildon) of the early part of the century, but he does not consider the issue of "universality" in their work significant. Michael argues, wrongly, that the English linguistic tradition shows no trace of the relationship between logic and language, between psychology and syntax, and his error is partly due to his failure to take seriously the impact of Wilkins, Port-Royal, and Locke on the linguists of the late seventeenth and early eighteenth centuries. Jean-Claude Chevalier, *Histoire de la syntaxe* (Geneva, 1968), offers a valuable discussion of the comparable problems in writing about the history of French grammars of this period (pp. 540–99). He notes the difficulty of reliably assessing the assumptions of works peculiarly self-conscious of their responsibility to deal with conflicting traditions. Chevalier's solution is to discuss changes as "mutations."

English linguists of the period have also fallen victim to the convenience of the "historical sweep," which grants importance to those toeing the prescribed line and ignores the rest. The "broad view" is what is taken by Morton W. Bloomfield and Leonard Newmark, *A Linguistic Introduction to the History of English* (New York, 1963), p. 296. What they find, however, is what they look for—the development of the doctrine of correctness and good usage in the period 1650 to 1850. The apparent triumph of their version of prescriptive grammar seems to justify selecting those few grammarians supporting their view and dismissing those who do not: "the recommendations of most eighteenth-century grammarians were in large part based on a Procrustean use of Latinish grammar, misapplied logic, or plain prejudice" (p. 318). The drive to prove the triumph of prescriptiveness also mars the relevant section of Albert Baugh's *A History of the English Language,* 2d ed. (New York, 1957), pp. 306–55; and Sterling Leonard, *The Doctrine of Correctness in English Usage* (Madison, 1929).

Marshall McLuhan uses a different broom, and his sweep is ampler still; for McLuhan, books are books and that is the fault of them all. There is *the* typographical mind, McLuhan argues, and it is represented all too well by the study of language in the eighteenth century: "Printed grammars since the eighteenth century created a fog based on the concept of correctness" ("The Effect of the Printed Book on Language in the Sixteenth Century," in Edmund Carpenter and Marshall McLuhan, eds., *Explorations in Communication* [Boston, 1960], p. 135). Also see McLuhan, *Gutenberg Galaxy: The Making of Typographic Man* (Toronto, 1962), pp. 229–35. To a lesser extent Walter J. Ong makes use of the same handle (see Chapter 1, note 27). Compare, for example, Ong's mistaken emphasis on the eighteenth-century associationists as mere geometers of ideas in a well-defined mental space (in "Psyche and the Geometers: Associationist Critical Theory," in *Rhetoric, Romance, and Technology: Studies in the Interaction of Expression and Culture* [Ithaca, 1971], pp. 213–36) and Land's discussion, in *From Signs to Propositions: The Concept of Form in Eighteenth-Century Semantic Theory* (London, 1974), of the contribution of some of these same associationists to the development of a "psychological model" of human thought and language (pp. 64–66).

2. In addition to the examples of the conventional wisdom of linguistic historians cited in the previous footnote, there are works by those who look more closely at primary sources but who also submit to the same bias. For both Hans Aarsleff, *The Study of Language in England, 1780–1860* (Princeton, 1967), and Land, *From Signs to Propositions,* there is a sense of triumph in the development of "scientific" linguistics that still dominates linguistic study in America. Aarsleff and Land evaluate the writers they elect for study according to their contribution to the "real" science of language. Land writes, for instance, that "as long as the theory of language depended upon a mentalistic or psychological component there could be no true science of language" (p. 75).

3. This attribution is widespread, but see the detailed work of K. G. Hamilton, *The Two Harmonies* (Oxford, 1963), and *John Dryden and the Poetry of Statement* (Brisbane, 1967).

4. Land, *From Signs to Propositions,* p. 73. See Introduction, note 29, for the similar views of Tuveson and note 15 below for a brief counterproposal.

5. I have suggested the specific appropriateness of these terms to Pope's poetic self-consciousness in an essay: "Versions of the Lock: Readers of 'The Rape of the Lock,' " *ELH* 43 (1976): 53–73. See, too, Ralph Cohen's remarks on the syntactic

features of Thomson's *The Seasons* in *The Unfolding of "The Seasons": A Study of James Thomson's Poem* (Baltimore, 1970), especially pp. 181–208, 251–52.

6. I relate Pope's invitation to his readerly company to "Expatiate free o'er all this scene of Man" in the manner of a well-planned walk through successive stages of his verse discourse to the patterns of perception Ronald Paulson has observed in his essay, "The Pictorial Circuit and Related Structures in Eighteenth-Century England," in Peter Hughes and David Williams, eds., *The Varied Pattern: Studies in the Eighteenth Century* (Toronto, 1971), pp. 165–87. Paulson's work on Hogarth's pictorial narratives and his suggestions about how to "read" Hogarth are also pertinent here: *Hogarth: His Life, Art, and Times,* 2 vols. (New Haven, 1971), 1: 263–76 and 2: 171–85.

7. The sublime has been well located by intellectual historians who have variously focused on its pertinence to aesthetics, natural history, theology, and literature, but see Land, *From Signs to Propositions,* for a valuable and brief discussion of the sublime in terms of the prevailing theories of meaning (pp. 36–50).

8. This important change, occurring in spite of apparent agreement, is another example of the independent significance of the manner in which ideas are presented— whether Ramistic diagrams, tables, or the format of books (see Chapter 1, note 27). I suggest in Chapter 1 that although the taxonomies of linguistic units were designed to represent the elements of reality, their effect was to dramatize the need for ways to *relate* the parts and, ultimately, to make the principles of relation the source of meaning. In this chapter, I try to show how the physical separation (and, later, the suppression) of the philosophical groundwork of language from practical grammar contributed to the idea that they were different. I offer these ideas as contributions to a history of the "phenomenology of the page."

9. [Charles Gildon], *A Grammar of the English Tongue, With Notes, Giving the Grounds and Reason of Grammar in General* (London, 1711), p. 1. This grammar was written for John Brightland and is commonly referred to as his, but Gildon's authorship is clear: see W. H. Mittens, "A Grammatical 'Battel Royal,'" *Durham University Journal* 11 (1970): 110–20. Mittens cites Gildon's references to Port-Royal but dismisses the attempt to correlate parts of speech and "universal laws of thought" as "forced" (p. 117). Gildon's grammar appeared with the approval of Isaac Bickerstaff stamped on the page opposite the title page: "as Grammar in general is on all hands allow'd the Foundation of All Arts and Sciences, so it appears to me, that this Grammar of the English Tongue has done that Justice to our Language which, 'till now, it never obtain'd." Although literary critics tend to treat Gildon in the same way Pope did, one of Gildon's works has been discussed with interesting and deserved care: John W. Yolton, *John Locke and the Way of Ideas* (Oxford, 1956), discusses Gildon's *Deist's Manual* (1705) as an important imitation and popularization of Locke's epistemology (pp. 161–62, 186–87).

10. James Greenwood, *An Essay Towards a Practical English Grammar. Describing the Genius and Nature of the English Tongue: Giving Likewise a Rational and Plain Account of Grammar in General* (London, 1711), p. 34. Greenwood appears to be the author of the letter to *The Tatler* (#234; *The Tatler,* ed. George A. Aitken, 4 vols. [New York, 1899], 4: 194–96) that responds to Swift's letter (#230) of the week before. Greenwood also composed *The London Vocabulary, English and Latin: put into a New Method proper to acquaint the Learner with Things* (London, 1713), an abridgment of Comenius's *Orbis.*

11. See note 9 above.

12. Greenwood's "Introduction" paraphrases Locke's *Essay* (3. 2. 1).

13. [Charles Gildon], *Bellum Grammaticale; or, The Grammatical Battel Royal* (London, 1712), p. 16.

14. [Thomas Wilson], *The Many Advantages of a Good Language to Any Nation* (London, 1724), p. 5.

15. Joseph Addison, in adapting Locke's distinction between wit and judgment, defines true wit and false wit in a way that also characterizes the two ideas of language in the seventeenth and eighteenth centuries: "As true Wit generally consists in this Resemblance and Congruity of Ideas, false Wit chiefly consists in the Resemblance and Congruity of single Letters, as in Anagrams, Chronograms, Lipograms, and Acrosticks: Sometimes of Syllables, as in Ecchos and Doggerel Rhymes: Sometimes of Words, as in Punns and Quibbles; and sometimes of whole Sentences or Poems, cast into the Figures of *Eggs, Axes, or Altars.*" *The Spectator,* ed. Donald F. Bond, 5 vols. (Oxford, 1965), 1: 265. Addison goes on to criticize (and misquote) Dryden's definition of wit: "Wit, as he defines it is 'a Propriety of Words and Thoughts adapted to the Subject.' If this be a true Definition of Wit, I am apt to think that Euclid was the greatest Wit that ever set Pen to Paper" (p. 267). Addison redeems Dryden from his definition, but the rejection of the dominant linguistic assumptions (and their literary manifestations) of the previous century is clear. The differences between metaphysical and Augustan poetry is also one of the subjects of Patricia Meyer Spacks's *An Argument of Images: The Poetry of Alexander Pope* (Cambridge, Mass., 1971). She bases her excellent reading of Pope on an insight into Pope's use of metaphor, a use perfectly correspondent with the linguistic changes I am describing. Spacks argues that Pope's images are more psychic than physical: "Many of his images stress function rather than appearance, often they record activity" (p. 11). The "function" or "activity" they represent is less the "power of wit" (p. 40) than the "powers of human perception" (p. 41). Seeing, for Pope, is itself a process of reasoning. I would add to Spacks's account what is usually missing from discussions of wit in Pope, that is, recognition of the difference between Sprat's call for the correspondence between words and things and Locke's insistence on the relationship between words and ideas. This distinction allows us to see the epistemological force of Pope's approval of a wit "whose Truth convinc'd at Sight we find, / That gives us back the Image of our Mind" (*Essay on Criticism,* 11. 299–300). Much of the related eighteenth-century critical discussion of the nature of description is usefully assembled by Ralph Cohen, "Things, Images, and Imagination: The Reconsideration of Description," in *The Art of Discrimination: Thomson's "The Seasons" and the Language of Criticism* (Berkeley, 1964), pp. 131–87.

16. A. Lane, *A Key to the Art of Letters: or, English a Learned Language* (London, 1700), p. 16. Lane also wrote another general grammar: *A Rational and Speedy Method of attaining to the Latine Tongue* (London, 1695).

17. In this, Greenwood follows the example of Claude Lancelot, *Nouvelle méthode pour facilement et en peu temps comprendre la langue latine* (1644).

18. See Chapter 1, note 28.

19. Thomas Dyche, *A Guide to the English Tongue* (London, 1707), A2$^\mathrm{v}$.

20. *The Needful Attempt, to Make Language and Divinity Plain and Easie* (London, 1711), p. 3.

21. Also, John Jones, *Practical Phonography* (London, 1701): "English Speech is the Art of Signifying the Mind by humane Voice, as it is commonly used in England, (particularly in London, the Universities, or at Court)" (p. 1).

22. Swift's language proposals are generally misinterpreted because historians
have not observed the critical change in ideas of language at this time. Swift's
*Proposal for Correcting, Improving and Ascertaining the English Tongue* (London,
1712) is usually listed with all the other linguistic projects of the previous century.
However, the language repairers of the Royal Society had in mind the creation,
perfection, or discovery of a language that would meet the needs of the international
(and atemporal) society of learned men and, for many of them, would reclaim the
brotherhood of man. Swift is interested in the society of his fellow-men. He wants
standards of communication in English rigorous enough to embarrass "modern
sparks" (p. 15). See, equally, *A Complete Collection of Genteel and Ingenious
Conversation According to the Most Polite Mode and Method Now Used at Court...
by Simon Wagstaff* (London, 1738). The relationship between proposals for
language reform in the early eighteenth century and the language programs
associated with the Royal Society ought to be reconsidered in terms of the different
core ideas of language predominant in each.

23. John Jones, *Practical Phonography*, p. 6.

24. Isaac Watts, *The Art of Reading and Writing English* (London, 1721), p. 83.
Watts is also the author of one of the most popular logics of the century, *Logick*
(London, 1725). His logic adapts Locke and, without citation, Arnauld: "As the
first Work of the Mind is Perception, whereby our Ideas are framed, and the second
is Judgment, which joins or disjoins our Ideas, and forms a Proposition, so the third
Operation of the Mind Reasoning, which joins several Propositions together, and
makes a Syllogism, that is, an Argument..." (p. 279). The fourth part of logic is the
"Art of Method" (p. 338). For a discussion of Watts's use of the Port-Royal logic,
see Wilbur Samuel Howell, *Eighteenth-Century British Logic and Rhetoric* (Princeton,
1971), pp. 334–45.

25. Watts recommends John Kersey, *A New English Dictionary; or, A Compleat
Collection of the Most Proper and Significant Words, Commonly Used in the
Language* (London, 1702). Kersey's is the first English dictionary not to make its
inclusion of "hard words" its main virtue. Instead, Kersey omits "obsolete, barbarous,
foreign and peculiar words" in favor of "the most proper and significant English
words, that are now commonly us'd either in Speech, or in the familiar way of
Writing Letters" (A2ʳ). Kersey advertises this difference between his dictionary and
those by John Bulloker (*An English Expositor* [London, 1616]) and Elisha Coles
(*An English Dictionary: Explaining the Difficult Terms... Containing Many
Thousands of Hard Words* [London, 1676]). The difference is an important one, for
the desire of the earlier dictionary-makers to collect all such words and to represent
language and things by lists contrasts with Kersey's emphasis on contemporary
communication.

26. Jenkin Thomas Philipps's *An Essay Towards an Universal and Rational
Grammar* (London, 1726) is, as the title page announces, largely drawn from James
Shirley's grammatical works, which include *The Rudiments of Grammar* (1656) and
*Manuductio, or a Leading of Children* (1660). Although Shirley's works define
punctuation marks primarily in terms of breaths, Philipps's own introduction makes
them a principal part of orthography: the first part of grammar "teaches the true
Spelling, and the Use of Stops in Reading, which is not only to give a proper Time for
Breathing, but to avoid Obscurity and Confusion of the Sense, in the joyning of
Words together in a Sentence" (p. iii). Philipps also adds the terms "Universal and
Rational" to Shirley's work, and what he means by them are the Lockean and Port-

Royal assumptions that there are four kinds of words "sufficient to express all the Ideas of Things, and the Judgments we make upon them, and render them intelligible to others, by Writing or Discourse" (p. iv). Isaac Watts, in *The Art of Reading and Writing English,* defines points as "marks used in Writing or Printing, to distinguish the several Parts of a Sentence, and the several Kinds of Sentences and Ways of Writing which are used" (p. 39). The phrases "Kinds of Sentences and Ways of Writing" suggest the impact of the Port-Royal grammar and logic. See note 24, above.

27. See Chapter 1, note 86; and Park Honan, "Eighteenth- and Nineteenth-Century English Punctuation Theory," *English Studies* 41 (1960): 92–102.

28. Michael Maittaire, *The English Grammar; or, An Essay on the Art of Grammar Applied to and Exemplified in the English Tongue* (London, 1712), p. 21.

29. Hugh Jones, *An Accidence to the English Tongue . . . Being a Grammatical Essay Upon our Language* (London, 1724), p. 41.

30. On couplet rhetoric see George Williamson, "The Rhetorical Pattern of Neoclassical Wit," *Modern Philology* 33 (1935): 55–81. See also Chapter 1, note 78.

31. William Loughton, *A Practical Grammar of the English Tongue; or, A Rational and Easy Introduction to Speaking and Writing English* (London, 1734), also suggests a mark for irony (an inverted exclamation point ¡). Both Greenwood and Loughton follow Wilkins's recommendation in *An Essay towards a Real Character, And a Philosophical Language* (London, 1668), pp. 356, 377. Loughton, in fact, uses Wilkins's mark. Francis Lodwick, in John Lowthorp, ed., *The Philosophical Transactions and Collections, to the End of the Year MDCC,* 3 vols., 5th ed. (London, 1749), 3: 377, recommends an inverted interrogative: ¿.

32. Complaints about the printers' habit of automatically capitalizing all nouns became common in the early eighteenth century. Thomas Tuite, *The Oxford Spelling Book* (London, 1726), criticizes English printers for this convention. So does Isaac Watts in *The Art of Reading and Writing English,* but his message is undercut by the printer's method: "It has been the growing Custom of this Age in printing . . . to begin every Name of a Thing . . . with a Great Letter; tho I cannot approve it so universally as it is practised" (p. 66).

33. These linguists combine the uses of capitalization with the visualization of the relationship between ideas (that is, words). In doing this, they contribute to what Earl R. Wasserman describes as the significance of personification in the eighteenth century: "The Inherent Values of Eighteenth-Century Personification," *PMLA* 65 (1950): 435–63. Wasserman shows that personification is the "most accurate linguistic means of expressing an abstraction as it appears to the human mind" (p. 460). It is also the rhetorical device most appropriate to the linguistic conviction that words are ideas, not things. Wasserman misjudges the intellectual context of the developing interest in personification, however, by assuming that eighteenth-century epistemology "followed in the tracks of the mechanism and materialism of Hobbes and Locke" (p. 448). The differences, real and historical, between Hobbes's materialism and Locke's sensationalism are more important than their similarities, and by not observing those differences, Wasserman misses the *function* of personifications. Instead, he stresses their status as static images. The idea of personifications as perceptions integrated into poetic discourse corresponds to Ronald Paulson's valuable analysis of the symbols (objects, documents, paintings) in Hogarth's art. See note 6 above.

34. Maittaire, in assuming the lower case "i," accommodates himself to the "Messieurs du Port-Royal," who, as Addison notes, "banished the way of speaking in the First Person out of all their Works, as arising from Vain-glory and Self-Conceit.

To show their particular Aversion to it, they branded this Form of Writing with the Name of an Egotism" *(The Spectator,* vol. 4, pp. 519–20).

35.  See Bertrand Harris Bronson, "Printing as an Index of Taste," in his *Facets of the Enlightenment: Studies in English Literature and Its Contexts* (Berkeley, 1968), pp. 326–65. Bronson cites the 1718 folio of Prior's works as an example of "an idiosyncratic and subjective attitude, capitalizing nouns, pronouns frequently, occasionally adjectives, setting personal names in caps-and-small-caps, with an additional refinement of italicizing place names. Such a procedure . . . makes for a homogeneous yet vivid, even dramatic, page" (p. 338). Bronson interprets the variations in printing habits as signs of lack of concern: "Little stress was laid on it [capitalization] in school, when even spelling was relatively unimportant and English not a subject of serious study" (p. 341). In fact, the serious study of English was based on spelling and grammar books all of which contained sections on capitalization. Still, Bronson uniquely provides a suggestive study of the significance of book size, binding, types, margin design, and illustration in the eighteenth century, and one which indicates significant differences among styles of printing in a typo-graphic culture.

36.  Richard Johnson, *Grammatical Commentaries: Being an Apparatus To a New National Grammar: By way of Animadversion Upon the Falsities, Obscurities, Redundancies, and Defects of Lilly's System* (London, 1706), p. 1.

37.  Addison, too, in *Spectator* #86, seems to agree that logic and grammar are not only compatible but that they are descriptions of the way the mind naturally works: "Every one that speaks or reasons is a Grammarian and a Logician, though he may be wholly unacquainted with the Rules of Grammar or Logick, as they are delivered in Books and Systems" *(The Spectator,* vol. 1, p. 365).

38.  Gildon, in the pages from which I am quoting here, is freely translating from the *Grammaire générale*. See Michael, *English Grammatical Categories,* pp. 289–91, 366–67, 454–56, for some of Gildon's other borrowings from Lancelot and Arnauld.

39.  See William K. Wimsatt, "Rhetoric and Poems," in *The Verbal Icon* (New York, 1960), pp. 164–82; Maynard Mack, "'Wit and Poetry and Pope': Some Observations on His Imagery," in James L. Clifford and Louis A. Landa, eds., *Pope and His Contemporaries* (Oxford, 1949), pp. 20–40; and my essay, "Versions of the Lock." Also see notes 6, 15, and 30 above.

40.  See note 8 above.

41.  Land, *From Signs to Propositions,* offers a pertinent history of some prominent instances of the application of mathematics to language in the seventeenth and eighteenth centuries (pp. 125–54).

42.  Modern critical discussions of metaphor in the late seventeenth and early eighteenth century fluctuate between compiling examples of hostility to figurative speech among those associated with the Royal Society and describing the abundance of figures in the literature (and sometimes in the writings of Royal Society members). The best sense critics have been able to make of this difference is a more or less sophisticated notion of the "poetry of statement." However, I think there is a more accurate, and more interesting, way to account for these problems and that is by considering the literary impact of the new idea of language developing in the late seventeenth century. In tracing its literary impact we might be able to account for the apparent contradiction between Swift's metaphoric sense and his condemnation of those who live their metaphors. For Swift, metaphors are not true of things but represent our ideas about things. Those who believe words are things become victims

162

of Swift's favorite satiric technique, literalization. It is from the problematics of figurative speech that the excitement in and of the literature of this time comes.

43. Robert Lowth, *Short Introduction to English Grammar With Critical Notes* (London, 1762), p. viii.

44. I discuss the work of James Harris in Chapter 3.

45. Paul Alkon, in "Critical and Logical Concepts of Method from Addison to Coleridge," *Eighteenth-Century Studies* 5 (1971): 97–121, usefully collects eighteenth-century references to "method." Alkon points to the emphasis, particularly in Watts's *Logick* (1725), on what Alkon calls "the role of connections" (p. 114) and "proper and decent forms of transition" (p. 115). Alkon himself stresses the difference between the concern for sequential order in the seventeenth century and the interest in presentational method among eighteenth-century logicians. Although he does not recognize the source of the difference and although he mis-interprets the emphasis on relations as indifference to order (he draws only from the last one-tenth of Watts's *Logick*), Alkon calls attention to a "neglected influence from logic on . . . the shape of eighteenth-century literature" (p. 120). Ralph Cohen, in an earlier essay, "Association of Ideas and Poetic Unity," *PQ* 36 (1957): 465–74, also finds, at least in the second half of the century, a literature that "exhibited that combination of ideas which was the characteristic of association . . . by creating a union of actions, passions, and thoughts" (p. 467). This is right, but the insight should be brought back to its origins in late seventeenth- and early eighteenth-century linguistic writings and to its earlier manifestations in Augustan literature.

46. Johnson, *Grammatical Commentaries*, p. 16.

47. It is Greenwood (and Lancelot, see note 17 above) who prevails, however.

48. Figure 7 is taken from the prospectus for *Practical Phonography* which was published three years earlier.

49. Jones expands on a method of learning which makes books the basis of learning:

> . . . To call to *Mind* how *Words* are *printed* (or *written,*) it will be (next to *actual seeing* them in the *Book*) a ready *Way* to shut your *Eyes,* and firmly imagine, that you distinctly see the *Word* in all its *Parts* in some *printed Book,* that you familiarly *use,* particularly in the upper line of the same to avoid *Confusion,* and *Distraction,* taking exact Notice of all its *Letters* during that imaginary *View,* which (as I have experienced in *several Persons*) will help you rightly to spell most *Words,* that you are well acquainted with the *Sight* of by often reading them, even to the *Amazement* of the *Standers* by, that otherwise knew your *Inability* of *Spelling;* but let me warn you to depend wholly upon the *imaginary Sight,* and not upon the prejudiced sounding of the *Word,* that you commonly use, which you must utterly forsake. (p. 12)

50. Wilson, *The Many Advantages,* proposes similar tables in a dictionary he promises to labor on if his essay is well received: "In this short Dictionary we propose to add to the first Themes or Original of Words, such of the Derivations as deserve Notice, and all the Derivatives which proceed from them. . . . By that Means the Senses of Words will be understood and remembered better . . . and when it shall be seen by what Ways the several Words are drawn from the Same Roots, the Grammarian will more easily sort them into their proper Kinds, and see by what Rules their Changes are made; and a better Grammar may be composed than we have as yet" (p. 41).

51. Solomon Lowe, *A Critique on the Etymology of the Westminster Grammar* (London, 1723), p. iv.

52. The illustration is from Solomon Lowe, *Latin and French Grammar Reformed Into a Small Compass* (London, 1727).

53. This development of typographical techniques parallels the history of the *ut pictora poesis* tradition as described by Jean Hagstrum, *The Sister Arts: The Tradition of Literary Pictorialism and English Poetry from Dryden to Gray* (Chicago, 1958): "in the eighteenth century the focus has shifted from the work to the mind" (p. 130). In the Renaissance, Hagstrum writes, the method of descriptive technique "enumerated detail after exquisite detail. . . . It was static and complete: item followed item until the whole was drawn." This is a good description of seventeenth-century linguistic practice as well. See, too, the valuable survey of the issue of poetry and imitation in the eighteenth century by Ralph Cohen, *The Art of Discrimination,* pp. 188–247.

54. The increase in varieties of education—for the poor, for tradesmen, for the nobility, for navigators, for the fair sex—in the eighteenth century has been documented by Richard S. Tompson, *Classics or Charity? The Dilemma of the Eighteenth-Century Grammar School* (Manchester, 1971).

55. John Milton's *On Education* (1644) is dedicated to Samuel Hartlib and refers to Comenius as "a person sent hither by some good providence from a far country to be the occasion and the incitement of great good to this island" (*The Works of John Milton,* ed. Allan Abbot, vol. 4, *Of Education* [New York, 1931], p. 275). Like Comenius, Milton defines education in theological terms: "The end then of Learning is to repair the ruines of our first Parents by regaining to know God aright" (p. 277). And the way to understand God is also the method of learning: "because our understanding cannot in this body found itself but on sensible things, nor arrive so clearly to the knowledge of God and things invisible, as by orderly conning over the visible and inferior creature, the same method is necessarily to be follow'd in all discreet teaching." For a summary of Puritan educational reforms see Charles Webster, "Science and the Challenge to the Scholastic Curriculum, 1640–1660," in *The Changing Curriculum* (London, 1971), pp. 21–36.

56. John Owen, *The Youth's Instructor in the English Tongue* (London, 1732), A1$^r$.

57. John Entick, *Speculum Latinum; or, Latin Made easy to Scholars* (London, 1728), p. 26.

58. John Henley, *The Compleat Linguist; or, An Universal Grammar to all the Considerable Tongues in Being* (London, 1719–26). *A Grammar of the Latin Tongue* (1720), p. ii. Henley's background as schoolmaster and grammarian is traced in Graham Midgley, *The Life of Orator Henley* (Cambridge, 1973); his life as the Orator is put into context by Howell, *Eighteenth-Century British Logic and Rhetoric,* pp. 193–203. Henley also translated the *Logique* (1712) of Jean-Pierre de Crousaz as *A New Treatise of the Art of Thinking; or, A Compleat System of Reflections, Concerning the Conduct and Improvement of the Mind* (1724). Crousaz was indebted to Arnauld and Locke (see Howell, pp. 304–31).

59. Isaac Barker, *An English Grammar Shewing the Nature and Grounds of the English Language* (London, 1733), p. 1.

60. Loughton, *A Practical Grammar of the English Tongue,* p. vi.

61. On the combined skills of the eighteenth-century writing masters see Ambrose Heal, *The English Writing-Masters and their Copy-Books, 1570–1800* (Cambridge, 1931).

62. Daniel Duncan, *A New English Grammar, Wherein the Grounds and Nature*

*of the Eight Parts of Speech, And their Construction is explain'd* (London, 1731), p. vi.

63. John Collyer, *The General Principles of Grammar; Especially Adapted to the English Tongue* (London, 1735), p. 94.

64. John Milner, *A Practical Grammar of the Latin Tongue . . . The whole establish'd upon Rational Principles* (London, 1729), p. 36.

65. I am aware that the dominant view of early eighteenth-century literature decidedly stresses the spatial: systems that are orderly, completed, and clearly symbolized. See, as a distinguished recent example of this opinion, Martin Battestin, *The Providence of Wit: Aspects of Form in Augustan Literature and the Arts* (Oxford, 1974). The linguistic evidence I have assembled in detail and the literary examples I am more sketchily proposing challenge, effectively I hope, this over-determined spatialization. See notes 15 and 39 above.

66. These oft-quoted terms come from Swift's letter to Pope, 29 September 1725. F. Elrington Ball, ed., *The Correspondence of Jonathan Swift,* 6 vols. (Oxford, 1910–14), 3: 209.

67. Fielding expertly draws the contrast between styles and manners of narration at every level, from sentences that begin pitched at the high style only to turn, on a phrase like "in plain English" or "in the common phrase," to simpler statement, to larger units like the domestic romance of the "History of Leonora" in *Joseph Andrews,* which is interrupted by the slapstick comedy of the splattered hogs' blood scene in the kitchen (book 2: iv–vi) or the experiment in the "Homerican Stile" in *Tom Jones,* which ends with a reference to the horse-whipping of an over-lathered Muse (book 4: vii).

68. Fielding characterizes this readerly responsibility quite clearly in *Tom Jones* (book 7: 1) when he likens the range of reader responses to Black George's theft of Tom's money to that of different groups of spectators in a theater. The right reader for Fielding is one who, narratorlike, responds to the life of a repertory theater and to actors who play different roles rather than to a particular scene or play or to a single role.

69. Fielding discusses the Ridiculous in the "Author's Preface" to *Joseph Andrews.* His comically complex definition of his work as a "comic epic poem in prose" is representative of his witty effort to collect traditionally specifying terms only to avoid restrictiveness. It is a deliberately indefinite definition, only as precise as its invisible Homeric model.

70. The reader's role in Fielding's novels has received some attention from John Preston, *The Created Self: The Reader's Role in Eighteenth-Century Fiction* (London, 1970), pp. 94–132; more suggestively, from Wolfgang Iser, *The Implied Reader: Patterns of Communication in Prose Fiction from Bunyan to Beckett* (Baltimore, 1974), pp. 29–56; and, most dearly, in my "Fictions of Judgment: Fielding and the Eighteenth-Century English Novel" (Ph.D. diss., The Johns Hopkins University, 1968).

71. Ralph Cohen, *The Unfolding of the Seasons,* p. 5.

72. See the recent work of Eric Rothstein, *Systems of Order and Systems of Inquiry in Eighteenth-Century Fiction* (Berkeley, 1975).

73. Among many agreeably unhappy instances see the representative self-criticism of Collins in "An Ode of the Popular Superstitions of the Highlands of Scotland, Considered as the Subject of Poetry." The subject of Collins's poem is the critical perspective of the title: how earlier poets actually "Believed the magic

wonders" that they sang (quoted from Roger Lonsdale, ed., *The Poems of Thomas Gray, William Collins, Oliver Goldsmith* [London, 1969], p. 517). *Their* poems satisfied their vision and incorporated their readers: "Melting it flows, pure, numerous, strong and clear, / And fills the impassioned heart and lulls the harmonious ear" (ll. 202–3); *his* verse pays tribute to what he recognizes "at [a] distance" (l. 207); and to where he may, one day, be taken, powerless as he is to get there by himself: "The time shall come when I perhaps may tread / Your lowly glens... by Fancy led" (ll. 208–10).

74. See Gray's meditations on these trials in, successively, "Elegy Written in a Country Churchyard," "Ode on a Distant Prospect of Eton College," and "The Progress of Poesy."

75. I take the phrase "burden of the past" and suggestions about its significance from W. Jackson Bate, *The Burden of the Past and the English Poet* (Cambridge, Mass., 1970).

## Chapter 3

1. For chronological lists of language texts the finest resource is R. C. Alston's *A Bibliography of the English Language from the Invention of Printing to the Year 1800,* 10 vols. and supplement (Leeds, 1965–73), to be supported by Ian Michael, *English Grammatical Categories and the Tradition to 1800* (Cambridge, 1970), especially the chronological lists, pp. 588–94, 277–78.

2. The sources for these lines are, in order, *Rasselas* (Chapter 11), Crabbe's *The Village* (I. 48), Cowper's *The Task* (I. 1), Burns's "The Cotter's Saturday Night" (1. 5), and Goldsmith's "The Deserted Village" (1. 411).

3. See, on Smart's pursuit of a "magical" language, Geoffrey H. Hartman, "Christopher Smart's *Magnificat:* Toward a Theory of Representation," *ELH* 41 (1974): 429–54; and, on Blake's poetic particularization, Donald Ault, *Visionary Physics: Blake's Response to Newton* (Chicago, 1974), especially pp. 57–95, 161–95.

4. James Buchanan, *An Essay towards Establishing a Standard for an Elegant and Uniform Pronunciation of the English Tongue Throughout the British Dominions, As practised by the Most Learned and Polite Speakers* (London, 1766), p. v. The geographic and social qualifications added to the ideal of standardization contribute to the distinctive context of later-eighteenth-century linguistics.

5. James Buchanan, *The Complete English Scholar* (London, 1753), p. xii.

6. James Gough, *A Practical Grammar of the English Tongue* (Dublin, 1754), also has rules "to be committed to Memory... printed in a larger character; and... Rules and Remarks which seemed less material to be printed in a lesser Letter" (p. v). Gough's use of print size to distinguish between more and less important rules contrasts with the graphic reinforcement of the theory of language by earlier linguists. The first grammar text published with a separate teacher's manual (in another volume and in smaller print) is the *Elementa Anglicana* (Stockport, 1792–96) by Peter Waldken Fogg.

7. Gough, *Practical Grammar,* p. iv.

8. Robert Lowth, *Short Introduction to English Grammar with Critical Notes* (London, 1762), p. i.

9. Lowth is anticipated in this by John Lawson, *Lectures Concerning Oratory* (Dublin, 1758). The fashion of teaching grammar by exercises requiring students to

correct false syntax begins with Ann Fisher, *A New Grammar* (Newcastle-upon-Tyne, 1750).

10.   Lowth's abundant evidence proving the frequent grammatical lapses of even his favored authors (Milton, Dryden, Swift, Pope, and others) also suggests that improvement of the language is a national responsibility to be shared by writers and young students, the established and the poor. Instead of providing different approaches to language, Lowth offers one concern—correctness—accommodated to all users of English.

11.   See G. K. Pullum, "Lowth's *Grammar:* A Re-Evaluation," *Linguistics* 137 (1974): 63-78. On the importance of the idea of linguistic relativism in the period see Land, *From Signs to Propositions: The Concept of Form in Eighteenth-Century Semantic Theory* (London, 1974), pp. 69-70. Thomas Blacklock, in *An Essay on Universal Etymology* (Edinburgh, 1756), similarly settles for convenience or convention in his syntactic definitions and distinctions while claiming, by reference to Harris's *Hermes,* the mental universals inherent in the analysis of sentences. See, too, William Ward's justification of traditional categories in his important contribution, *An Essay on Grammar* (London, 1765), vi-viii.

12.   James Harris, *Hermes; or, A Philosophical Inquiry concerning Language and Universal Grammar* (London, 1751), p. 138.

13.   In his perceptive and precise presentation of Harris's views, Noam Chomsky, *Cartesian Linguistics: A Chapter in the History of Rationalist Thought* (New York, 1966), willingly ignores the context in which Harris makes his case. By isolating the insights common to the Port-Royalists, Harris, and William von Humboldt, Chomsky provides distinguished precedents for his own theory of language, but he sacrifices the striking differences between the methods, purposes, and receptions of those earlier linguists. These are aspects of the history of linguistics in which Chomsky takes little interest: "Questions of current interest will . . . determine the general form of this sketch; that is, I will make no attempt to characterize Cartesian linguistics as it saw itself, but rather will concentrate on the development of ideas that have reemerged, quite independently, in current work" (p. 2). However, we should note that Harris's view of language as context-free and logical (rather than social and communicative) makes him interesting to Chomsky, and impressive, but exotic and distant to his contemporaries and successors.

14.   James Burnet [Lord Monboddo], *Of the Origin and Progress of Language,* 2d ed. Edinburgh, 1774), vol. 1, vigorously supports Harris on the basis of the latter's acceptance of Plato's classification of ideas and his rejection of Locke's. Platonic absolutes and a prioris dominate Harris's presentation. For a fine discussion of Monboddo on language see Land, *From Signs to Propositions,* pp. 92-101.

15.   Contrast Lowth's view that linguistic universality "cannot be taught abstractly." A significant similarity between theory, after Harris, and practice in the period is that neither can deal with any but existing languages. The importance of this restriction appears in the distinctive development of philology in the last decades of the century. See Hans Aarsleff, *The Study of Language in England, 1780–1860* (Princeton, 1967), pp. 115–61.

16.   James Beattie, "The Theory of Language," in *Dissertations Moral and Critical* (London, 1783), p. 343. On Beattie see Stephen K. Land, "James Beattie on Language," *PQ* 51 (1972): 887-904.

17.   John Horne Tooke, *Epeá Pteroenta; or, The Diversions of Purley,* ed.

Richard Taylor (London, 1840), pp. 608–9. Ward, *Grammar,* is more moderate in his protection of students and his opinion of schoolmasters (pp. x–xii).

18. Joseph Priestley, *A Course of Lectures on the Theory of Language, and Universal Grammar* (Warrington, 1762), attempts, as we shall see, to redefine universality in order to accommodate it to living languages. He refers to Harris as a distinguished but remote philosopher, one whose observations on the genitive and dative cases, for instance, are "ingenious" but "too philosophical for so vague and irregular an use as is actually made of those cases" (p. 77). For Monboddo, too, Harris is a distinguished philosopher of language, while Lowth's "excellent grammar" is recommended as the best source for preserving the language (*Origin,* 2: 495). Monboddo notes that for Harris there are four parts of speech corresponding to four categories of existence, while for Lowth there are nine sorts of words according to the "common Division." Monboddo agrees with both systems: the conventional division is appropriate for "ordinary grammar," the other for a philosophical analysis (2: 28).

19. Richard Wynne, *An Universal Grammar* (London, 1775), p. 4. Similar sentiments are expressed by Gough, *Practical Grammar;* W. R., *A Series of Letters on English Grammar,* in *Oxford Magazine* (London), July 1768–September 1769; Thomas Smetham, *The Practical Grammar* (London, 1774); H. Ward, *A Short but clear System of Grammar* (Whitehaven, 1777); and [Monboddo], see note 18 above.

20. Lindley Murray, *An English Grammar: Comprehending the Principles and Rules of the Language* (New York, 1810), p. 28. Murray prefers supplying defects and abridging superfluities by notes rather "than by disorganizing, or altering, a system which has been long established, and generally approved" (pp. 56–57). See, for instance, his discussions of moods (pp. 60–69) and syntax (pp. 130 ff.). On Murray's grammar as a summary account of some late-eighteenth-century assumptions, see George H. McKnight, *Modern English in the Making* (New York, 1928), pp. 393–99.

21. Oliver Goldsmith, "'The Preface,' to *A Complete English Grammar on a New Plan,*" in Arthur Friedman, ed., *Collected Works of Oliver Goldsmith,* 5 vols. (Oxford, 1966), 5: 305.

22. The dramatic differences between the discussions of grammar in the first and third editions of the *Encyclopaedia Britannica* demonstrate the separation of grammar from theory in the period. In the first edition (1771), the Scottish publication draws chiefly from James Harris. See *Encyclopaedia Britannica; or, A Dictionary of Arts and Sciences* (Edinburgh, 1771), 2: 728. By the third edition (Edinburgh, 1797), the science of grammar, which in 1771 was defined as the "analogy and relation between words and things," is the analysis of language "only as it is significant of thought" (p. 37). The third edition accepts the common division of the parts of speech as the "most proper" (p. 38) and characterizes the philosophical discussion in the first edition as "absolute nonsense."

23. See George Campbell's reliance on Priestley in *Philosophy of Rhetoric* (London, 1776), 2: 362.

24. See Goldsmith's desire to avoid any indication of "needless affectation" ("Preface," p. 306).

25. According to Thomas Merriman, *A Compendious English Grammar* (London, 1750), tradition is, simply, "better than innovation" (p. iii).

26. Joseph Priestley, *The Rudiments of English Grammar; Adapted to the Use of Schools with Observations on Style* (London, 1761), p. vi.

27. Robert Baker, *Reflections on the English Language* (London, 1770), p. xiv.

28. Edward Search [Abraham Tucker], *Vocal Sounds* (London, 1773), p. 113. Also see Campbell, *Philosophy of Rhetoric:* "the grammarian's only business is to note, collect, and methodise" the laws of each language (1:341).

29. Thomas Sheridan specifies such a restriction on his elaborate scheme to perfect the pronunciation of English, in his *Dissertation on the Causes of the Difficulties, Which occur, in learning the English Tongue. With a Scheme for publishing An English Grammar and Dictionary Upon a Plan entirely New. The Object of which shall be, to facilitate the Attainment of the English Tongue, and establish a Perpetual Standard of Pronunciation* (London, 1761): "... in the present scheme it is not proposed that there should be the least change in our alphabet, or alteration made in the mode of writing or spelling English. The object of it is, to fix such a standard of pronunciation ... that it may be in the power of every one, to acquire an accurate manner of uttering ..." (p. 30). For substantial spelling reforms proposed by James Elphinston, see note 106.

30. Robert Nares, *Elements of Orthoepy: Containing a Distinct View of the Whole Analogy of the English Language. So Far as it Relates to Pronunciation, Accent, and Quantity* (London, 1784), p. xix.

31. John Walker, *The Rhyming Dictionary of the English Language* (London, 1775), pp. lxi–lxii. In his *General Idea of a Pronouncing Dictionary of the English Language* (London, 1774), Walker disavows reform since language "is not more than the totality of such usages as form a relation between signs and ideas, these relations can only be understood as usage or custom has explained them. So that custom is not only the law of language but strictly speaking it is language itself" (quoted in McKnight, *Modern English in the Making,* pp. 438–39).

32. Priestley, *Course of Lectures on the Theory of Language,* p. 186.

33. See Howard Weinbrot, "Samuel Johnson's *Plan* and 'Preface' to the 'Dictionary': The Growth of a Lexicographer's Mind," in Weinbrot, ed., *New Aspects of Lexicography* (Carbondale, 1972), pp. 73–94.

34. Samuel Johnson, *The Plan of a Dictionary of the English Language* (London, 1747), pp. 1–2.

35. Samuel Johnson, "Preface" to *A Dictionary of the English Language,* in E. L. McAdam, Jr., and George Milne, eds., *Johnson's Dictionary* (New York, 1963), p. 6. The principal lesson Johnson draws from compiling his massive work is that tradition is better than change. He advises his readers "not to disturb, upon narrow views, or for minute propriety, the orthography of their fathers. It has been asserted, that for the law to be *known,* is of more importance than to be *right*" (p. 8). At the same time Johnson knows that what he has compiled is a record of change, but change inherent in the history of his people rather than surveyed without reference to their habits and circumstances.

36. Johnson writes convincingly of the perils of having to define words by other words which, if they were purely explanatory, would merely repeat the original words. As it is, the lexicographer confronts the obscurity of some terms, the evanescence or indeterminancy of others, his own ignorance and fatigue, proximate meanings, the interpenetration of original and derivative words or literal and metaphoric usages, and the fact that "some explanations are unavoidably reciprocal or circular" (p. 16). The only thorough corrective to these necessary faults of explanation would be to supply the usages the lexicographer is trying to summarize.

37. See, too, Noah Webster, *Dissertations on the English Language: With Notes,*

*Historical and Critical* (Boston, 1789): "The Principal business of a compiler of a grammar is, to separate *local* or *partial* practice from the *general custom* of speaking; and reject what is *local* . . . and recommend that which is universal, or general; or which conforms to the analogies of structure in a language" (p. ix). Webster draws the limits of universality at the general (non-dialect) characteristics of a particular language.

38. Nares, *Orthoepy,* p. xvii.

39. The linguistic compiler is one of several types of the collector in the period, which had become, as Pope bitterly predicted in the fourth book of the *Dunciad* (1741), an age in which "by some object ev'ry brain is stirred." Words in a book, like countries on a tour or poems in an anthology or plays in an endless series or matching books on a shelf, became the standing orders of the day.

40. John Fell, *An Essay Towards an English Grammar* (London, 1748), p. x. Complaints about the confinement of style and recommendations of stylistic richness and variety are familiar in the Scottish rhetoricians. See Campbell, *Philosophy of Rhetoric,* 1: 365; Hugh Blair, *Lectures on Rhetoric and Belles Lettres* (London, 1783); and Henry Home, Lord Kames, *Elements of Criticism* (Edinburgh, 1762), chapter 9.

41. Johnson, "Preface," also hopes that "the spirit of English liberty" will stop any academy intended to cultivate style (p. 24).

42. William Kenrick, *A Rhetorical Grammar of the English Language. Wherein the Elements of Speech in General and those of the English Tongue in Particular are analyzed; and the Rudiments of Articulation, Pronunciation, and Prosody Inteligibly Displayed* (London, 1784), p. 6. Lindley Murray, *An English Grammar,* draws from Campbell to provide authority for the idea that the standard of language reflects "reputable, national, and present use" (p. 123). See Campbell, *Philosophy of Rhetoric,* 1: 139. Webster, *Dissertations on the English Language,* also draws on Campbell's criteria (pp. 204-5). See, too, John Rice, *An Introduction to the Art of Reading with Energy and Propriety* (London, 1765): "Custom alone is the Criterion of Pronunciation" (p. 194).

43. [Tucker], *Vocal Sounds,* finds a similar use for his recommended phonetic transcriptions: "By this method our language would be transmitted down entire to future generations. New dictionaries, or new editions of dictionaries are produced every twenty years, and in them such among posterity as shall think it worth their while to examine, may see exactly how their ancestors spoke as well as wrote in every successive twenty years . . ." (p. 124).

44. The fact that languages are inevitably mutable means, to Priestley, that they reflect characteristics of their users, not qualities independent of time and society. Language "is a thing not exempt from the influence of fashion and caprice: whereas true science is the same in all places, and in all times, and admits of unbounded improvements" (*Rudiments,* p. 58). Also, Gregory Sharpe, in his fascinating *Two Dissertations: I. Upon the Origin, Construction, Division, and Relation of Languages. II. Upon the Original Powers of Letters* (London, 1751), investigates the correlation between changes in the forms and sounds of words and developments in a society. Different "modes of speaking" will naturally develop "among men using the same language in different provinces" (p. 32). Sharpe, by tracing words back "step by step," tries to isolate the "peculiarities of each language," since each group of speakers will adopt words to its prevailing "mode" of speaking at a particular time.

45. V. J. Peyton, *The History of the English Language; Deduced from its Origin, and Traced Through its Different Stages and Revolutions: In Which Its Excellence and Superiority over the other European Tongues are evidently demonstrated, As well as the Source of those Revolutions: Being very interesting for Persons ignorant of the Infant State of their own Country and those Revolutions; And for the Benefit of those who aspire to the Perfect Knowledge of their Mother Tongue* (London, 1771), p. 29. The full title suggests the importance of historicist and nationalistic assumptions to later eighteenth-century linguistics. We witness in the linguistics of the period a shift from a static or idealized to an evolutionary or progressive view of time.

46. Daniel Fenning, *A New Grammar of the English Language* (London, 1771), p. vi. Gough, *Practical Grammar,* argues that Latin is "over-valued, and thought to be of more Service than it really is" (p. viii). One who masters English learning is a scholar despite his ignorance of every other language, according to Gough. For Goldsmith ("Preface") one does not need Latin to write English "with correctness, elegance, and precision" (p. 306). See, too, Anselm Bayly, *The English Accidence* (London, 1771), p. 31; Ralph Harrison, *Institutes of English Grammar* (Manchester, 1777), p. v; and George Neville Ussher, *The Elements of English Grammar, Methodically Arranged for the Use of Those who Study English Grammatically Without a Previous Knowledge of the Learned Languages* (Gloucester, 1785).

47. Buchanan, *Complete English Scholar,* p. xv.

48. Anselm Bayly, *An Introduction to Languages, Literary and Philosophical . . . Exhibiting at one view their Grammar, Rationale, Analogy and Idiom* (London, 1758), p. 40.

49. James Parsons, *Remains of Japhet: Being Historical Enquiries into the Affinity and Origin of the European Languages* (London, 1767), p. 356. Sharpe, *Two Dissertations,* cites the seventeenth-century idea that Chinese is the original language: "This is amusement only" (p. 6). Sharpe mocks Kircher, too, as a "man of genius and learning for the time in which he lived" (p. 24). Seth Ward, in *Vindiciae Academiarum* (1654), also rejects a hieroglyphic model because of its mysteries, but he does not substitute a historical argument (p. 18). For the historicization of the study of hieroglyphs in the eighteenth century, see Madeleine David, *Le débat sur les écritures et l'hiéroglyphie aux XVII<sup>e</sup> et XVIII<sup>e</sup> siècles* (Paris, 1965), pp. 96–102.

50. Beattie, "Theory of Language," p. 240.

51. [Monboddo], *Origin,* 2: 428.

52. Surveys of the languages scattered after Babel were common to learned grammars of the sixteenth and seventeenth centuries. See, for instance, J. C. Scaliger, *De causis Linguae latinae libri tredecim* (1540) and John Wallis, *Grammatica linguae Anglicanae* (Oxford, 1653). Distinguished attempts were also made, especially in the late seventeenth century, to bring evidence of England's linguistic past into the tradition: William Somner, *Dictionarium Saxonico-Latino-Anglicum* (Oxford, 1659); and the enduring work of George Hickes, especially *Linguarum vett. septentrionalium thesaurus grammatico-criticus et archaeologicus* (Oxford, 1703–5).

53. Kenrick, *Rhetorical Grammar,* p. 62.

54. Gough, *Practical Grammar,* p. v. See also Fell, *Essay,* p. vi; Fenning, *New Grammar,* p. iii; Goldsmith, "Preface," p. 304; and Lowth, *Grammar,* p. i.

55. Ussher, *Grammar,* p. vi.

56. Daniel Farro, *The Royal Universal British Grammar and Vocabulary* (London, 1754), p. 1.

57. James Buchanan, *The British Grammar* (London, 1762), p. 1. See also John Bell, *A Concise and Comprehensive System of English Grammar* (Edinburgh, 1769). A reversion to the older definition and to Lily's Latin grammar is Thomas Bowles's *Aristarchus; or, A Compendius and Rational Institution of the Latin Tongue* (Oxford, 1748).

58. See Ussher, *Grammar,* p. 1, and Mark Anthony Meilan, *A Grammar of the English Language* (London, 1771). Both Thomas Blacklock, *An Essay on Universal Etymology,* and James Elphinston, *The Principles of the English Language Digested* (London, 1765), assume that language universals are represented in the traditional system of the parts of speech.

59. Anselm Bayly's *A Plain and Complete Grammar of the English Language* (London, 1772) is a similar "attempt to write a universal grammar" (p. vi). The universals are those "general rules, in which all languages agree" (p. vii). Bayly never resolves what kind of work he wishes to write, and this results in a number of contradictory statements in all his linguistic works. In the *Grammar,* he seeks a "rational and familiar grammar" (p. 97) that could introduce all languages without sacrificing the genius of English. He struggles to discover general rules for verbs, for instance, and acknowledges that "it may be difficult, if not impossible to reduce common speech to rule, and indeed it is beneath a grammarian's attempt" (p. 43). Bayly is interestingly perplexed about how much a grammarian can claim for the sort of detailed study of a particular language he himself provides. He even argues that it is the distinctive genius of a language that is "the gift of nature, and is fixed," while "language is a thing which changes" (p. 61). Monboddo faces a comparable problem when he debates whether there could ever have been natural connections between words and ideas (see *Origin,* 2: 199–219).

60. Farro, *Grammar,* p. xv. See also Bayly, *Plain and Complete Grammar,* p. 97. John Williams (*Thoughts on the Origin and on the Most Rational Method of Teaching the Languages: With Some Observations on the Necessity of One Universal Language for All Works of Science* [London, 1783]) wants Latin to be the universal language, not for any philosophical reasons, but because it is, practically speaking, already more widely known than any other.

61. Elphinston, *Principles,* p. xi.

62. John Henley, *The Compleat Linguist; or, An Universal Grammar to all the Considerable Tongues in Being* (London, 1719–26), also makes the system of classification the means of discovering universals (see Chapter 2), but, unlike Elphinston, he is not as interested in linguistic differences. For Elphinston's emphasis on differences, see note 12.

63. Beattie, "Theory of Language," p. 320.

64. L. D. Nelme, *An Essay Towards An Investigation of the Elements of Language and Letters* (London, 1772), offers a method of discovering universals that he calls "De-composition," and, stranger still, W. P. Russel devotes his efforts to *Verbotomy; or, A classical improved Vocabulary, and Self-Interpreting Spelling-Book* (London, 1805). Russel calls himself a Verbotomist, or, Word Dissector.

65. Aldo Scaglione, in *The Classical Theory of Composition From Its Origins to the Present: A Historical Survey* (Chapel Hill, 1972), documents the shift, after the mid-eighteenth century on the continent, from linguistic to stylistic characterizations of composition.

66. Priestley adapts the Port-Royalists' favorite sentence ("The invisible God made the visible world") to his own purposes. Instead of discussing the sentence in

terms of its "deep" and "surface" structures, Priestley discriminates between more and less emphatic arrangement of clauses (*Lectures on the Theory of Language,* pp. 147-48). He goes on to elaborate the stylistic (rather than logical) basis of discourse:

> It is in these forms of transition from sentence to sentence, and paragraph to paragraph, or the connexion of the different sentences and parts of a discourse, that the chief difficulty of composition, in point of elegance, consists. Some connect the materials of their compositions in a more obvious and direct, others in a more concealed and indirect manner; some enlarge upon the relations of the several parts, and thereby make their discourse more diffuse; others in a manner suppress the connecting particles, and by that means are concise; and it requires judgment to determine when the one method, and when the other is preferable (p. 152).

67. Murray, *An English Grammar,* p. viii.

68. These principles are central to the work of the linguistic oriented rhetoricians and associationists of the period—Reid, Hartley, Kames, Campbell, Blair, and Beattie. See the survey by Martin Kallich, *The Association of Ideas and Critical Theory in Eighteenth-Century England* (The Hague, 1970); and the editors' introduction to Priestley's *A Course of Lectures on Oratory and Criticism,* Vincent M. Bevilacqua and Richard Murphy, eds. (Carbondale, 1965).

69. Rice, *Art of Reading,* p. 3. See also John Mason, *An Essay on Elocution or Pronunciation. Intended chiefly for the Assistance of those who instruct others in the Art of Reading* (London, 1748); Thomas Sheridan, *Elements of English: Being a New Method of Teaching the Whole Art of Reading* (London, 1786); and Noah Webster, *A Grammatical Institute of the English Language. Part III: Containing the Necessary Rules of Reading and Speaking* (Hartford, 1785).

70. John Walker, *A Rhetorical Grammar, or Course of Lessons in Elocution* (London, 1785), p. 101.

71. For a more elaborate discussion of the idea see Blair, *Lectures.* Blair associates word order and harmony so that sound and sense are reunited but on a purely rhetorical rather than on a physical or epistemological basis.

72. Buchanan, *British Grammar,* p. 49.

73. See Joseph Robertson, *An Essay on Punctuation* (London, 1785) and Ward, *Grammar,* p. 9.

74. John Herries, *The Elements of Speech* (London, 1773), p. 5.

75. It is, notes Herries, the "Creator in whom we live, move, *breathe,* and have our being" (p. 21).

76. Kenrick, *Rhetorical Grammar,* p. 4.

77. Bayly, *Plain and Complete Grammar,* p. 61. Also, Sharpe, in *Two Dissertations,* bases his discussion of the history of languages on the laws of sound changes peculiar to each language. Consonants and vowels change for one another "according to affinity or nearness of sound" and "often change places or are transposed" (p. 43). Sharpe, by discovering "tribes of mutable consonants" (p. 50) and other classifications "according to the organs of speech" (p. 53), can relate these "observations upon the relation, change, and mixture of the letters" to the "laws of derivation" (p. 54).

78. Thomas Sheridan, *A Rhetorical Grammar* (Dublin, 1781), p. 100.

79. Bertram Harris Bronson, "Some Aspects of Music and Literature," in his *Facets of the Enlightenment: Studies in English Literature and Its Contexts* (Berkeley, 1968), p. 118.

80. The story of the sad fate of the once sheltered hare is in *The Task,* 3. 334–51, and the reference to Babel is in 5. 193–201.

81. On the elocutionary movement see Wilbur Samuel Howell, *Eighteenth-Century British Logic and Rhetoric* (Princeton, 1971), especially pp. 145–256. Howell uses some scattered texts to prove that the elocutionary movement begins in 1702 (with the first English translation of Le Faucheur's *Traitté de l'action de l'orateur*) if not in 1646 (with John Wilkins's *Ecclesiastes*). However, it is clear that the widespread agreement about the importance of sounds to language texts and the discussion of sounds in rhetorical terms are mid- and late-century phenomena.

82. Buchanan, *British Grammar,* p. 3. Also see Elphinston, *Principles,* I, pp. 1–217; Goldsmith, "Preface," p. 309; Anon., *A General View of English Pronunciation* (London, 1784); and Noah Webster, *A Grammatical Institute of the English Language, Comprising An Easy, Concise, and Systematic Method of Education . . . Part I: Containing a New and Accurate Standard of Pronunciation* (Hartford, 1783). In *Dissertations,* Webster announces that his first goal is "critically to investigate the rules of pronunciation in our language" (p. 36).

83. Fenning, *New Grammar,* and John Walker, *A Key to the Classical Pronunciation,* 7th ed. (London, 1822), agree that it is not presently possible to teach sounds by writing. Fenning thinks that the "true sound of the letters can only be learned by practice, and by the assistance of a master" (p. 16).

84. Elphinston, *Principles,* p. xii. Also, John Ash, *Grammatical Institutes; or, An Easy Introduction to Dr. Lowth's English Grammar, Designed for the Use of Schools,* 4th ed. (London, 1763), and Sayer Rudd, *Prodromos; or, Observations on the English Letters* (London, 1755).

85. Goldsmith, "Preface," p. 309.

86. Solomon Lowe, *The Critical Spelling-Book; An Introduction to Reading and Writing readily and correctly* (London, 1755), p. 10. On Webster's response to Dilworth, see Ervin C. Shoemaker, *Noah Webster: Pioneer of Learning* (New York, 1935), pp. 64–78.

87. Bayly, *English Accidence,* p. 10.

88. Benjamin Martin, *Institutions of Language; Containing, A Physico-Grammatical Essay on the Propriety and Rationale of the English Tongue. Deduced from a General Idea of the Nature and Necessity of Speech for Human Society* (London, 1748), p. 24.

89. William Kenrick, *A New Dictionary of the English Language: Containing not only the Explanation of Words, with their Orthography, Etymology, and Idiomatical Use in Writing; But likewise, their Orthoepia or Pronunciation in Speech, according to the present Practice of polished Speakers in the Metropolis* (London, 1773). Also see William Johnston, *A Pronouncing and Spelling Dictionary* (London, 1764), and John Burn, *A Pronouncing Dictionary of the English Language* (Glasgow, 1786). Johnston demonstrates his method as he explains his purposes in his preface: his dictionary provides the "full detail, description, and notation, of the literal sounds" (p. vi).

90. Herries, *Elements of Speech,* p. 25.

91. Rice, *Art of Reading,* p. 70.

92. Rice commonly uses terms like *time, force,* and *velocity* to discuss individual sounds: "even as in the Composition of Motion, the Matter and Velocity may reciprocally supply the Place of each other in forming the Momentum of the Whole, a small Quantity of Matter moving with a great Velocity, being equal to a greater Quantity moving proportionably slow" (ibid, p. 57).

*Notes to Pages 109–12*

93. Tucker, *Vocal Sounds,* p. 2.

94. Nares, *Elements of Orthoepy,* p. xvii.

95. Baker, *Reflections upon Learning,* pp. xvi–xvii. See Howell, *British Logic and Rhetoric,* for some connections between the elocutionary movement and acting. The theatrical context of Sheridan's proposals is documented by Esther K. Sheldon, *Thomas Sheridan of Smock-Alley* (Princeton, 1967).

96. Sheridan, *Dissertation on the Causes,* p. 3.

97. See Robertson, *Essay on Punctuation,* on the "pleasures" of respiration which are enjoyed as much by the hearer as by the speaker (p. 75).

98. John Walker summarizes these assumptions in his *Rhetorical Grammar:* "The art of speaking, though founded on grammar, has principles of its own: principles that arise from the nature of the living voice, from the perception of harmony in the ear, and from a certain superaddition to the sense of language": (p. 30).

99. Adam Smith, *Essays Philosophical and Literary* (London, 1880), p. 310. The essay on the origin of language was first published in 1761 and subsequently included in *The Theory of Moral Sentiments,* 3rd ed. (1767).

100. [Monboddo], *Origin,* 2: 117.

101. *An Essay Towards Establishing the Melody and Measure of Speech* (London, 1775). Steele published a new edition in 1779 retitled *Prosodia Rationalis.* On Steele see David Abercrombie, "Steele, Monboddo and Garrick," in his *Studies in Phonetics and Linguistics* (Oxford, 1965), pp. 35–44.

102. See Howell, *British Logic and Rhetoric,* pp. 191–92, 204–8 on Mason.

103. See Herries, *Elements of Speech,* p. 60; Sheridan, *Dissertation on the Causes,* p. 19, and *Rhetorical Grammar,* p. xviii; William Cockin, *The Art of Delivering Written Language* (London, 1775), p. 121; John Walker, *The Melody of Speaking Delineated; or, Elocution taught like Music, by Visible Signs* (London, 1787). The title of another book by Anselm Bayly collects some of the assumptions behind language study at the time: *A Practical Treatise on Singing and Playing with just expression and real elegance, Being an essay on I: Grammar. II. Pronunciation; or, The art of just speaking. III. Singing—its graces—their application* (London, 1771).

104. Walker, *Rhetorical Grammar,* p. 61.

105. Sheridan, *Rhetorical Grammar,* p. xviii.

106. Kenrick, *New Dictionary,* p. ii.

107. Other phonetic marks are proposed by Thomas Gibbons, *Rhetoric* (London, 1767); Rudd, *Prodromos;* William Ward, *An Essay on Grammar* (London, 1765); Burn, *Pronouncing Dictionary;* Webster, *Grammatical Institute, Part I.* Sharpe, *Two Dissertations,* adopts "marks and characters to the parts of sound as they are formed by the organs of speech" (p. 57). He also associates letters on the basis of likeness of sound (as *d* and *t*) and stresses the difference between this system and the kinds of universal characters used by decipherers.

108. Buchanan's design is repeated by Sheridan, *Dissertation on the Causes,* p. 30.

109. Walker, *Rhetorical Grammar,* p. 4.

110. Sheridan, *Rhetorical Grammar,* p. 113. Walker, in his *Rhetorical Grammar,* echoes Sheridan: emphasis gives the light and shade "necessary to form a strong picture of the thought" (p. 99).

111. Thomas Spence, *The Important Trial of Thomas Spence* (London, 1803), p. 94, referring to his *Grand Repository of the English Language* (Newcastle-upon-Tyne, 1775). On Spence see Abercrombie, *Studies in Phonetics,* pp. 68–75.

112. Noah Webster, *Dissertations on the English Language.* Webster's suggestions for spelling reform, in which he was preceded and encouraged by Benjamin Franklin, have little to do with the theory of language. Rather, Webster writes, *"Now* is the time, and *this* the country, in which we may expect success, in attempting changes favorable to language, science and government. . . . Let us then seize the present moment and establish a *national language,* as well as a national government" (p. 406). On the political context of Webster's language work see Shoemaker, *Noah Webster.* The most substantial spelling reforms in England are those proposed, late in his career, by James Elphinston, in *Propriety Ascertained in her Picture; or, Inglish Speech and Spelling Rendered Mutual Guides* (London, 1786); *Inglish Orthography Epittomized: and Propriety's Pocket-Diccionary, Containing dhe Inglish Roots Arranged and Explained,* 2 vols. (London, 1790); and *A Minniature ov Inglish Orthoggraphy* (London, 1795). Like some earlier reformers, Elphinston wants to reduce pronunciation to science based on the principle that "Orthoggraphy iz the mirror ov Orthoeppy: propper immage, ov propper sound" (*Propriety,* p. ix). However, the scientific pronunciation of English reveals not its universality but its distinctive features:

> Evvery tung iz independant ov evvery oddher. Hooevver seeks dhe anallogy (or nattural rule) ov anny tung, must dherfore find it at home: nor wil dhe seeker seek in vain. Inglish diccion dhen haz no laws, but her own. Yet, in her picturage, and consequently in much ov her livving practice; hav anny oddher laws, or anny lawlesness, been prefferably regarded. No more can anny language adopt dhe system ov anny oddher; dhan anny nacion, dhe hoal pollity ov anoddher nacion: for such adopter wer no more a distinct nacion or language; wer but a mongrel, or an eccoe. (p. i)

Elphinston's phonetic system is based on an important assumption of late-eighteenth-century linguistic work: "Ov dhis Propriety," he writes, "dhe ear, not dhe eye, iz dhe judge: for dhe ear iz dhe eye ov dhe mind" (p. xii). For the elaborate phonetic work proving "vocality" is the "soul, and articulation the body of sound" see his *Principles,* 1: 3.

113. Walker, *Rhetorical Grammar,* p. v.

114. Herries, *Elements of Speech;* p. 220; Cockin, *Art of Delivering,* pp. 40–44; and Beattie, "Theory of Language," pp. 275-76. Also, see Elphinston, *Principles,* 2: 206–20.

115. Herries, *Elements of Speech,* p. 224.

116. [Monboddo], *Origin,* 2: 339.

117. Tooke, *Diversions of Purley,* p. 25.

118. George Brown, *The New English Letter-Writer* (London, 1779), p. 17. Also, William Ward, *Essay:* grammar is the "art of applying these sounds and letters consistently for the purpose of communicating the thoughts of one man to another" (p. 3).

119. Fenning, *New Grammar,* p. 1; and Farro, *Grammar,* p. 27.

120. Priestley, *Course of Lectures on the Theory of Language,* p. 13.

121. Mason, *Essay on Elocution,* p. 5.

122. Rice, *Art of Reading,* p. 4. The art of reading is "a just and unaffected Imitation of Natural Speech" (p. 19).

123. Sheridan, *Rhetorical Grammar,* p. 106.

124. See the ample survey and documentation of Arno Borst, *Der Turmbau von*

*Babel: Geschichte der Meinungen über Ursprung und Vielfalt der Sprachen und Völker,* 6 vols. (Stuttgart, 1957–63). Hans Aarsleff documents some of the pertinent history for my purposes in "The Tradition of Condillac: The Problem of the Origin of Language in the Eighteenth Century and the Debate in the Berlin Academy before Herder," in Dell Hymes, ed., *Studies in the History of Linguistics* (Bloomington, 1974), pp. 93–156. A useful general bibliography has been assembled by Gordon Winant Hewes, *Language Origins: A Bibliography,* 2d ed., rev. (The Hague, 1975).

125. David, *Le débat sur les écritures,* while discussing Warburton's *Divine Legation of Moses* (1747), argues for a "discovery of history" around mid-century by distinguishing Warburton's interest in hieroglyphs from the fascination with them the century before. For Warburton, "la vision du signe ancien est désormais devenue inseparable d'un noeud de facteurs historiques" (p. 102).

126. Priestley, *Course of Lectures on the Theory of Language,* p. 30.

127. [Monboddo], *Origin,* 1: 12.

128. Kenrick, *Rhetorical Grammar,* p. 1.

129. Williams, *Thoughts* (see note 60, above) similarly entertains both ideas. Whether language is divine or acquired cannot be finally settled, says Williams; both "are, in part, true" (p. 5). However, any original language is surely lost. Sharpe, *Two Dissertations,* proposes to determine whether the first language was God's gift or the "offspring of necessity and convenience" (p. 1). In any case, the question should not be violently disputed since there is "a great probability at least, that the truth is not in either extreme" (p. 2). Also see *Encyclopaedia Britannica,* 3d ed., 3: 37.

130. Priestley, *Course of Lectures on the Theory of Language,* p. 155.

131. Priestley's other examples of cycles in the human arts are architecture and dress which, with language, exemplify the general progress of human life "from poverty to riches, and ruin" (p. 173). Priestley's cyclical interpretation suggests the work of Vico. For the debate on Vico's vogue (or availability) in the period see the contributions of George Wells, René Wellek, and Enrico de Mas in Giorgio Tagliacozzo and Hayden V. White, eds., *Giambattista Vico: An International Symposium* (Baltimore, 1969), and Land, *From Signs to Propositions,* pp. 54–57 and passim.

132. Bayly, *Introduction to Languages,* p. 24. See John Kirkby, *The Capacity and Extent of the Human Understanding* (1745), in Henry Weber, ed., *Popular Romances,* (Edinburgh, 1833), vol. 2.

133. Beattie, "Theory of Language," p. 269. Murray, in his *An English Grammar,* uses this passage from Beattie without citation (p. 128). Also see Campbell, *Philosophy of Rhetoric:* "Language is purely a species of fashion" formed "by the general, but tacit consent of the people" (1: 340).

134. Martin, *Institutions of Language,* p. 27.

135. Priestley, *Course of Lectures on the Theory of Language,* p. 238. Also see Sharpe, *Two Dissertations,* p. 43.

136. [Monboddo], *Origin,* 1: 190. In a later work, *Hermes Unmasked; or, The Art of Speech Founded on the Association of Words and Ideas* (London, 1795), Thomas Gunter Browne discovers the "mighty metaphysical secret" of the power of association as the key to the relations between words and ideas. To discuss the principles of association governing the development of any language, one must "know the local situations, the customs and the opinions" of the people (p. 42). One gains "insight into the situation of any country, by an accurate examination of the state of their language" (p. 47), and Browne's favorite technique is to "appeal to

the nursery . . . I listen to the child; I watch his actions and his looks, as well as the active and passive terminations of his verbs" (pp. 90–91).

137. Bayly, *Introduction to Languages,* p. 26.

138. [Monboddo], *Origin,* 2: 577.

139. Williams, *Thoughts,* p. 35. Sharpe, *Two Dissertations,* makes a similar suggestion (pp. xi–xii).

140. Priestley, *Course of Lectures on the Theory of Language,* pp. 216 ff.

141. Sheridan, *Dissertation on the Causes,* p. 36.

142. Both Lawrence Lipking, *The Ordering of the Arts in Eighteenth-Century England* (Princeton, 1970), pp. 327–462; and Leo Braudy, *Narrative Form in History and Fiction* (Princeton, 1970), interestingly trace some of the evidence of the new, vital, and distinctive interest in history around mid-century. Michel Foucault, *The Order of Things: An Archaeology of the Human Sciences* (New York, 1970), offers the most suggestive discussion of the impact of historicist attitudes on language, economics, and biology (see pp. 250–300).

143. Lipking, *The Ordering of the Arts,* briefly discusses the ambivalence of Thomas Warton's admiration for antique poetic and linguistic forms and confidence that only contemporary speech is poetically appropriate (pp. 384–87).

144. Shelley's syncretic myth-remaking is the subject of Earl R. Wasserman's *Shelley's Prometheus Unbound: A Critical Reading* (Baltimore, 1965). Wasserman glances at the relationship between what he calls Shelley's "mentalistic ontology" and late-eighteenth-century linguistics (pp. 49–53).

145. Priestley, *Course of Lectures on the Theory of Language,* p. 269. Sharpe, *Two Dissertations,* seeks the "national properties of every language" (p. 56).

146. Martin, *Institutions of Language,* p. 10.

147. Bayly, *Plain and Complete Grammar,* p. 99. On nontranslatability see Ward, *Grammar,* pp. 36–38.

148. Buchanan, *Essay,* p. xii.

149. See also Tucker, *Vocal Sounds:* each language has its distinctive sounds "so that it is impossible to frame a universal alphabet, unless one could know and find characters for all the various tones that are in currency among all the nations upon earth" (p. 40). Walker, in *Key,* recommends that, as a consequence of having lost the distinctive sounds of the dead languages, we "preserve a pronunciation which has naturally sprung up in our own soil, and is congenial to our native language" (p. xv).

150. Buchanan, *British Grammar,* p. 73.

151. Fell, *English Grammar,* p. x. See note 37.

152. Rice, *Art of Reading,* p. 254.

153. Tucker, *Vocal Sounds,* p. 11. Also see Bayly, *Plain and Complete Grammar,* p. 59; and Murray, *An English Grammar:* "Ancient usage is not the text by which the correctness of modern language is to be tried. The origin of things is certainly a proper and gratifying subject of inquiry; and it is particularly curious and pleasing to trace the words of our language to their remote sources. This pleasure should, however, be confined to speculation" (p. 123). Elphinston (*Propriety,* p. vii) and Webster (*Dissertations,* p. 402) express similar attitudes.

154. Peyton, *History of the English Language,* p. 21.

155. See note 52 above.

156. Martin, *Institutions of Language,* p. 111.

157. Williams, *Thoughts,* pp. 11–13.

158. See Aarsleff, *Study of Language,* pp. 115–61.

159. [Monboddo], *Origin,* 2: 221.

160. On the continental influences see Aarsleff, *Study of Language,* pp. 44–72.

161. John Horne Tooke, *Letter to John Dunning* (London, 1778), p. 13.

162. Tooke, *Diversions of Purley,* p. 171.

163. Nelme, *Essay,* p. i.

164. John Cleland, *The Way to Things by Words, and To Words by Things, being a Sketch of an Attempt at the Retrieval of the Antient Celtic, or, Primitive Language of Europe* (London, 1766), p. ii. Much of this linguistic work is tied intimately to interest in primitive folk cultures, particularly the Celtic. On Cleland's derivitiveness in this context see William H. Epstein, *John Cleland: Images of a Life* (New York, 1974), pp. 161–65.

165. Rowland Jones, *The Origin of Language and Nations, Hieroglyfically, Etymologically, and Topografically Defined and Fixed* (London, 1764), A2ʳ.

166. In his *Postscript to the Origin of Language and Nations* (London, n.d.), Jones defends his analysis against charges by Cleland that it is "laid too deep" (p. 4). For Jones, the "very best of modern grammarians" is James Harris. (Jones, *Hieroglyfic; or, A Grammatical Introduction to An Universal Hieroglyfic Language* [London, 1768], a5ʳ).

167. Rowland Jones, *The Io-Triads; or the Tenth Muse, wherein the Origin, Nature and Connection of the sacred Symbols, Sounds, Words, and Ideas and Things, are discovered and investigated according to the Platonic Numbers. And the Principles of all Human knowledge, as well as the First Language, are retrieved in the English. Together with the Origin of Language and Nations, an Hieroglyfical Grammar, the Philosophy of Words; and the Circles of Gomer* (London, 1773), B1ʳ. Much of his *Philosophy of Words, in Two Dialogues Between the Author and Crito* (London, 1769), consists of a continuous complaint by Jones that he had been ignored, dismissed, or ridiculed.

168. Tooke, *Diversions of Purley,* p. 19.

# INDEX

THE JOHNS HOPKINS UNIVERSITY PRESS

This book was composed in Aldine Roman with Caslon Oldstyle display by Horne Associates, and printed on International 50 lb. Cream White Bookmark paper. It was printed and bound by Thomson-Shore.

Library of Congress Cataloging in Publication Data

Cohen, Murray.
    Sensible words.

    Includes bibliographical references and index.
    1. English language—Early modern, 1500–1700.
2. English language—18th century. 3. Linguistics
—England. 4. Language and culture. I. Title.
PE1081.C6       427'.00941       77-1856
ISBN 0-8018-1924-5